A Small Furry Hope

By the same author

The Angle Quickest for Flight

West of Jesus: Surfing, Science, and the
Origins of Belief

A Small Furry Hope

Dog Rescue and the Meaning of Life

STEVEN KOTLER

B L O O M S B U R Y

LONDON · BERLIN · NEW YORK · SYDNEY

Copyright © 2010 by Steven Kotler

First published in Great Britain 2010

The moral right of the author has been asserted

Bloomsbury Publishing Plc
36 Soho Square, London W1D 3QY
Bloomsbury Publishing, London, Berlin, New York and Sydney

A CIP catalogue record for this book is available from the British Library

ISBN 978 1 4088 1022 4 (hardback)
ISBN 978 1 4088 1738 4 (trade paperback)

10 9 8 7 6 5 4 3 2 1

Printed and bound in Great Britain by Clays Ltd, St Ives plc.

www.bloomsbury.com/stevenkotler

For Joy Nicholson

Preface

It is cold night and dark skies and I am sitting in an old rocking chair on the back porch of a small adobe in the mountains of northern New Mexico watching the moon rise through the slats of a dilapidated barn and trying to make sense of the dying. Inside the house, my wife is asleep, as are most of the dogs. People like to ask how many we have and after exploring other options I've come to understatement as the best approach. "Six hundred and thirty-seven," is what I usually say, "you know, give or take." The real number seems closer to eighteen, but this is tentative supposition based on indirect evidence—how much room there is in the bed at night, the timbre of the barking when the neighbors let their horses out to pasture, the amount of fecal matter found in the morning on pee pads set out the evening prior for those too young or too old to wait. Tentative supposition, that is, because once the dying started I lost all desire to count.

I have completely lost track of time as well. My guess is it's April 2008, but it's mostly a guess. Later I will realize this is one of the advantages to sitting shivah, the Jewish rite of mourning, where tradition dictates seven days for the process. Without any similar ritual for animals, grief has no anchor. And no barrier. It can last a week, a month; perhaps it will never end. No relatives fly in from far away to cook meals, no friends drive through the night to attend the service. There's no one to bring me a tumbler of whiskey, none to quietly let me know when I've had too much. Definitely not my wife. When we first met, she used to say that the trouble with us is that when we're alone together, there's no adult in the room. It was funny then—and lately I miss those days.

Scientists who study what is now known as "companion animal bereavement" often point out that the grief following the death of a pet can be far worse than that of a person, even if that person is a close friend or family member. Psychologist Lorri Greene, the author of *Saying Good-bye to the Pet You Love*, co-founder of the San Diego County Pet Bereavement Program, and an internationally recognized expert on the subject, once told me this is why vets have such a high suicide rate. Another is that bereavement is frequently compounded by the facts of euthanasia and the guilt that often follows. Personally, because of the unusual circumstances that surround the dogs in my care, I have not felt that particular regret, though what was true for bluesman Kansas Joe McCoy in 1929 remains so today: *If it keeps on rainin', levee's goin' to break.*

By now, perhaps, you have come to understand what you are getting. You are getting a guy who placed a bet he could not cover. Someone who wandered too far from the mothership and won't be back in time to catch the last flight out. I have begun to doubt what philosophers call "first principles," defined as "those that cannot be deduced from any other." These are foundational assumptions, a priori truths, axioms in mathematics. It was Aristotle who formulated the *first* first principle, the tautology denoted as A=A. I have always had some difficulty distinguishing optimism from fantasy and chose as my first principle the metaphysical certainty that everything would work out because I was doing the right thing. Of course, my wife, who has significantly more experience in such matters, told me differently. Of course, I didn't listen.

A year ago my wife and I moved to these mountains to run a dog sanctuary. We specialize in dogs with special needs: the very old, the very sick, the really retarded. Many of the animals we take in will need years of work before they are eligible for adoption. Many will never be eligible. We believe that how an animal dies is important, so we've become purveyors of a few great months and a very good death. Not many rescuers do this sort of hospice work, as most find it too trying. My wife is tough enough to take it. My excuse is a predilection toward risk and a history of lucky—which, I assumed, would have some predictive value. Let's just say, in this case, A did not equal A.

One of the lucky things I assumed had predictive value was that my first year and a half in this cause had been remarkably death free. Dogs would arrive in our care in dire shape with dire warnings: three weeks to live, a month at most. But there is a difference between how long a dog is supposed to live and how long that dog does live, and in a great many cases that difference is my wife. Again she tried to tell me otherwise; again I didn't listen. By February 2008 I had developed a false sense of confidence—which was about when the universe decided to make up for lost time.

We now have a small pet cemetery in our backyard. The graves are laid out in a line. If I stand directly in the center of them, my best friend's grave is two to my left, my wife's best friend two to my right. We lost a lot of love that winter. Seven dogs total. Seven dogs dead in seven weeks. Vinnie was among them. He was a schnauzer, sweet and old and prone to the shivers. Once the winter arrived, we began wrapping him in comforters and sweaters and anything else we could think of to keep him warm. After we buried him, I couldn't shake the concern. Two nights ago, my wife found me standing above Vinnie's grave with a blanket in one hand and a shovel in the other. When she asked me what I was doing there, I told her what was most likely the truth: that I didn't really know. Judging by appearances, my plan was to dig up his body and wrap him up tighter.

"You know he's dead, right?" she asked after a while.

"Uh–huh," I said. "I was worried he was cold."

There's a small cherry tree shading our graveyard. I remember how hopeful we felt when we planted it. Our world was shiny and new back then. Nothing was irrevocable, everything was possible. I had not yet concluded that the bet I could not cover involved my own happiness, as I had not yet come to understand that the life I was living was, in fact, real. My wife laid the shovel beneath the cherry tree, took my hand, and led me toward the house. "It's late. Why don't you come back to bed." She was about to tell me that everything would be better in the morning, but I watched her swallow those words. She's a realist. It's been a very long time since anything was better in the morning.

PART ONE

Walking on water wasn't built in a day.

—Jack Kerouac

1

Not too long ago, I took all the money I had in the world and bought a postage stamp of a farm in Chimayo, New Mexico. It was an impulse buy. I didn't know much about country living, had never entertained secret pastoral fantasies. One moment I was a money-grubbing bastard, the next a guy negotiating for a donkey. Sure, there was the recent conclusion that nothing in common remained between the life I had imagined and the one I was leading—but did farm animals solve this particular problem?

It wasn't much of a problem. Just another existential crisis in the early spring of 2007, and they were in fashion that year. It was the season of nowhere to hide. The economy was lousy, the ice caps melting. There were water wars on the horizon and oil wars under way, and those bees kept dying. Global pandemic came back on the menu. We were freakishly short of food. And this, the experts said, was just the warm-up round. The term scientists have coined for our current planetary die-off is the "Sixth Great Extinction." I couldn't remember ever not feeling tired. All that seemed clear was that at some point we had butchered the job and begun to call up down and right left, and just about everybody I knew could no longer find their way home.

Like others, I had learned the necessary stagecraft. During my waking hours I was a competent enough act as far as such things were concerned: a journalist by trade; a taker of notes, meetings, and an acceptable level of nonprescription pharmaceuticals; a waterer of house plants; fully capable of handling most cutlery; able to recall Spencer Tracy's advice on thesping—"remember your lines and don't walk into the furniture"—during those times of need. As I turned forty that year, there had been plenty of times of need.

In four decades I'd managed to accumulate some hard facts, but little true wisdom. I can say for certain that the Fifth Great Extinction was the one that killed off the dinosaurs, but didn't think to ask anyone a question about Chimayo before moving there. I was unaware that my new home sits in the heart of the Española Valley and that the *Rio Grande Sun* is the newspaper that serves that valley. I did not know that the *Sun*'s weekly police blotter had lately become something of a national amusement. Jay Leno liked the woman who smuggled heroin inside a burrito to her boyfriend in jail. National Public Radio liked the man "in a white Dodge chasing people around with a sword" and the guy wearing "a blue sweater and blue pants talking to the robotic horse in front of the grocery store," and the one who "challenged his entire family to a fight and was presently hitting his mother."

It had also escaped notice that Chimayo has one of the highest rates of drug addiction in the country and that a significant portion of the local population was arrested in September 1999 when Operation Tar Pit swept through town. Nor did I hear the August 18, 2005, NPR broadcast that included the commentary of local clean-living activist Dr. Fernando Bayardo, who pointed out that such abuse has been entrenched in this area for over fifty years. "You have a grandmother shooting up with a grandchild. You have family members shooting up together. It's not something the teenage son hides from other family members. How are you going to change those unhealthy lifestyles and habits and develop new norms?"

I had no idea how to develop new norms. All that was certain was that my girlfriend and I had been thrown out of our house in

Los Angeles with no other options beyond the just plain dumb. In our case, the just plain dumb was deciding to bet everything on a bunch of dogs and a pie-in-the-sky list of homesteading desires. The dogs we'll get to in a moment. The desires were organized into a wish list of sorts, written the night after we'd learned we were being booted, in a state of not so quiet desperation. A number of the items on that list were critical. My girlfriend had lupus. I had Lyme. Together we were two tenors with multiple sclerosis shy of an auto-immune quartet. We needed long days of brilliant sunshine because we needed to walk. Few zoning restrictions and lots of space were also important because we had a bunch of animals and plans for more. Unfortunately, what we didn't have was all that much money.

The only location in America that fit all our desires was Santa Fe, New Mexico, but Santa Fe was nearly as expensive as Los Angeles. Maybe an outlying community that had escaped the housing boom was the pipe dream. Oprah Winfrey had a ten-million-dollar mansion in the only outlying community we'd heard about, so maybe this was the crack-pipe dream. There were forty items on our wish list. We had the budget for ten. The thing about Chimayo—we got thirty-nine. I should have known there was a pretty good reason for this, but by the time that puzzle was solved, talking to a robotic horse in front of the grocery store made as much sense as anything else I could think up.

2

About six weeks before I bought the farm, I decided that life weighed too much. So I gave away three thousand books, six garbage bags of clothing, four bookcases, three chairs, three backpacks, two tables, two pairs of skis, two surfboards, two computers, an old skateboard, a torn tent, a packed filing cabinet, a small comic book collection, some entomological gear left over from the bug-collecting phase, a bit of pornography—two-thirds of everything by the end. I had decided to move in with my girlfriend. She lived in a very small house.

My girlfriend's name is Joy. Her small house sat just south of the Santa Monica Mountains, just north of Hollywood, in the township of Los Feliz—two words that translate from Spanish to English as "the happy." Nearby is the Griffith Park Observatory, the Greek Theater, and the three thousand other acres that collectively make up Griffith Park. The park was bequeathed to the city of Los Angeles in December 1896, a sort of Christmas present from the appropriately named Griffith J. Griffith. His gift came with only one condition: "It must be made a place of recreation and rest for the masses, a resort for the rank and file, for the plain people." We were the plain people and—for a short while—we lived in *the happy*.

Our house was rented, cheap, possibly haunted, and measured out to exactly 666 square feet. It perched atop a steep cliff, surrounded by a dense thicket of tall trees. Inside, a small living room gave way to a smaller bedroom and on into a kitchen the size of a ship's galley. Everywhere, the paint peeled and pipes broke. There were cracks in the walls, holes in the floor, and doors that wouldn't quite shut. Even the stairs leading up that cliff were not much more than a makeshift ladder of rotting wood, but life at the top was quiet and calm and the living room was a wall of windows. We had fallen in love looking out those windows, looking at our view of the happy.

Mahatma Gandhi once said, "There is more to life than increasing its speed," and while I agree completely, two weeks after Joy and I moved in together, we moved out together. There was no other choice. Our landlord had bought too many properties back when the getting was good. In person, he'd told us ours was the last he'd planned on developing. "Two years at least—and a six-month warning before I give you the boot," was what he'd said. We had been going on faith here, as none of this was in writing. In writing was an already expired lease followed by a month-to-month contract. That contract gave us thirty days to vacate and no recourse. When we mentioned lawyers, he mentioned the ASPCA. That, as they say, was the end of that.

Our problems were more than a few. The first was simple economics. We were broke. Certainly I had the money to buy that house in New Mexico, but that was the entirety of my savings account, and we'd been living off that savings account for much of the past year. We were both writers. The magazine industry was in the tank, and the publishing industry wasn't far behind. It was a silly time to try to make a living out of words, but it was a silly time in general. Anyway, our real problem was the dogs.

The reason we lived in a broken-down house atop a steep cliff was that that house came with an exceptionally large yard and exceptionally few neighbors and we needed both because there are seven animal shelters in Los Angeles and dozens more in surrounding communities. At capacity the bigger ones hold about two hundred animals, and they're almost always at capacity. There's only one way to make more space. Canines may be man's best friend, but most of these shelters still have ninety percent kill rates. They euthanize more than a thousand dogs a month in the City of Angels, and Joy spent much of her time trying to even those odds.

Dog rescue involves plucking a dog off death row in the hopes of eventually finding the animal a home. Most of these animals arrive in pretty poor shape. Rehab takes months of hard work. It often takes thousands of dollars in medical care—much of which comes out of the rescuer's pocket. Occasionally, after all that, some of these dogs end up too sick or too difficult to be adoptable. Dog rescuers call these "lifers." In my late twenties, an old girlfriend awoke one morning to end our relationship. "I want eight kids, you don't want any," was her reasoning. While I couldn't fault her logic, she'd long known of my antipathy toward children. It had taken her over a year to realize there was no changing my mind. Not much later, for advertising purposes, I printed up a T-shirt reading *Dogs Not Kids*. I still feel that way—but lifers add a whole other dimension to the equation.

Years back, Joy had started out rescuing English bull terriers. For those unfamiliar, these are squat white beasts created by some eighteenth-century madman intent on crossing a bulldog, a pit bull, and a Dalmatian. They were bred for bull baiting, a process that involved leaping at the underbelly of a bull, clamping jaws to testicles, and applying something like sixteen hundred pounds per square inch of pressure to said testicles. Eventually the bull fell down. Then the dogs released the balls and tore out the throat. Until it was outlawed in 1835, this is what passed for fun in Britain.

Afterward, bull terriers became fighting dogs, meaning they

were still bred for aggression. Their albino coats are highly prized, but the inbreeding required for such coloration leaves them with compromised immune systems and limited social skills. They also have an extremely short intestinal tract, which leads to bad digestion and worse gas. The results are an aggressive, easily agitated, stubborn, single-minded fireplug of a fart machine so damn macho that the only other dogs Joy's bull terrier wouldn't attack on sight were Chihuahuas—thus she had five of them.

And there was also some kind of dachshund-beagle hybrid, and then my half-husky, half-Rottweiler got added into the mix. We totaled out at eight—and they were all lifers. This was a little tricky since Los Angeles's canines-per-household law specifies three as the legal limit. Trying to find a landlord willing to bend this rule under the best of circumstances was difficult. Then the real estate market stalled and the rental market soared. The city's occupancy rate stood at 96 percent. Under such conditions, finding an affordable apartment that took eight dogs was right up there with world peace and ample leg room in coach class on the list of things that weren't going to happen anytime soon.

It was a Sunday when we found out our house was being sold. I came back from running errands to find Joy crying on the couch. She told me the landlord had dropped the hammer, and then told me she had made a decision. She was moving to Mexico, where life was cheap and they didn't care how many dogs one owned. I had no desire to live in Mexico. I had no chance to revive my career in Mexico. This wasn't, it is worth pointing out, her first choice. It was her last chance. She knew I couldn't move to Mexico with her, but it had taken over two years of constant looking to find our small house and we didn't have two years. We had less than a month—and almost no money. She couldn't stand the thought of being a burden. "You want a life in the city, a great career, and you're not going to get that with me and my dogs."

All of which might be true. It was also true that I didn't want those things anymore. What I wanted was to feel like something in this world mattered, even if it had been a long time since that had been the case. What was the case was that I've been downright silly for Joy ever since the day we met. I gave away a lot of stuff to move in with her, and truthfully, it all could have gone. Most days, my gal and her dogs were the only things around worth keeping. So no, none of us were going to Mexico, though all of us were going somewhere—that much for sure.

3

"I have measured out my life with coffee spoons" are nine words that T. S. Eliot once wrote. During the period of time I'm talking about I would often repeat these words to myself as some kind of talisman, meant to ward off . . . well, I was never quite sure. They were often stuck in my head when I was stuck in traffic, among the hundred-foot billboards, the thousand-dollar haircuts, the everybody with their shopping bags, the endless repetition of strip malls and strip clubs and suntans—this whole mad crush that was often Los Angeles. These words were my way of putting into perspective the feeling that had become much of my day. I was forty years old and no longer sure my life meant much of anything.

I had come into adulthood equipped with the essentially romantic delusion that life would get easier. It had not gotten easier, but had gotten something. I began making choices. I gave up cooking for thirty seconds in the microwave. I wrote books but stopped reading. I missed the days when the drugs did the work. I wasn't unhappy so much as unsure. Just the constant sensation that whatever else might be true, this was definitely not what I'd ordered.

It was a time when I wasn't alone in questioning the way I was living. Joy and I had been having philosophical differences. When being polite, we called these differences "art versus altruism." We were not always polite. I believed in creativity, the act of making something from nothing, the high-minded transfer of inspiration, and other such claptrap. She felt the making of art was inherently selfish, and instead trumpeted the quiet generosity of laying it all on the line for every blessed creature. It doesn't sound like much of a fight—but it was.

What seemed to be at stake was the best way to live in the world; what was really at stake was the best way to live together. Dog rescue is often emotionally exhausting and physically time-swallowing, while freelance writing is more of the same. Love doesn't always hold up under those conditions. Joy's had both ex-boyfriends and ex-husbands grow jealous of her dogs—which helps explain how they became exes—while I hadn't managed a long-term relationship in decades.

Then there was our financial future. Neither of our causes came with a great paycheck, a downside I combated with the traditional metaphysics: *do what you love and the rest will follow.* But with both of us doing what we loved, would the rest really follow? And if one of us had to get a real job? Since her higher calling involved living creatures and mine involved putting words together in a straight line, common sense said I should be the one to make the sacrifice. Unfortunately, in my experience, common sense and higher callings are contradictions in terms.

It was into this debate that a dog named Damien arrived. He was not much over ten pounds, flea-bit and back broke. His entire life had been spent tied to a radiator, his home range a two-foot patch of hard-packed dirt, his collar a thin metal chain dug so deep into his flesh it required surgery to remove. There were plenty of available comforts lying around; Damien was past the point of available comforts. For his first three months with us, he stayed beneath the house, living inside an old truck tire, trying to kill anything that came close. And more and more, I was coming around to his perspective.

It was clearly time for a change. Joy's side of the argument hinged on the crucial fact that besides doing animal rescue she was also a writer, with two books to her name and more success than had ever come my way. She had lived the art and preferred the altruism. Until I'd done the same, in her opinion, my opinion remained suspect.

"Now wait just a minute," I tried to protest. "I definitely have some experience with altruism."

"Which is?"

"Like everybody else who backpacked through Asia after college, I had sex with a Peace Corps volunteer."

"Uh-huh," she said, "absolutely, that counts."

So I guess you could say that when I traded forty years of the mostly ordinary for a world made of dog, I was trying to prove her wrong. Or me right. Or something else entirely. Turns out it was something else entirely.

But what that something is—is a bit of a longer story.

4

Chimayo has always been a place people came to in times of confusion and despair, though sometimes their arrival was not entirely voluntary. Its earliest inhabitants were outlaws, sent to this backwater as punishment. The town began in 1680, established as a penal colony for the Spanish Empire, and has never completely escaped this past. It sits thirty miles north of Santa Fe, in the middle of the Sangre de Cristo Mountains, on what is locally considered the "high road" to Taos. The high road also turns out to be something of an apt moniker, as Chimayo is further known for being the black tar heroin overdose capital of these United States and, well, for miracles.

Those overdoses occur at four times the national average. Those miracles occur at El Santuario, a small church said to be the "Lourdes of America." Lourdes is the spot in southwestern France where the Virgin Mary appeared to St. Bernadette in 1858. In the years since, its waters have become the stuff of therapeutic wonder. While the Virgin has yet to appear in New Mexico, sometime around 1810, Don Bernardo Abeita saw a light bursting from a nearby hillside. The record is unclear about whether Abeita was a farmer working in his fields or a local friar performing penances, but we are certain that after digging in the spot where the glow emerged, he unearthed a peculiar crucifix: *Nuestro Señor de Esquipulas*, known colloquially as the "Black Christ."

The Black Christ is a religious icon native to Guatemala. Not sure what it was doing in northern New Mexico, Abeita called in the local priest, Friar Sebastián Álvarez, who brought the cross nine miles down the road to an altar in a church in neighboring Santa Cruz. Overnight, the crucifix disappeared from the altar and reappeared in its original hole. The next day, Álvarez brought it back to Santa Cruz and back it went to Chimayo. When this happened a third time, folks decided to leave well enough alone. A small chapel was built near the hillside, the Black Christ installed on the altar.

Not soon after, the miraculous healings began. In a letter to the Episcopal See of Durango, dated November 16, 1813, Friar Álvarez told of people traveling hundreds of miles to "to seek cures for their ailment." By 1816, these healings had became so numerous that they needed to replace the small shrine with a larger adobe mission. The mission has since become a National Historic Landmark, with pilgrims still showing up in droves. Every year, nearly three hundred thousand make the trek, some traveling on foot from as far away as Albuquerque. The crucifix remains on the chapel altar, though its curative abilities have recently been overshadowed by *El Posito*—the sacred sand pit.

The sand pit is the original hole from which the crucifix was unearthed, the dirt said to be the source of its power. While El Santuario is among the holiest Catholic sites in America, this is actually a bit of divine appropriation. When the Tewa Indians lived nearby, they called the place *Tsimajopokwi*, which technically means "waters," but nominally means "medicinal hot springs." The Tewa were slaughtered by the conquistadors, the hot springs long dried up. When it came to naming the spot, the Spanish dubbed it Chimayo, for "good flaking stone," a reference to the local abundance of obsidian. Whatever the case, just off the main chapel, there's a little alcove known as the "healing room," littered with cast-off crutches and canes and thousands of notes of gratitude for the thaumaturgy performed by this holy mud.

It's a long thirteen hours from California to New Mexico, and by the time I got there I was tired and sore and could have used some of that mud. Worse, I'd left LA in a hurry, throwing on whatever was around and jumping in my truck and only later realizing that whatever was around was perhaps not appropriate. Some dogs, they'll piss on anything. By the time I'd noticed the stains the road had been hit and the hours logged and it was late evening and pouring rain. I had arrived in downtown Santa Fe, parked, and gone in search of coffee. I was crossing a gas station parking lot when a voice called out to me. I stopped and turned and found a homeless man sitting on the side of the curb. He was dirty and skinny and missing most teeth and both shoes, but took one look at me and said: "Jesus—you got a place to sleep?"

I had yet to choose a motel, so shook my head no.

"Shelter's two blocks up and one block left," he said, then looked me over again and added, "I don't mean to be rude, but I've got some clean pants you can have."

There was no need of pants; there was some need of booze. I bought us a six-pack at the gas station. With no dry spots to be found, we headed over to a nearby park to drink beer under the dead branches of an old tree. Along the way, he recounted a recent speed binge in Tijuana. He was Native American himself, apparently didn't have much truck with Mexicans.

"Fuck-fuckers, throat-slitting, piss-takers," was how he put it—whatever the hell that means. "But tell you what," he continued, "damn Mexicans finally figured out how to cook themselves some meth."

I didn't know what to say to that, so we sat in silence for a while. Eventually he took another swig of beer and asked what I was doing in Santa Fe. I didn't know what to say to that either: There are some demons we kill and some that kill us, and after a while these too become hard to distinguish? Instead, I settled on the truth.

"I came for the dogs."

"Sure as shit," he said, "ain't no shortage of those women in this town."

5

I bought the house two days later, but by the time the banks were dealt with and the papers signed and the long hours driven back to Los Angeles, we had less than two weeks to spare. Ten days to dismantle our lives and pack up our house and bid our farewells and nobody was getting much sleep, not even the dogs. The phone rang constantly. Whenever anyone asked, Joy said we were leaving California to go run a "real rescue" in New Mexico. A lot of people asked. Eventually I asked as well.

"We've got eight dogs, two humans, and a shoe box for a house—but this isn't a real rescue?"

"Fancy a road trip?" she said.

This was about five days before we were supposed to leave and I didn't really fancy a road trip, but what if I didn't fancy a real rescue either? I had been to Chimayo already and knew that whatever we might find there, it was going to take a while to find it. Our new home had been chosen because of its distance from, not proximity to, civilization. I was about to be up close and personal with this woman and her dreams and not much else. I got dressed. I decided to see what a "real rescue" entailed.

There are a half dozen real rescues spread across the California's Central Valley, with actress Tippi Hedren's Shambala Preserve being the most famous. Shambala is Sanskrit for "peace" and "harmony," which in Hedren's case meant "lions" and "tigers." I have some fond memories of the Ringling Bros. Circus, so a big-cat sanctuary sounded great to me. Joy thought circuses cruel and, since we were moving to save dogs, figured we should see something in the canid family.

"Plus," she said, "Tippi's rich."

"So?"

"We're not."

Joy chose the Wolf Mountain Sanctuary because it was one of the few where you could actually "interact" with the wolves. I didn't know what interact meant, but the sanctuary turned out to be a small house and some large pens on the dusty edge of the Mojave Desert. This was California's Lucerne Valley, a hinterland so hot that in 1912 the town council voted unanimously to hold Fourth of July celebrations every year—just in the safer, cooler months of autumn. Even in the autumn, safer is a matter of per-spective. When we turned off the freeway and I got my first look, I knew immediately what Joy had meant by "we're not."

Rich rescuers can afford lots of space in lots of upmarket loca-tions. Real rescuers cannot. The Lucerne Valley is the kind of place they end up instead. And it's the kind of place things go wrong. This was pioneer country, the West those young men once went. These days that tradition is mainly upheld by chemists pioneering new ways to cook meth. The desert is full of their detritus, the bars thick with their customers. Even the rattlesnakes are nervous. Anyway, the sanctuary wasn't much to see, save the wolves.

The wolves, though, they were something else. Describing ani-mal encounters is often tricky because animals are frequently the basis for our descriptions. If I say a German shepherd is as big as a wolf, you know exactly what I'm talking about. But standing in a pen with a real wolf for the first time, my reaction was: "Holy shit, that thing's as big as a wolf." So what, exactly, was I talking about?

The thing I was talking about weighed in at ninety pounds and stood a few inches away from me. Another was right behind it. When Joy and I entered the pen for our "interaction," the wolves were out of sight in a far corner. We'd been told to belly up to a raised wooden platform in a different corner so the animals could come over and introduce themselves. What anyone failed to mention was that because of the height of the platform and the size of the wolves that meeting was going to take place face-to-face.

Large dogs have never bothered me. I'm happy to wade into a pack of pit bulls or Rottweilers or whatever. I thought the same would hold true with wolves. It didn't hold. When the wolves walked across the pen and jumped up on the platform I was again reminded that mortal dread is not a comfortable feeling. Occasionally, we'd been warned, a wolf may attempt to adopt a visitor into the pack. In this auspicious ceremony, the animal will rub his muzzle along the human's neck, transferring pheromones, marking us as friend, not foe. After the wolf in front of me decided I was worthy of adoption and closed the gap between his jaws and my neck to start that process, mortal dread is really what I felt.

When Stephen Jay Gould said, "Consider the earth's history as the old measure of the English yard, the distance from the King's nose to the tip of his outstretched hand. One stroke of a nail file on his middle finger erases human history," he was trying to offer some insight into what scientists call *deep time*. This is both the concept of geological history and the incredible shrinking sensation that occurs when confronting geological history. I've had this feeling only once before, hiking a 200-million-year-old canyon in southern Utah, but that was deep time at some remove, not wrapped around my neck. The second the wolf made contact, primordial lightning struck. At least it felt like lightning. Suffice it to say a large quantity of electricity shot up from the bottom of my ass and out through the top of my head. I wanted to gasp, was terrified to move. The only reason

I didn't wet my pants was because the sensation zapped the piss right out of me. If this was what a real rescue was like—hell, I should have started one years ago.

We left the pen and walked over to the gift shop, not really a gift shop, actually an old card table covered in cheap cloth and tribal jewelry and parked against a corner of an overcrowded back porch. There was one young Indian girl sitting behind the table, with an older white woman standing beside her. I studied the jewelry, Joy struck up the conversation. The woman was the sanctuary's owner, the girl her daughter. The owner told us about business—good during the summer months, not so good other times. Occasionally the wolves found pickup work in Hollywood, dancing with Kevin Costner among other jobs.

"Mostly, though . . ."

Joy waited for the woman to finish that thought. I waited for her to finish that thought. The woman picked up a small silver bracelet and spun it around her finger.

"Mostly it takes a lot of jewelry to feed sixteen wolves."

Joy asked if it was only the two of them doing all the work. Both mother and daughter started laughing.

"I've got help," said the woman.

"Yeah," said her daughter, "she's got thirty-six children."

Turned out wayward wolves weren't all this woman had been adopting.

"There's not many options around here," the woman said, "but there's a lot of meth. Same old story: Dad's in jail or dead or on his way, Mom's not far behind. Not many of the kids they leave behind are right in the head. Either I adopt them or they go feral."

I looked up at her house. It wasn't much bigger than our house. We were living on top of each other with our eight dogs. This woman had sixteen wolves and thirty-six kids. This was about the time I realized that a "real rescue" might require real sacrifice, and this seemed different from the kind I was familiar with—the kind that gets you laid when you talk about it in bars.

6

The thermometer started to climb on our drive home from Wolf Mountain and kept climbing throughout the night. By the following afternoon, the canines were agitated, the humans were agitated, the temperature was in the low hundreds and rising fast. In a few days, the resulting combination of dry timber and blistering heat would burn one-quarter of Griffith Park to the ground, but before that happened we had to maneuver two old cars and eight old dogs across Death Valley on our way to New Mexico. The cars were prone to heatstroke. The dogs were prone to heatstroke. We were trying to outrun the front end of a massive heat wave by driving across the hottest desert in America—there may be a moral here, either for my decision to give dog rescue a try or for decisions in general. Like many things, it was too soon to tell.

Elise was Joy's good friend, occasional dog rescue partner, and something of a speed demon. Elise was driving. Joy rode shotgun. There were six small dogs in their car. I had the bigger dogs and more boxes than one should ever pack into a truck. Otis, the bull terrier, was one of the bigger dogs. One of the other things that distinguishes bull terriers is their need for human company. If he had his way, Otis liked to be touching a human, and because he was a bull terrier, he often had his way. When Joy wasn't around, he liked to sleep under my desk, beneath my feet, no matter what he had to destroy to get there.

There is a learning curve with dogs, and on the drive to New Mexico I learned that Otis had some difficulty distinguishing between my office and a moving vehicle. In the moving vehicle, he was supposed to sleep in a makeshift bed in the back of the truck. Somewhere outside of Needles, California, Otis decided things were not to his liking, smashed a box into my chest, a stereo into my head, and a cactus onto my lap, then dove for his favorite spot, directly beneath my feet. We were doing around seventy-five at the time. When I finally got him off the gas pedal we were sliding off the shoulder at a blurry one hundred and ten.

"Love me, love my dogs," Joy had said not long after we met. I didn't love her dogs, or not at first. As a rule, small dogs are yappy and pesky, and after five years in Los Angeles—where the well-heeled set like to treat pets as fashion accessories—difficult to abide merely on principle. But if I wanted to do something completely different with the second half of my life than I'd done with the first, than I wanted to make different mistakes. One dog is a pet, eight is a pack. I'd never been part of a pack before, so decided this might be a different mistake.

There were some drawbacks. Take Gidget. Dog rescuers often specialize in both types of dogs and types of dog problems. Joy started out with bull terriers but soon realized she was better at working with small dogs and best at small dogs with serious immunological problems. Gidget was one of those problems. She arrived one winter morning, about three months before our move to New Mexico. The smallest dog I'd ever seen, she was not much more than two pounds, and looked as if someone had dipped those pounds into a vat of boiling oil. Gidget had demodectic mange. Her coat was destroyed, her eyes bulging out, her brain not quite right. Maybe it was the mange, maybe she was a few spoons shy of a place setting, maybe she just felt the funk—whatever the reason—this dog had to dance. Her dance involved standing in one place and moving her paws straight up and straight down, not unlike a marionette on mescaline. Trying to have sex with Gidget doing the last tango in Paris on my head, that was one of the drawbacks.

The Buddha taught four noble truths: life is suffering, suffering has a cause, the end of suffering is the goal of life, thus the removal of the cause of suffering is how we should pass our days. These facts are meant to be understood not as pessimism but rather as practicality. While Joy isn't a Buddhist, no other notion so captures both her worldview and her way of being—especially when it came to dogs. A little while back, Joy made some money off her first book. She took that money and moved to Mexico and opened a no-kill dog shelter. It was an idea better in principle than in practice. Mexico is a Catholic country, and Catholic doctrine teaches that dogs have no soul. In Mexico, anything without a soul isn't worth the effort. The Church also teaches that prophylactics are a sin against God and it also strikes me as significantly harder to care for animals when one has so many children that there's not enough money to feed them all.

The locals shunned her work, stole her medicines, threatened her person. After five years of trying, the money was gone. Joy moved her operation from the safer center of town to the dangerous outskirts of the barrio. Her nights were spent sleeping on the floor of the shelter, cuddling an axe for protection. She did this for three months straight, then filed for bankruptcy. This may not have been what the Buddha had in mind, but when Joy talks about ending suffering, this is exactly the kind of commitment she intends.

Along similar lines, we stopped for the night in the town of Kingman, Arizona. It was Saturday night and nearly every hotel in town was booked solid. The Laughlin River Run was going on. The Laughlin River Run is a motorcycle rally of some renown, and since 2007 marked their greatest turnout ever, some seventy-five thousand enthusiasts had shown up. The streets, sidewalks, parking lots, and damn near every other inch of available real estate were packed with bikes and bikers, and our motel was no exception.

Kingman is a mountain town and thus was impervious to the heat wave baking the rest of the West. Early the next morning, temperatures were in the low thirties. Chihuahuas are desert mammals and aren't adapted for serious cold. It takes almost no time for a small dog to freeze to death in the mountains. Ever since we'd decided to move to Chimayo—which sits around six thousand feet—Joy had been trying to figure out how to keep our animals alive under these conditions. Then she solved the dilemma by raiding the going-out-of-business sale of a typical LA pet store. It was a brilliant solution up until that cold Kingman morning when Joy asked me to walk the dogs.

Our room was tucked in an out-of-the-way corner of the motel. I walked the dogs out of that room, down a staircase, around a corner, and around another, trying for a small grassy area behind the parking lot. As I rounded that last corner, I found twenty-five black-leather-clad motorcycle enthusiasts of the Hell's Angel variety lining the parking lot. During the 2003 Laughlin River Run, these same Angels had started a riot that claimed three lives and led to forty-two arrests. In her favor, when Joy first said "Love me, love my dogs," perhaps she hadn't known that would eventually include parading three sweater-clad Chihuahuas and one Gidget—decked out in her pink rhinestone Playboy Bunny special—past twenty-five Hell's Angels.

7

In his book *Finite and Infinite Games*, the New York University professor of religion James Carse distinguishes between the two kinds of games played here on earth, with finite games being activities such as politics, sport, and war, where rules are followed, boundaries exist, and a consensus winner is declared. Infinite games are those where rules are fluid, outcomes unreachable, and a participant's only goal is the continuation of play. All relationships are a finite game when treated as items on a checklist. Carse believes they become infinite when "it can only be said that these persons played with each other and in such a way that what they began cannot be finished."

Which brings us to my dog Ahab.

Ahab and I met in the middle of the third year of this new millennium and the middle of my third year fighting Lyme disease. Back then, I was a seriously abused human. Ahab was a seriously abused dog. I had spent the better part of those years in bed; Ahab arrived by a rougher road. By the time we got together, his back had been broken, his tail snapped, and most of his teeth knocked out. There were cigarette burns running down his spine. I nursed him back to health and he nursed me back to health and the end result felt a lot like what Carse considered an infinite game.

Before moving in with Joy, Ahab and I shared a small apartment about a block off Hollywood Boulevard, less than a hundred feet from the spot where I once watched a woman get her throat slit in a lover's quarrel and just up the street from the site of a contract killing. The contract killing occurred inside an old dive, the kind of nondescript bar that friends of mine from the Ohio of my childhood would have called a "stop-and-fight." The gunman executed his victim with a double tap to the chest and a coup de grâce to the forehead, which, as one witness later remarked, is the kind of precision not often found in this neighborhood.

One night back then, after a well-spent evening seeing the Pogues play the Wiltern, I turned my truck down my street and found a crowd of people standing in front of my apartment building. While there's nothing unusual about crowded sidewalks in Los Angeles, finding a crowd in my neighborhood often meant nothing good. As I drove past, I noticed that all of these people were pointing, shouting, and staring straight at the sky. I followed their gaze up three stories to a small window ledge, not much more than five inches wide, tucked near the corner of the building, where a large dog was standing—apparently contemplating a life-ending leap of some kind.

It took me about ten seconds to realize the ledge in question was the one directly outside my living room window, and ten more to conclude that the dog in question was Ahab. I don't quite know what happened next—somehow my car got parked—but I have no memory of such things. What I recall is banging through that assembled crowd, thinking Don't look up, don't look up, as people shouted, "Is that your dog?" There was a suggestion about using a taut blanket as a crash pad and a question about my fitness for pet ownership—but I didn't have time for either discussion.

The hubbub continued as I shoulder-bashed some gentleman out of the way, but faded as I tore up three flights of steps. When I got to my floor, I found a security guard—who knows where he'd come from—standing in the hallway outside my door. My guess was that he was unwilling to break inside for fear of startling Ahab, but again, I didn't stick around long enough to ask. When I got the door open I noticed a number of things at once. Before I'd left for the concert, there had been a *New Zealand Herald* article sitting on my desk, atop a stack of other curiosities. While the rest of those items were still on the desk, the article was now lying in the middle of my floor. It told the strange story of a historic bridge on the west coast of Scotland that had lately become the site of an unprecedented series of canine suicides. In the months preceding the article, so many dogs had leaped over the railing and plunged to their deaths that locals started calling the spot "Rover's Leap."

A second after I saw the *Herald* article in the middle of my floor, I noticed my front window—which had been closed and locked before I left for the concert—now halfway open. Ahab was perched on the other side of that window. Indecision came next. After the sweaty palms and the stutter steps and the growing realization that I didn't have a plan came the heart pounding and the almost puking and the decision to just try to grab the beast. The beast had other ideas. Before I could reach him, Ahab lifted his head to meet my gaze, then casually nudged his snout beneath the bottom of the window, grunted once, and lifted the pane a few more inches so he could drop neatly to the floor. Down on the street I heard cheering. Back in the apartment, Ahab went over to his water bowl, had a couple of gulps, and lay down for a nap. This too might be some kind of infinite game. Then again, it might not. There was no one around to ask, and even if there had been, how exactly do you frame that question?

8

Something changed after that evening. In the moments it took Ahab to climb off that ledge and drop back into my apartment, my vision focused and my head cleared, and it was the roll of this wave that I rode right out of my old life in California and into my new life in Chimayo. I traded the finite games of the big city for the infinite games of the country and did so because there seemed to be some kind of cosmic lesson unfolding, a lesson that bound my quest for meaning and my girlfriend's love of animals to larger and stronger forces that are hard to reduce to the narrative construction of simple sentences.

Along similar lines, the donkey I'd negotiated for was named Fuzzy. In the days after the purchase and before our arrival, Fuzzy became the symbolic center of my new decision to find the meaning of life in the world of zoology. I didn't yet know the full specifics of that symbolism, but planned on asking my donkey as soon as we got the chance to talk.

That chance arrived right after we arrived in Chimayo. While Joy looked over her new digs and Elise started unpacking the truck, I dashed down to the pasture to check on Fuzzy. My concern right then was less about answers to my questions and more about donkeys being equines. Equines are social animals. Most social animals are social because they are prey species. Prey species confront danger best through numbers. Think of zebra herds crossing the Serengeti and you have a close approximation of the numbers that make equines most comfortable. To this end, Fuzzy once passed her days in the company of a doting owner and a healthy assortment of barnyard critters. Then I bought her house and that owner went off to greener pastures and that assortment went off to greener pastures and Fuzzy was left alone in a pen for the time it took us to drive across the Southwest.

The first thing I noticed was that Fuzzy was snorting, braying, stomping, and rather unhappy about her few days of enforced solitude. The second thing I noticed was that Fuzzy was a significantly larger donkey than the one I remembered. I remembered a skinny, two-hundred-pound animal. She was close to double that, very little of it flab. Her neck was a long braid of muscle, her hindquarters stronger than her neck. Before leaving California, I'd figured I could wrangle this beast. Before leaving California, I'd had no idea what kind of country moron I would soon prove to be.

I eased the gate open, stepped into the pen, and gave Fuzzy a good scratch between the ears. That scratch seemed to be working, so I was scrubbing my way down her back when Elise walked over to say hello. The pen's gate hung on tall wooden posts loosely wrapped in chicken wire. Elise had gotten two steps inside the gate when the petting zoo closed for the day. Fuzzy lowered her head, snorted once, rocked backward, then shot forward. The full weight of her charge hit me square in the back. She knocked me ass over teakettle and drove that teakettle straight up into the air. On my way down, she rammed me right into the gate. I took chicken wire to the face and a fence post through the chest, and that's about when the honeymoon ended.

In the next moment, Fuzzy gave me another smash to the back, then noticed Elise. She caught her in the shoulder and spun her to the dirt, missing head with hoof by millimeters, before galloping hell's bells for Joy—who went face-first into a hedge of rosebushes to get out of the way. This was something of a blessing, as it spared her the sight of what happened next. Next, Fuzzy tried to stomp the small dogs to death, and when they proved too elusive to kill, went at the bigger ones. She reared up and crashed down, missing Ahab on her first try and Otis on her second. Before she got a chance at a third we got a rope around her neck and a prayer off to the gods, and one or the other seemed to do the trick.

After we dragged Fuzzy back into her pen, she began to bray and bray and didn't stop. The sound was extraterrestrial, like a fog-horn being tortured. We knew she needed company, but company wasn't easy to come by. The dogs clearly weren't fitting the bill. Goats were the obvious choice, except we had a small orchard and wanted to keep those fruit trees. Goats ate bark and killed fruit trees. So company meant another equine—which we couldn't af-ford. We'd come to New Mexico to help animals and quickly real-ized there was only one way to help Fuzzy.

"We have to find her a new home," said Joy.

"It's the only way," seconded Elise.

The dog rescuers were resigned to their decision; the signifi-cant other was nowhere close. Sure, it had taken us all of five min-utes in the country to get our asses kicked by an ass, but wasn't that the party we'd come for? Giving up on the totem animal just days after meeting the totem animal seemed a bad precedent to set. Martin Luther King Jr. had a dream. I had a donkey—and couldn't even hold on to that. Oh yeah, my meaning-of-life quest was turn-ing out exactly as planned.

PART TWO

We do not seem to be getting to the point.

—Joan Didion

9

In 2002, after my first two years of illness, countless doctors, and no real cures, I stumbled upon a nearly forgotten list of things to do before I died. The list was fifteen years old and fourteen items long. A number of those items had already been checked off, a number were no longer relevant, and the vast majority required a level of health and fitness no longer mine. The only one left with any real potential was "get a dog," but by real potential I meant sometime in the distant future, not later in the same afternoon.

Back then, the only dog I'd ever had was a golden retriever named Corky. He arrived on my thirteenth birthday and died around my twenty-second and in the years since I'd consistently missed his company, but pet ownership required a more sedentary lifestyle than journalism permitted and, once I got sick, a more active one than my disease allowed. My good friend Joe Donnelly felt differently. He felt that way because a stray had shown up on his front doorstep and refused to leave. As Joe already had a dog of his own, and a landlord decree of one pet per apartment, keeping him wasn't an option. So he did what just about every other person in Los Angeles did when they found a stray that needed a home—he called his friend Joy.

"You have to find him a home," Joy said.

"What about—"

"A nearly destroyed Rottweiler mix? Take him to the shelter and they'll just kill him."

Finding a nearly destroyed Rottweiler mix a home is a difficult task under normal circumstances, made worse by the fact that this dog had been badly beaten and tended to bite anyone who moved too quickly, including me on first meeting. The reason that meeting took place was because I'd found that list of things to do before I died and realized there was nothing left on it I had any real chance of doing. So I followed that realization out of the house and down to the liquor store and started hyperventilating somewhere between the whiskey and the wine coolers, promptly bought several large bottles of "I don't want to feel anything anymore," and ran into Joe in the parking lot. He was canvassing the neighborhood for a home for his stray, and canvassed me as well. "Get a dog," my fifteen-year-old list had said. I was out of other ideas—so I did.

To say I didn't know what I was doing with my new ward would be polite understatement. Joe tried to explain, telling me to go to the store and buy a leash, a collar, a bag of food, a toy for him to chew on, and two bowls—one for water, another for food.

"You're going too fast," I said.

He lifted his right hand and spread his first two fingers into a peace sign.

"Two bowls," he said.

In the end, I made him write it all down. On my way home, during what would technically be my first walk with Ahab, I remember pulling out that list and staring at it, and realizing that the care of a living creature could be reduced to items one through fourteen, with one of those items being "rub belly frequently."

As time passed, my initial trepidation was replaced by a more ongoing consternation. Let's just say, that man-and-dog bonding thing, ours took a while to happen. Like a great many traumatized animals, and not that different from a great many traumatized humans, Ahab employed diffidence as a survival strategy. Months on end he kept himself apart, spending most of the day sitting on a cushion in the corner, staring straight at a wall. He always kept his back toward me, never made eye contact, barely tolerated my affection. Forget belly rubs—we were stuck on "brush shoulder without inciting violence."

This standoff was made worse by his separation anxiety. While Ahab didn't much like my company, he truly hated being left alone. When I was gone, he expressed his displeasure by strewing garbage across my apartment, tearing apart clothes, and chewing up the furniture. At first I was frustrated; then I was stumped. Should I take the advice of most dog trainers and ignore the disease of emotional trauma in favor of curing the symptom of bad behavior? Or should I take the advice of animal rescuers and ignore the behavior in favor of treating the underlying trauma? How much was my furniture really worth to me? How much was a cure really worth to me?

All this caught me a little by surprise. These were ethical questions. I lived in LA—like who the hell thought about ethical questions in LA? But with Ahab around, I thought about them constantly. How humans and animals should live peacefully together was the core of my concern. Should the goal be for Ahab and me to merge our lives, or should I follow the biblical dominion-over-the-beasts ethos and just try to wedge him into mine? If I chose the path of freedom, whose needs trumped whose? When I had a busy day at work, should Ahab get shorter walks because of it? When I had a free afternoon, did I go to the movies or did Ahab go to the beach? And what about his separation anxiety? What did responsibility really mean?

In the beginning, having no idea what responsibility really meant, I tried to change Ahab's behavior. I would return from the store to find a shredded pillow and lead him over to the mess and firmly say "No!" while trying to remain calm. After he took apart my new couch, I lost touch with calm. I was angry, and when this didn't produce the desired result, even angrier. But I hadn't gotten a dog to be mad at that dog, and scolding Ahab really wasn't getting the job done. Instead, I decided to review the facts.

These were the facts: Every time I came home to disaster, Ahab looked guilty. When I shouted at him, he looked sorry. If I could trust my read of his emotions, then he knew that what he was doing was wrong but still did it anyway. Armchair psychology said this meant one of two things: either he was so terrified of abandonment that he couldn't help himself—and what I had been interpreting as political protest was actually pure panic—or else the damage was dog language for "I'm terrified of being left alone, you stupid schmuck!" Either way, he was terrified.

Since there was no way to stop leaving him alone, I started comforting him when I got home. I would ignore the mess, apologize for my absence, and smother him with affection. I mean *smother* him. The bigger the disaster, the more love he got. I was going on instinct here, as my plan ran contrary to the advice of most dog trainers. That advice covered the gamut, but a typical example was the 2009 ABC News story "How to Cure Your Dog's Separation Anxiety." They suggest more discipline—thus cementing my position as "team leader"—or less affection—thus breaking him of his "owner addiction." Across the board, the experts were certain that my strategy— coming home and treating him, for lack of a better phrase, like a human being—would only reward and reinforce his bad behavior. As often happens in dog rescue, the experts were wrong.

Within a week, Ahab stopped destroying the furniture. Within two, he left the garbage alone. At the start of the third, he got up from the corner, walked over to the couch where I was sitting, and put a paw on the cushion. He was trembling slightly, trying to hide it, but trembling. It took him a little while to work up his nerve, but eventually he pulled himself the rest of the way up and belly-crawled over. He stopped a few inches away to gather himself. The quivering ceased, his fur lay back down, and he lifted his head to face me directly. Martin Buber once said, "An animal's eyes have the power to speak a great language," and this time no different. It really was the first time Ahab had ever held my gaze, I'm not sure what I'd been expecting—maybe fear, wariness, a hint of hope—but what I got was the weight of tradition, a combination of great furry love and truly sober nobility. It felt like Ahab was both offering me his heart and telling me of an ancient trust between our species, a sacred covenant, an honor code I didn't yet know existed. I'm pretty sure he was also telling me not to screw it up.

Then, our ethics lesson over, Ahab put his head in my lap, sighed once, and fell asleep. Not ten seconds later, he was snoring loudly. I started laughing. It had been such a profound performance. The months of buildup, the fear and trembling, the meaningful look—and for an encore, the melodic sounds of a Panzer tank in the middle of a coughing fit.

Oh, how I came to love those snores: a rumble of contentment, a rolling chortle, a great magic. These were the sounds that woke me on my second morning in Chimayo. As our furniture was still somewhere in transit, Joy and I had slept that night on the porch, in a pile of anything soft we could find. Ahab slept beside us. It had been a lovely May evening when everyone went to bed, but when that Panzer melody roused me from my slumber it was just daybreak and the ground was buried beneath a foot of snow. How had this happened? Just yesterday, my view had been sunshine and skyscrapers. Now there were snow-capped mountains in the distance and snow-covered fields in the foreground and a donkey in the middle. I was disoriented. Also freezing. I grabbed an old coat from the pile, put it on, and blinked about. It was then that I put my hand in the pocket of the coat and found Joe's old note: his advice, items one through fourteen, for the care and feeding of another living creature. I hadn't seen the note in years, but reading it again, I knew the answer to my question. I knew exactly how this had happened. I'd walked through a door marked "rub belly frequently" and never looked back.

10

Of course, there are those occasional situations where "rub belly frequently" isn't much use. Fuzzy was one of those situations. She was still miserable, but at least there was an end in sight: a note on the bulletin board at the feed store was all it had taken to find our donkey a new home. But that good fortune ran out about the time we tried to get her to that new home.

Locally, our donkey is known as a *burro verde*, which should translate to "green ass," though the title seems to be applied to the full spectrum of equines. The term is shorthand for never broken, never ridden, and never acquainted with the ways of the horse trailer. Since those unacquainted tend to get pissy when they find themselves trapped in a steel cage for the first time, some assistance was required.

Assistance came in the form of a sister of a cousin of a neighbor of a friend of an uncle, or some other infinite regress of the way things work in Chimayo. Her name was Cindy. She was full-blooded Cherokee by birth and donkey whisperer by trade and arrived one hot afternoon in a truck the size of the Dakotas, black hair and rail thin, wearing jeans and scuffed boots. Out of the corner of her mouth dangled one of what would prove to be a steady stream of Marlboros. She puffed in unapologetic celebration. While many tribes regard tobacco as a sacred plant, this was not what Cindy had in mind. She'd had open-heart surgery about three weeks back and was just celebrating her survival.

Loading a green donkey onto a horse trailer requires a delicate two-step: push from the back, lure from the front. Pushing involved locking arms across hindquarters and digging in for the long haul. Luring was done by waving oats in front of mouth and walking backward. The danger with the first was that my testicles were directly in the line of fire. The danger with the second was the love of my life being smothered in green ass. There were no other options. We dug in and lured on. We pushed and pulled, coaxed and begged. Fuzzy would not be moved. We got our backs bent and boots caked, and when neither did the trick, Cindy tied a bandana around her head, shoved another cigarette in her mouth, and squatted down with her lips inches from Fuzzy's rear end. Then she started whispering.

Her voice was soft and low and ass is not a language I speak, but my concerns just then were less about the contents of the conversation and more about Cindy's lit cigarette bobbing millimeters from Fuzzy's butt. Cindy did not seem concerned. She seemed connected. The feeling turned out to be mutual. After about five minutes of whispering, Fuzzy started nodding. Eventually she lifted one foot to test the edge of the trailer. I wasn't quite sure if I was witnessing minor miracles or Monty Python, but Cindy kept whispering and Fuzzy kept nodding. Eventually she nudged that first foot in deeper, lifted her other one, and then did this little hop-step number straight on inside like she'd been doing it on Broadway for years. I didn't get kicked, Joy didn't get crushed, the donkey whisperer jumped into her pickup and smoked on home.

It was a man named Chris Malloy who helped me make sense of the whole affair. I'd met Chris about six months back, when I was writing an article about him for a magazine and he was transitioning from his old life as a professional surfer into his new life as an organic rancher. Because he was the only person I knew who had any experience living in the country, he was the first person I called for advice after buying the house in Chimayo. It was his stories of fence building and food raising and other hardscrabble, earthbound delights that helped reinforce my decision to move. To let him know how that decision was playing out I called him not long after my encounter with the donkey whisperer. When I finished telling him the story, he started laughing and didn't stop for quite some time.

"Animals," he said finally. "They just have no time for normal people."

11

In retrospect, there weren't too many normal people around—ourselves included—though perhaps that will become clearer as we go along. I suppose I am talking about consequences, about what can happen when you decide that anything is better than more of the same, about why large quantities of alcohol should not be cocktailed with ideas about what to do with the entirety of one's savings account. Mostly I'm talking about the inherent difficulties in chasing down a dream, but perhaps that too will become clearer as we go along.

What was immediately clear was that snow in May wasn't the only thing different about our new home. As the crow flies there were less than eight hundred miles between us and anything familiar, but down here on the ground those distances were astronomically greater. The local landscape was all terra incognita, a whorl of mesas and buttes and hoodoos and fairy chimneys and slot canyons and none of it making much sense. Riverbeds that hadn't sprung to life in two hundred years would suddenly flood; deep springs would vanish even faster. Everything seemed to have a nebulous quality that tilted the world, burned away the familiar, and rearranged fundamental properties according to laws of physics as yet undiscovered. Perhaps this is what D. H. Lawrence meant when he wrote: "It was New Mexico that liberated me from the present era of civilization."

And nowhere in this dread state are these forces stronger than in northern New Mexico. Here they seep in through cracks in the floor and catch you while you're sleeping, making off with whatever might be left of your mind. You want proof? Just north of my front door is the Hog Farm, which Wavy Gravy once dubbed "a mobile hallucinogen-extended family"—both America's longest-running hippie commune and the spot where the acid trip scene in *Easy Rider* was filmed. Just south puts you in Los Alamos, where the first atomic bomb was built, site of a small museum where you can stand before exact replicas of Fat Man and Little Boy and feel, at least in my case, damn unsure what should be meant by the word *humanity*.

In between these spots stretches our little valley, Rio Arriba County, ground zero for an entirely different kind of bomb. Northern New Mexico is some of the most serious outlaw territory in the lower forty-eight, populated entirely, as Kerouac would say, by "the mad ones." Bikers and bandits and beatniks. Guys who still ride horses to work; guys who can strip a car in no time flat; guys who haven't been sober since Nixon. Everybody has a secret to hide and a knife in his boot. It's an area where work wear runs from Carhartt to Dickies, weekend style from Harley to Davidson. Jailhouse tattoos are also popular. Not long after we arrived, I was standing in the checkout line at our grocery store when the clerk asked the woman in front of me how her brothers were doing.

"Ramón got himself shot, José's upstate for a nickel, and Juan just broke his parole."

"What about Arturo?"

"Oh," she said with a smile, "they haven't caught him yet."

And none of this, none of this was anything new.

New Mexico became a territory in 1850, yet wasn't granted statehood until 1912. Utah came first, as did Nevada, Colorado, Idaho, Montana, Wyoming, and both Dakotas. Known as "Robber's

Roost," Oklahoma still beat out this place by five years. In fact, my new home was the fourth last state—only Arizona, Alaska, and Hawaii came later. But New Mexico's sixty-two-year waiting period between territory and statehood represents the longest such stretch in U.S. history—and not without good reason.

The Indian battles fought here were among the country's bloodiest. None of the tribes went gently into that good night, and the first "settlers" weren't much calmer. There were wars fought over timber and wars fought over land—known as the Tall Tree Wars and the Land Grant Wars, respectively—and more war over cows—the Lincoln County War—and banditry, mostly known as Billy the Kid, but really, he wasn't alone. The reason it took New Mexico so long to become a state was that everyone with a lick of sense and a say in these matters was just too damned scared of the place.

Which brings us to our neighbors. In dog rescue, because dogs make plenty of noise and have a tendency to go missing, having a good relationship with one's neighbors is critical to success. So on the afternoon of our third day in Chimayo, Joy decided it was time to meet ours. She snipped a few flowers from the garden and started walking down the road. Shortly thereafter, a car came flying past. The cops came next. They caught the guy in front of our neighbor's driveway and pulled him over fifty feet beyond. Joy figured speeding ticket and kept walking. Around the time she knocked on our neighbor's door, a second squad car arrived. Then a third. Suddenly the street was filled with cops. A moment later there were men pouring out of the woods and coming down from the hills, their blue windbreakers reading *DEA* in big yellow letters. Joy's jaw dropped, her feet froze; she was the only person in sight not carrying a firearm. Not surprisingly, our neighbor didn't answer his door.

Instead, he cracked a window, parting the curtains an inch.

"What the hell do you want?"

"Um," said Joy, "just moved in next door." Then, pointing toward the drug bust, "But, uh, don't have anything to do with that."

The window opened another crack, the curtains parted slightly more.

"Who are you?"

"Your new neighbor."

"What?"

"Obviously, this is not a good time."

"What are you doing here?"

"I came to say hello." Then, holding out the flowers, "And to give you these."

There was a long pause. Our new neighbor glanced from Joy to the flowers and back again. He glanced at the military action in the distance. Apparently, the DEA wasn't there for him, rather had been using his property as a staging area for a raid down the street. This didn't improve his mood.

"We can just wave to each other over the fence," he said finally. "We'll be neighbors like that."

Over the years, an exceptionally talented photographer named Christopher Wray McCann has joined me on a number of jobs that involve too much travel and not much sleep, and Christopher occasionally responds to such trying conditions by limiting the majority of his communication to Irish whiskey and *Apocalypse Now* quotes—"There are mines over there, there's mines over there, and watch out, those goddamn monkeys bite" being but one example. I mention this because the day after the drug bust we met another one of our neighbors. He dropped by early the next morning, wearing a pink bathrobe and blue shower sandals, to let us know of a pack of pit bulls rampaging in the area.

"Possibly rabid," he said, "definitely attacking local dogs."

I hadn't had coffee yet and wasn't quite sure what he was telling me.

"You know," he said, "one pit bull bites the head, another the ass, a third tries to tear out the entrails. It's usually over pretty quickly. Anyway, welcome to the neighborhood."

It was right about then I recalled another of Christopher's favorite *Apocalypse Now* quotes: "I wanted a mission, and for my sins, they gave me one."

12

Squirt was our first rescue in Chimayo, arriving our first weekend in town. She had been sprung from a shelter in LA, then driven across the Southwest because no one in California wanted a dachshund-pug hybrid with a weight problem. At least we'd been told it was a weight problem. The truth was Squirt looked like three bowling balls stuffed inside a tube sock. Worse, all that weight made her fearless. She was a brawler with a short fuse and a roamer with no common sense, and in those early weeks in New Mexico that was a lousy combination.

We had coyotes in the hills, wild dogs in the streets, and no fences surrounding our property. I was in charge of putting up those fences—and failing miserably. I started failing on our second day in town; by the sixth I was head to toe with scratches and again on the phone with Chris Malloy. At the time, he was at the airport about to board a plane for Tahiti.

"Seriously," I said, "surfing's for pussies. The tropics suck. Why not trade it for a week stringing fences in the lovely American Southwest?"

"Seriously," he said, "you have to get a grip."

A week later, I still didn't have a grip—though we almost had a fence. The property was entirely enclosed except for the front gate, which I had yet to figure out how to install. But I forgot about that detail and banged into the house to brag about my success.

I also forgot to close the door. Thirty seconds later, from somewhere near our neighbor's fields, we heard a frantic bark, a blizzard of growls, and a scream that still keeps me up nights. By the time we found her, Squirt was in tatters. The gashes started up by her neck and ran down toward her belly, and that was the last time I forgot to close a door.

It was also the first time we met Kathleen Ramsay—though nobody calls her that. She's Doc: a middle-aged, salt-and-pepper-haired woman, slender and small, given to bright scrubs and blunt talk. Doc was born in Los Alamos at a time when seventy-five percent of the town's adult population had postgraduate degrees and security clearances. Her mother did geothermal research, her father worked on detonation sequences. This was not long after the war, and Los Alamos was still a "closed city." During those years, parental duties were neglected for national emergencies, so most of Doc's childhood was spent on horseback, alone in the Jemez Mountains.

When she was twelve, her father took a job in Saudi Arabia, but she went to high school in Lebanon. The 1982 Beirut embassy bombing relocated her to Bahrain, then she came back to New Mexico for college. She studied metallurgy and biochemistry and was all set to do more of the same at the graduate level when she realized that the only jobs open to her afterward were in big cities, and having come to hate big cities, instead took a hard left turn and a considerably harder path and went back to school and eventually became, to the limited number of people who know and understand the rather special work she now does, a kind of legend.

For the past twenty-five years, Doc has run the Cottonwood Veterinary Clinic and the New Mexico Wildlife Center, both with the goal of "helping any injured animal that comes in the door." What comes in the door at the clinic are mostly dogs and cats and birds. What comes in the door at the center are black bears, mountain lions, and bald eagles. Also frogs, snakes, lizards, hawks, eagles, lots of owls, bobcats, elk, deer, and the rest of the ark. Not surprisingly, Doc hasn't slept more than three hours a night in a very long time.

The New Mexico Wildlife Center began as the Northern New Mexico Raptor and Rehabilitation Center back when raptor medicine wasn't a field anyone knew much about. "When I was in school," recalls Doc, "it was dogs, cats, cows, sheep, goats, period." But when she got out, while working in a clinic in Los Alamos, some guy brought in a golden eagle caught in a foothold trap. "He was dangling from a chain, thrashing and screaming. I took one look at the bird and decided if I did anything with my life, I wanted to be able to give these guys a second chance." So she quit the traditional clinic and opened the Wildlife Center and quickly expanded the operation to include other animals beside raptors because, well, other animals kept showing up.

In doing so, Doc put herself on the front end of a wave that's been cresting for nearly two hundred years. The first official animal welfare organization was the Society for the Prevention of Cruelty to Animals, founded in Britain in 1824 by a group of twenty-two reformers who liked to meet at the appropriately named Old Slaughter coffeehouse in London. They were led by parliamentarian Richard Martin, a man whose philanthropic actions earned him some fame, much notoriety, and the nickname "Humanity Dick." The society's initial thrust was to support Martin's Act, an 1822 law that attempted to curb cruelty to farm animals. In 1840, Queen Victoria became hip to the cause and granted them official status, and their name was changed to the Royal Society for the Prevention of Cruelty to Animals.

In 1866, a former diplomat to the Russian court of Czar Alexander II, Henry Bergh, carried this fight to America, where he began to plead on behalf of "the mute servants of all mankind." He next drafted a "Declaration of the Rights of Animals" and brought it to the New York State Legislature. The result was the creation of the American Society for the Prevention of Cruelty to Animals (ASPCA) and the passage of an anticruelty law that the society was authorized to enforce. In 1867, the ASPCA began operating the first ever ambulance service for injured horses; also the year David Heath became the first person prosecuted under the new law, receiving ten days in prison and a fine of twenty-five dollars for beating a cat to death. Thirty years later, New York dogcatchers were still rounding up three hundred strays a day, packing them into cages, and hurling those cages into the East River. Since these catchers were paid by the dog and not the hour, abuses were frequent and house pets were missing. To fight against this, in 1894 the ASPCA was placed in charge of animal control duties, and a more "humane" method of euthanasia was found inside the gas chamber.

Pet ownership, in its earliest modern form, began as a Victorian hobby. The nouveau middle class, suddenly flush with leisure time as a result of the Industrial Revolution, discovered a passion for genetics that quickly turned forty core dog breeds into four hundred varieties. The results of this were adopted by working-class Americans in the years after World War II, when the development of canned food, kitty litter, and other such conveniences made pet ownership affordable for the masses. But more convenience meant more pets and more pets meant more work for the ASPCA.

According to the official numbers, shelters take in somewhere between six million and eight million dogs and cats every year and euthanize about half of them. And this is an improvement. While it was back in the 1970s that the HSUS began trying to raise awareness of the benefits of spaying and neutering, it wasn't until the 1990s that their catchy tag line, "Less born, less killed, less cruelty," really caught on. In the 1980s, shelters were euthanizing twenty million animals each year. But then birth rates dropped and admission rates dropped, and today, while the three to four million animals they kill annually is a slaughter, it's also a significant improvement over the massacre that came before.

Of course, veterinarians also have to put dogs down, sometimes at alarming rates. After sewing up Squirt's wounds, Doc told me her morning had been spent euthanizing puppies.

"It's the season for it," she said.

"Euthanasia has a season?"

"Distemper has a season."

Distemper, I learned, is an always painful, always fatal disease that affects young dogs the worst. Spring is the season for puppies, so spring is the season for distemper. It turns out the disease is entirely preventable provided dogs are vaccinated—a treatment that costs about seven bucks.

"Sixty percent poverty rate in this valley," said Doc. "When you have three jobs and three kids, and eight hundred dollars a month is your income, do you spend it on groceries or the dog?"

Then she told me it really wasn't about the money. What was going on came down to culture.

"This area has a few Caucasians," she said, "but they're farmers and farmers are a different type. Mostly we have a large Mexican and Spanish population. In those cultures, the animal is a commodity, something put here for human use. It's hard to fight against that. I try to look at the broader picture."

"There's a broader picture?"

"I may not like having to put down seven dogs, but at least I get to put them down. Ten years ago, if I told someone their dog needed to be euthanized, they'd take it out back and shoot it in the head."

"So things are looking up?"

"Welcome to New Mexico," she said.

13

We had been in New Mexico about three weeks and Joy had been to the local animal shelter about six times. She first went to introduce herself, then came back to volunteer. She walked dogs and cleaned cages, and always tried to get me to come along. I never came along. I wanted nothing to do with the place. Or anyplace like it. Shelters scared me. In hindsight, I think it was fear of empathy, of feeling too much, of the level of commitment that might come from feeling too much, keeping me away. At the time, though, it was just lower-belly dread—the very real sense that whatever emotional fortitude I'd developed in my forty years wasn't enough to handle rows of dogs in cages, most of them destined for euthanasia.

Joy felt otherwise. She felt that seeing a shelter was an initiation, an important rescuer rite of passage, and wouldn't shut up about it. In LA I'd made up excuses. Then we moved to New Mexico to run a dog sanctuary—of all things—and how could I run a dog sanctuary without knowing why I was running a dog sanctuary? I was out of excuses. In the middle of our fourth week in New Mexico, I paid a visit to the Española Humane Society and made what rescuers commonly refer to as "Sophie's choice."

The Española shelter is a long, low brick building comprised of a main reception room, a few offices, a small vet clinic, and a warehouse of dogs. Making Sophie's choice involves combing that warehouse to select one dog who will live from the hundreds who will die, and doing so requires paying considerable attention to detail at a time when it's not necessarily comfortable to do so. The goal is to find an adoptable dog who would otherwise go unnoticed. Dogs in shelters go unnoticed for a variety of reasons. Most people come looking for puppies and purebreds, so older mutts are at a considerable disadvantage. Beige dogs are often overlooked, brown dogs ignored. Black dogs are so hated that rescuers refer to their trouble as "black dog syndrome," which oddly extends beyond the boundaries of race: even black people don't like black dogs. Ugly dogs, sick dogs, handicapped dogs, retarded dogs, shy dogs, fat dogs—those too don't stand a chance. Pit bulls are out of the question, Rottweilers as well. Dogs that need too much house training, dogs with bad coats, dogs that like to chew, dig, drool, et cetera. As it turns out, what makes a dog adoptable has very little to do with dogs, a great deal to do with humans.

Yet the above preferences are mostly fetishes, as our real attraction comes from *neoteny*. Developmental biologists use the word to refer to the retention of childlike characteristics by mature members of a species. These characteristics include physical attributes such as dimples, floppy ears, and large eyes and personality dispositions such as playfulness, curiosity, and helplessness—all of which fall under an analytical model in ethology known as "cuteness." In 1949, the Nobel Prize–winning zoologist Konrad Lorenz introduced the concept to science, arguing that "infantile features produced nurturing responses in adults." The way he saw it, cuteness was the secret weapon evolution came up with to ensure that parents cared for their children. And neoteny is the biology behind cuteness, a biology to which humans are particularly susceptible. As *New York Times* science writer Natalie Angier pointed out, the reasons humans are so attracted to cuteness are simple: "As a species whose youngest members are so pathetically helpless they can't lift their heads to suckle without adult supervision, human beings must be wired to respond quickly and gamely to any and all signs of infantile desire." And the reason shelters scared me so much is also simple: dogs, more than any other species, have infantile desire down to an art.

At the Española shelter, the strays occupy a small hangar, about fifty feet long and twenty feet wide. Puppies are kept in a wire pen in the center, bigger dogs alone, in pairs, or occasionally in trios, in cages around the sides. The lighting is fluorescent, the air stinks of piss, the floors are cold concrete. At first, not wanting to look at any of the dogs directly, I kept my eyes on those floors. But diverting my gaze only made their barking, whining, and whimpering that much more emphatic. Eventually I had to look.

The first dog I saw was a chestnut brown pit bull. She was directly to my right, jumping up and down, wagging her tail, completely desperate for a playmate. I walked over and let her lick my hand through the bars. It was the ears maybe, perhaps the shape of her muzzle, but I remember thinking how much she reminded me of my friend Tara's pit bull. That was my first mistake. Pretty soon I was walking down the line of cages, letting any dog that wanted to lick my hand do so, and finding out that all of these dogs reminded me of other dogs. There was the shaggy terrier with the same sideways head cant and nervous tongue flick as the shaggy terrier Ahab used to play with at the dog park in LA. There was my friend Barry's Australian shepherd, my friend Amy's German shepherd. I felt sick to my stomach. There wasn't anything wrong with these dogs. I wanted to take them all home with me. The whole damn warehouse of misery. Just strap it to my back and get the fuck out of the way.

There are two competing theories as to why my feelings were so strong, as there are two competing theories as to how canine domestication occurred. The first idea is that early hominids stole cute wolf pups from their mother's dens and raised them as pets. The wolves that were friendlier, calmer, and more socially adept around humans were kept; the wilder ones were either driven off or killed outright. The remaining "tamer" wolves were bred together and produced even tamer offspring, but as James Serpell, professor of humane ethics and animal welfare at the University of Pennsylvania School of Veterinary Medicine, writes in *The Domestic Dog*: "No one . . . could have foreseen the bizarre ontogenetic ramifications of this simple process of selecting for tameness. When this same process was . . . applied systematically to captive foxes at a Siberian fur farm, weird things started happening. As expected, the selected lines became tamer, but they also began to look and behave increasingly like dogs, even to the extent of developing piebald coats, drooping ears and dioestrus reproductive cycles." Domesticated dogs, it appears, are not just expert at neoteny, they're nature's most complete blueprint for the process.

In the stealing-wolf-cub version of this story, mankind domesticated dogs, and this version is another often cited reason for our species' specialness: humans are the only species to have "tamed" another species. And this was the only version of the story until Hampshire College biologist Raymond Coppinger realized that if you want to steal a wolf cub to raise as a pet, you have thirteen days to do it, because afterward wolves are virtually untamable. Since thirteen days is a pretty tight window for roving hunter-gatherer bands to climb through, Coppinger proposed a different, somewhat stranger idea: that wolves domesticated themselves.

How this happened comes down to "flight distance." How close an animal will allow something dangerous—like a human being—to get before fleeing is flight distance. The reason it's important is because as humans learned to live in fixed settlements, even if those settlements were nothing more than a cave for the winter, we produced a lot of garbage. Our refuse included prime wolf chow such as rotting vegetables, fruit seeds, and discarded carcasses. Once wolves discovered they loved our leftovers, biology took over. The wolves with shorter flight distances got more of those leftovers than the ones without. Better-fed wolves had more pups, and those pups were also born with shorter flight distances. As Coppinger points out: "My argument is that what *domesticated*—or tame—means is 'to be able to eat in the presence of human beings.' That is the thing that wild wolves can't do."

No one is quite sure how to settle this domestic dispute, but we do know that the act of selecting for tameness triggered a further cascade of neoteny in wolves. And then humans, already perfectly designed to respond to this cascade, pushed things even further. The cute pups were the more beloved pups, so they were kept inside, fed better, and allowed to have offspring. As this process made them healthier, these select few were more likely to have larger litters. And the cuter pups from those larger litters would get the same preferential treatment the next time around. Which is why these days adult dogs act far more like puppy wolves than adult wolves, and also why going to a shelter and choosing a dog to rescue can be so damn hard: it involves trying to overlook the very animals several millions of years of evolution have shaped us to notice.

In attempting to do just that, I tried to set my biases aside. I was looking for a dog who, under normal conditions, I might never quite see. I found him cowering in a cage in the corner. His name was Leo, and he was just about the saddest sack I'd ever met. My personal preference is for friendly and fuzzy, and Leo was neither of these. Some generations ago, he had started out as a German shepherd, but things had gone haywire ever since. His coat was stringy, his eyes sunken, his weight about thirty pounds below normal. He had the spunk of a big rock at the bottom of a deep lake, was already red-listed—destined to be euthanized within twenty-four hours—and in no danger of being adopted before his time was up.

Then again, neither were many of the other dogs in cages. I was having a hard time breathing. I glanced back at Leo. There really was nothing appealing about him. There was really no way I could stay in this room another minute.

"Perfect," I said, "I'll take him."

Not so fast. Leo still had his balls. The problem at most shelters comes down to overcrowding, and overcrowding comes down to too many dogs who still have their balls. So before I could spring him from the pound he had to be neutered, and this took an extra few days and didn't go as planned. During the surgery, the vets found out Leo was a hemophiliac. After the surgery, they also discovered he was smart enough to be able to rip off his plastic neck cone and dumb enough to tear out his stitches. They couldn't risk another procedure without risking him bleeding to death, so they shrugged and sent him home to me—with a hole the size of a tennis ball where his testicles used to be.

Since Leo could still get out of a cone, during the two weeks it took that hole to heal, he spent his days under careful supervision and his nights stockaded, tied by leashes between two vigas on our back porch. The vigas were the only things around strong enough to hold him. As there are wild dogs and coyotes and cougars in the area—all of which can smell blood at a distance and can quite easily hop our fences—I spent those same nights sleeping on the porch for purposes of his protection, a heavy shovel within arm's reach.

As a man whose primary response to children has always been the desire to run fast in the other direction, I assumed a certain immunity to neoteny. Moreover, Leo wasn't really my kind of dog to begin with, and spending my nights on protection detail was not my idea of a good time, but humans' response to helplessness is innate and completely automatic. A switch flipped, a cascade followed. Sympathy became empathy and empathy is always the point of no return. Pretty soon I was more than a little attached.

My first real rescue was complete. The thing I had been afraid of ever since Joy mentioned visiting a shelter was now behind me. It didn't take too long for Leo to gain back some of that weight and begin coming out of his shell. The difference was magnificent. He had started out barely walking and soon was barely containable. In a few weeks' time, he'd be ready for adoption. I felt like something significant had occurred.

On the one-month anniversary of my springing him from the shelter, I went into town to buy Leo a bone to celebrate, and that chestnut-coated pit bull popped back into my mind. I decided to drive over and check up on her, but when I got to the shelter she was gone. In her cage was an old hound dog. I asked the woman at the front desk if someone had adopted her. Her face fell, just a little, but I knew. The dog had been euthanized, put down because of our personal fetishes, the shelter's lack of space, and a whole series of reasons that no longer made much sense to me.

"No one adopts a pit bull," she said, as if that cleared everything up.

PART THREE

And probably you had no business being out in the rain in the first place.

—Alan Furst

14

Salty is a three-pound Chihuahua, handsome, blonde, shell-shocked, and not too unlike Michael Caine near the ragged end of *The Man Who Would Be King.* Who knows why he was dumped at the Espanola shelter, but that's where Joy met him. He was enough of a looker that once the shock wore off she figured finding him a home was not going to be much of an issue. Then the vets discovered Salty had heartworm. Untreated, the disease is always fatal, but the cure is arsenic, which is almost as bad. Dying worms can clog the bloodstream. To avoid death by circulation shock, doses are kept low and delivery stretched out—often six months to a year. Even then, few make it through. The secret to survival is keeping the heart rate low and the dog calm, but a year is a long time and few people have the patience to try and few shelters have the space required. Mostly heartworm means euthanasia.

Of course, Joy wanted to try. I wasn't so sure. We had arrived in New Mexico with eight dogs. Squirt made nine. Leo was ten. Ten had been our agreed-upon cutoff point. Joy put me in charge of enforcing that limit. After bankrupting herself in Mexico, she felt that I should be in charge of admissions. Her difficulty there had been that she couldn't say no to dogs in need. My difficulty here was that after visiting a shelter I was starting to share her opinion. Pretty soon we were up to eleven, then twelve, then "How many dogs do you have this week?" became funny to my friends, then thirteen, then I found myself standing in an aisle at Petco, wondering if it was normal to be this terrified buying dog food.

I must have been standing there a while. The manager walked by twice. Some guy in a blue uniform and a name tag reading "Bob" walked by three times. Then they both walked over to see if they could help.

"Might be a little late for that," is what I said.

My cell phone took this opportunity to ring, and I took this opportunity to answer it. Bob and the manager were not amused. I told them I was about to spend five hundred dollars on dog food, then held up the phone up for emphasis: "But I need to speak to my therapist first."

That was about the point where Bob and the manager walked away. I put the phone back to my ear. It was my friend Joe Donnelly, sounding incredulous.

"Five hundred dollars on dog food?"

"Uh-huh."

"It's a one-time expense?"

"It's this month—who knows how many dogs we'll have next month."

And then I told him about Salty and my misgivings and how the shelter was going to euthanize him the next morning, so I needed to make up my mind quickly.

"Ten was the limit?" he asked.

"Uh-huh."

"Financial or emotional?"

"Little of both."

"And Salty makes fourteen?"

"Uh-huh."

"So why are you doing this to yourself?"

I had no answer for him. I had a thousand answers for him.

Every one of them sounded stupid aloud. But Joe had introduced me to Ahab and later introduced me to Joy. I felt like he was owed an explanation.

"I fell in love with Joy," I said. "She was the perfect storm."

15

I called Joy from the Petco parking lot and told her to drive over to the shelter and adopt Salty. She started cheering. I started laughing. But when I hung up the phone, Joe's question, or a version of it, popped back into my mind. What I wanted to know wasn't why I was doing this to myself; it was why Joy was doing this to herself.

Every time we get a new dog, Joy disappears down a drain of concern. If there are emotional or physiological problems—and everyone in our pack has these problems—she can't rest until the dog's on the road to recovery. Her focus is unbreakable, the toll on her well-being considerable. Usually this period lasts a month, occasionally two. But Salty needed a year's worth of vigilance just to keep him alive, and nothing about that year would be easy on her. What I realized in the parking lot is that Joy knew all this and was still cheering about a chance to save him.

I'm inquisitive by nature and a journalist by trade, and my willingness to spend five hundred dollars on dog food coupled with Joy's eagerness to spend a year on Salty had my attention. So I did what many reporters do when faced by ideas they can't quite understand: ludicrous amounts of research. What I was trying to wrap my head around was altruism. Joy gave all of herself to her cause, and why did that happen? Where does this urge toward altruism come from? Is it biological, psychological, or cultural? All of the above? What about spiritual? The Hebrew word *mitzvah* means both "good deed" and "sacred commandment," while the early Christians made Leviticus's Holiness Code—love thy neighbor as thyself—a central component of their faith. Does this extend to animals? Even more fundamental, were these religious rules written down to promote an urge that genetically existed or to create a moral good where one was desperately needed?

I quickly discovered a lot of people with similar concerns. The first philosophers to consider altruism were the Greeks, and they considered it unlikely. In *The Republic*, Plato wrote, "One loves something most when one believes that what is good for it is good for oneself," and everyone from Aristotle to Marcus Aurelius agreed. Epictetus took an even stronger stance: "Did you never see little dogs caressing and playing with one another, so that you might say, there is nothing more friendly? But that you may know what friendship is, throw a bit of flesh among them, and you will learn."

This bit of back-and-forth between early egoist philosophers and early altruist theosophists became the opening blows in a battle that's been raging ever since. In the eleventh century, Thomas Aquinas tried to win a round by arguing that man's selfish impulses must always bow before divine law. In the nineteenth, John Stuart Mill thought the difference was not duty to deity; rather, triumph of good schooling: "Why am I bound to promote general happiness? If my own happiness lies in something else, why may I not give it preference?" he asked in *Utilitarianism*, later answered: "By the improvement of education, the feeling of unity with our fellow-creatures shall be . . . deeply rooted in our character." By the turn of the twentieth, in *Ecce Homo*, Nietzsche called all such talk rot: "Morality . . . has falsified everything psychological, from the beginning to the end; it has demoralized everything, even to the terrible nonsense of making love 'altruistic.'"

Nietzsche was the last to ponder the question without the aid of biology, as Charles Darwin had already joined the discussion. In his *The Descent of Man,* Darwin moved beyond morality and examined altruism through the lens of evolution. He considered it a question of where in the biological hierarchy natural selection exerts pressure. Was selection a multitiered effect, or did one tier have prominence? Were individuals favored over groups or vice versa? Could it work at the level of whole ecosystems? If selection acts exclusively at the individual level, Darwin reasoned, then altruism can't evolve: "He who was ready to sacrifice his life, as many a savage has been, rather than betray his comrades, would often leave no offspring to inherit his noble nature." But altruism makes sense at the group level: "Although a high standard of morality gives but a slight or no advantage to each individual man and his children over the other men of the same tribe . . . an advancement in the standard of morality will certainly give an immense advantage to one tribe over another. . . . [A tribe] always ready to aid one another, and to sacrifice themselves for the common good, would be victorious over most other tribes; and this would be natural selection."

This was the invention of an idea called *group selection* and for the next hundred years it held fast. It fell fast in the 1960s when mathematical models were introduced to evolutionary biology. Once scientists started modeling altruism, free riders became the problem. "Even if altruism is advantageous at the group level," says the *Stanford Encyclopedia of Philosophy,*

> within any group altruists are liable to be exploited by self-ish "free-riders" who refrain from behaving altruistically. These free-riders will have an obvious fitness advantage: they benefit from the altruism of others, but do not incur any of the costs. So even if a group is composed exclusively of altruists, all behaving nicely towards each other, it only takes a single selfish mutant to bring an end to this happy idyll. By virtue of its relative fitness advantage within the group, the

selfish mutant will out-reproduce the altruists, hence selfishness will eventually swamp altruism. Since the generation
time of individual organisms is likely to be much shorter
than that of groups, the probability that a selfish mutant will
arise and spread is very high, according to this line of argument.

In 1976, Oxford evolutionary biologist Richard Dawkins reduced things further, arguing in *The Selfish Gene* that it didn't
really matter on what level evolution occurred: genes were the
"fundamental unit of selection," and since a gene's only function is
the inherently selfish self-replication, any selection pressure applied
at the group level would be completely negated at the individual
level. Altruism became *kin selection*—we help those who are closely
related to us—or *reciprocal altruism*—we help those who help us—and
the world became a crueler place.

While Dawkins's ideas still dominate today, dog rescue—or
what's technically known as cross-species altruism—isn't easily explained by selfish genetics. Since dogs are not our species, kin selection immediately falls apart. Meanwhile, reciprocal altruism
runs into an entirely different wall. Because genes are the fundamental unit of selection, the cornerstone of reciprocal altruism isn't
just that we help those who help us—it's that we help those who
help us pass on our genes. But no matter what rescuers do for animals, none of it is going to help them pass along their genes.

To get around this, the few researchers who have considered
cross-species altruism argue for "reputation models": the idea that
being kind to animals enhances one's reputation in the community
and that enhancement is beneficial to survival. Unfortunately, no
one I knew thought allocating a considerable chunk of my income
to dogs was a particularly good idea. Plus, because of animal zoning laws and pets-per-household limits, most rescuers live in places

with a sparse human population, so you can enhance their reputations all you want, but there's still no one around to notice.

And that's it. The end of the scientific line. The extent of our best thinking on the matter. Perhaps this wouldn't all be so perplexing if animal rescue was just a tiny movement, but a 2002 and 2003 survey conducted by the Humane Society of the United States identified ten thousand animal protection groups, a number that, according to People for the Ethical Treatment of Animals (PETA), has since risen above twelve thousand. Some are mom-and-pop shops similar to what Joy and I had started; many are significantly larger. More than three thousand have freestanding buildings for their animals. One hundred and fifty private shelters and three hundred public ones have operating budgets in excess of one million dollars. In total, Americans spend about two and a half billion dollars on animal advocacy and sheltering each year—and what all this research is saying is that no one has yet to figure out why.

16

It's late June and late afternoon. Outside, it's monsoon season: dark skies, thumping thunder, curtains of rain. Inside, I'm cozy on the couch, buried beneath a pile of dogs. My body is stretched out lengthwise. Ahab is asleep between my legs, his head resting on my belt buckle. Farrah lays on my chest, Hugo on my feet, while Dagmar and Squirt perch on pillows behind my head, Dagmar draping down my right shoulder, Squirt hugging my left. Leo, meanwhile, is wedged between my side and the back of the couch, his hind legs lying over mine. From above, we look like a stack of fur-covered pickup sticks. From below, I can barely move.

Then there's Otis. Our resident alpha is both a bastard of a boss and now snoring on a pillow beside the couch. It doesn't take much to wake him. Sneezing, coughing, even strolling through his field of vision while he's trying to nap will rouse his ire. What bugs him most is being touched by another dog. When he's wide awake, the only one allowed any contact is Hugo, and all he's allowed to do is lick Otis's ass. But when he's asleep, even brushing against him can be a capital crime.

All this concerns me slightly. We added too many dogs too quickly and the new pack has yet to gel. Dagmar and Squirt have been fighting for weeks, and the fact that they are now inches apart and straddling my face is both an answered prayer and slightly unnerving. Meanwhile, Ahab is jealous of the attention I've been paying Leo, and Farrah is terrified of both of them. As long as Leo stays put, things should be okay, but the thunder scares him. With every boom, he jerks and Farrah jumps, and sooner or later she's going to land on Ahab and tip onto Otis and, well, I've already spent too much on vet bills this month.

That was because of Gidget. She's never been very healthy, but in early May she lost control of her limbs and started having seizures. Most were ten to twenty seconds in length, minorly terrifying, but over quickly enough. Occasionally they lasted longer. The worst it got was about twenty minutes: her body a cacophony of spasm, eyes rolled back in her head, yellow froth pouring out of her mouth. We took her to see Doc a half dozen times, but epilepsy often accompanies mange and there wasn't much she could do. Instead, Joy started carrying Gidget around kangaroo-style, in a pouch strapped across her chest. Some of this was because dogs find the sound of a heartbeat soothing; most of it was that Joy didn't want Gidget to die alone.

Either way, the pouch worked wonders. By the first week of June, Gidget could stumble about. By the second week, she was running—at least wobbling fast. Unfortunately, despite the physical recovery, Gidget came to us fairly fried, and those long seizures torched her brain even more. With her wobbling about for the first time, we quickly discovered she had almost no ability to recognize social cues, and a complete block when it came to pack order. That order is also pretty confusing right now, and with this much tension in the air and her being barely two pounds, all it's going to take to get her in trouble is not much at all.

There's another thunderclap. Leo jerks, Farrah jumps, and something scurries across the corner of my vision. From my position pinned to the couch it's hard to say for sure—maybe it's Gidget sprinting toward Otis, but no dog can be that dumb. I crank my neck for a second look. Turns out Gidget is exactly that dumb. Not only did she sprint toward Otis, now she's stepping onto his thigh. This doesn't make any sense, and then it does. Gidget doesn't like thunder either. She usually spends storms inside her pouch, safe against Joy's breast. When Joy's not available—and she's currently in town running errands—then Gidget goes for the middle of my chest. Since Farrah currently occupies that spot, her addled mind somehow decided Otis was where to go for comfort.

"Gidget," I hiss, trying to keep my voice quiet. She ignores me, climbing from thigh to hip. I call her again, a little louder, but that was the wrong decision. Otis's eyes slam open. Anger in all mammals tends to contract the pupils, and his are now dark points. I hear a low growl and see fur rise. Any other dog would be long gone, but Gidget isn't any other dog. Either she doesn't notice the signals or they don't compute. She puts one paw in front of the other, climbs to the middle of Otis's back, and then—as if it were the most normal thing in the world—spins a tight circle and lies down for a nap.

I think it's the shock that keeps Gidget alive. Otis goes from growling to gobsmacked in no time flat. Gobsmacked is something to see, like a cartoon—Goofy the moment after being broadsided by a two-by-four: brow ridiculously raised, ears at wild angles, eyes popping out of his head. Then those brows pull together, as if an idea is forming in his head and just a moment while he thinks it through. I've never seen this sort of deductive logic in a dog before, but Otis connects the dots: Gidget has to be crazy to be on his back, and if she's crazy, then the normal rules don't apply. Instead of attacking, Otis shakes his head once, snorts loudly, and goes back to sleep.

Over the next few weeks, the entire pack began to follow Otis's lead. Gidget was now allowed to sleep on anyone. One day it was Leo, the next it was Squirt. Because Ahab's coat was so thick and he overheated quickly, it was only in the dead of winter that he allowed me—and only ever me—to sleep near him. But a week after Gidget climbed onto Otis, in the middle of a very hot summer, I walked into the living room and found her perched atop Ahab as well.

Somehow a collective decision had been reached: Gidget was crazy, thus to be treated with compassion. It spread through the pack and united the pack. Until then, many of our animals were strangers to one another. They all had bad pasts and trust issues and found themselves thrown into a novel setting with uncertain rules. And we didn't impose many rules. Joy believed the secret to dog rescue was to let the dogs be dogs and love them for it. I believed Joy. Our method was allowing them to decide for themselves. That summer they made some pretty interesting decisions.

Our bed is the most coveted real estate in our house. The dogs treat it as their den, and dogs in dens always follow one commandment: never walk on anyone. This is a basic safety concern—dogs can get crushed—so it's deeply ingrained. Gidget has a favorite spot in the bed: she either nestles in the crook of Joy's neck or gets very frustrated. But being so little, it takes her a moment to climb up there. Usually, by the time she arrives, most of the other dogs have staked a claim. This means that clambering to her favorite spot requires clambering over others' backs. The usual reaction was a small riot. Gidget gets bashed and bitten and flung to the floor. But after Otis made his decision, Gidget was allowed to walk across anyone, and no one so much as groaned.

A bigger change came during meals. With fifteen dogs, feeding time at the zoo had always required a complicated geometry. To avoid fights, the bigger ones had to be separated out: Otis in the bathroom, Ahab in the front fields, Leo in the back fields. Dagmar and Damien also liked to scrap for snacks, so she'd go in Joy's office, while he got the bedroom. The rest of the Chihuahuas got split between the kitchen and the living room, but even then, keeping the peace required constant patrols. Yet a few weeks after Gidget climbed up on Otis, Joy saw her snatch a bone from between his paws, a truly unbelievable feat of daring; even zanier was that he let her have it. A few days later, I watched Gidget pluck food out of Dagmar's mouth—and she too permitted it. This led us to a risky experiment: we decided to alter our feeding strategy and see how far this goodwill had really spread. With me standing guard, Joy scattered dog food across the back porch like chicken feed. The first time it hit the floor there was a moment of profound befuddlement— dogs are not known for their desire to share—but once that wore off, sharing is what went on. Everyone just got down to dinner. No growling, no fighting, no problem.

And all this empathetic behavior had a ripple effect. From that point on, whenever we added dogs to the pack who were ill or old or just plain nuts, they were treated with courtesy similar to what was being extended to Gidget. During meals, with newcomers, we also started seeing our bigger dogs put their bodies between the others and the recent arrivals—who are usually stunned the first few times they get fed via the scattershot method—to ensure that the newbies get enough to eat. Even on something as simple as a walk through the woods, when the pack spreads out along the trail and the older dogs lag at the rear, after Otis's change of heart we began to notice the younger dogs routinely doubling back to check up on their aged friends.

Caring for the sick, protecting the meek, defending the elderly—these are all examples of altruistic behavior. After I'd spent a month researching the roots of this behavior in human beings and not finding many answers, seeing it turn up in my dogs was perplexing. Until very recently, scientists believed altruism the sole province of human beings. In his 1997 book *Good-Natured: The Origins of Right and Wrong in Humans and Other Animals*, legendary primatologist Frans de Waal goes even further, arguing that cognitive empathy—which is the ability to put oneself in another's place and the mental precursor to altruistic behavior—"may be absent in other animals" except for people and, perhaps, the great apes.

This opinion has since begun to change, but only slightly and only in the past few years. As University of Colorado cognitive ethologist Marc Bekoff and author Jessica Pierce explain in their 2003 *Wild Justice*, what facilitated the shift was an outpouring of data that didn't fit with established dogma:

> Eleven elephants rescue a group of captive antelope in KwaZulu-Natal; the matriarch undoes all the latches on the gates of the enclosure with her trunk and lets the gate swing open so the antelope can escape. A rat in a cage refuses to push a lever for food when it sees that another rat receives an electric shock as a result. A male Diana monkey who has learned to insert a token into a slot to obtain food helps a female who can't get the hang of the trick, inserting the token for her and allowing her to eat the food reward. A female fruit-eating bat helps an unrelated female give birth by showing her how to hang in the proper way. A cat named Libby leads her elderly, deaf, blind dog friend, Cashew, away from obstacles and to food.

The scientific reception to this new information has been cautious. While many researchers now suspect that animals engage in ethical behaviors more frequently than was once assumed, others have pointed out that these examples are primarily anomalous incidents, not widespread patterns. But Joy and I weren't just seeing anomalous incidents. We were seeing a complete shift in moral behavior, and, at least according to common consensus, that's not something you see every day.

At the time, just six months into my adventure in dog rescue, I was still surprised by this. Back then, I still held fast to a common misconception: that humans actually understood animals, or mostly understood animals; even if we didn't quite yet understand all animals, we certainly understood dogs. But somehow we have managed to live with dogs, to entirely intertwine our lives with them, without noticing something as straightforward as their capacity for moral behavior? This struck me as troubling. So much of modern life is built on the backs of animals—our convenient food supply, our basic clothing materials, our entire habitat (which was clearly once their habitat)—and all of this, we feel, is permissible because humans are a special species. We have long lists of reasons supporting our specialness, with "humans are the only species to exhibit real moral behavior" topping most of those lists, and altruism is widely considered the pinnacle of all moral behavior. But if we have no solid understanding of altruistic behavior in humans and have been almost completely blind to altruistic behaviors in other animals, then how can we be so sure of anything?

Oh yeah, this definitely struck me as troubling.

17

In early July, a writing assignment sent me back to the sunshine and star maps of Los Angeles. It had been three months since I'd been away, and I was excited about getting a break from the dogs. A little quiet, a few nights in a bed by myself, not having to share my dinner with a dozen roommates—you know, the standard stuff forty-one-year-old men are usually excited about. Even the timing seemed fortuitous: a friend of mine had just had a baby, and my plan was to spend five days reporting the story and one day meeting his baby and, well, so much for my plan.

The problem was the dogs. Forget needing a break—even before my plane departed Albuquerque, I was missing them. By the time I was in Los Angeles, I was certain a small hole had been augered through my chest. No one was more surprised by this than me, but the feeling continued to grow. Later that evening, despite being out to dinner with old friends, it expanded into something I hadn't felt since high school—sort of the *I know I'm going to always be alone because I'll never get a girlfriend because my hair is weird and I can't catch a baseball and who would ever like me anyway so I'll probably kill myself when done listening to the Sisters of Mercy sing "This Corrosion" three hundred times in a row* blues. The next day, it was worse.

It wasn't just loneliness. There was also an awkward vulnerability, a weakness of sorts. For three months I hadn't been anywhere without my posse. Sure, my posse was mostly crippled Chihuahuas, but you'd be surprised how much ass a crippled Chihuahua can kick. In a very real sense, the dogs had become extensions of my senses. I no longer had to look for danger; all I had to do was listen for their barks. Because dogs have better hearing, the natural division of labor made security their job. On top of which, there's no denying a certain *Reservoir Dogs* je ne sais quoi that comes from traveling as a pack. All I can tell you is that with the pack gone, my whole kung fu was off.

I lasted until the middle of my second morning in LA before I found myself canceling a couple of meetings, turning my rental car around, and driving directly to the nearest dog park for some therapy. The nearest dog park happened to be the same one that Ahab and I used to frequent. When I arrived, no one I knew was around, but even the sight of other people's pets calmed me down. I spent the next few hours trying to fondle these pets—and trying not to be too creepy about it—before a friend and his pit bulls showed up. I was so happy to see familiar dogs that I choked up at the sight, then canceled a couple more meetings so I could spend the next few hours in their company.

But after leaving the dog park, the bad feelings came rushing back. I felt a little lost, a little underwater, and very far from normal. Besides the loneliness, I found myself unable to stop worrying about the dogs. Scenarios were forming in my mind. I imagined earthquakes, tornados, nuclear wars. I started calling Joy three times an hour. All night I dreamed dogs were in trouble and I was too far away to help. By morning I knew what was going on. The symptoms were unmistakable. I had seen this problem in other rescuers . . . and in my own mom. I was turning into an overprotective mess. This was Jewish mother syndrome gone doggie-style.

And that was the end of my trip. I just didn't want to be in LA anymore. It was back to New Mexico on the next flight out. I never met my friend's baby and never finished that assignment, and both were pretty unusual for me. Not meeting his kid was just bad form, and having been raised in the Midwest—proud standard-bearer of the work-hard-and-don't-lie ethos—I'd never not finished an assignment before. I hadn't ever felt this out of sorts before, though, truthfully, I wasn't all that surprised.

I'd always assumed there'd be emotional fallout from doing dog rescue. There's just too much history between our species and too much biology woven through that history. At the core sits a question that has bugged ethologists for years: why did humans pick wolves to turn into man's best friend? We hung out with a lot of other species before we started hanging out with wolves, but we never bothered intertwining our lives with theirs. So what happened? Did one of our forebears happen to glance over at the one-hundred-and-eighty pound man-eater and think, This guy—with the fangs and the snarl and the drool—he's the one I want as my best friend? Did we instinctively know our two species would bond so well? And if we knew this instinctively, then why did we know this instinctively?

For a long time the answer has been tangled up in supposition. Archeologists have fourteen-thousand-year-old skeletons of humans and dogs sharing the same grave sites and so adopted 12,000 BCE as the start date for our cohabitation. Then we discovered that the mitochondrial strand of DNA, a sort of genetic constant inherited from one's mother, allowed for deeper analysis. Since mutations are also passed along with the mitochondrial DNA, scientists use these mutations to track backward through time. If two different species share a common mutation, they also share a common ancestor, allowing researchers to estimate how far back that common ancestor lived.

In 1997, UCLA biologist Carles Vilà used this technique to discover that all domestic dogs are direct descendents of the wolf, rather than the motley assortment of previously suspected canids.

Since the split between wolf and dog was the direct result of our cohabitation, he used this new information to figure out how long humans and dogs have been living together. The results were startling. It now appears we've been cohabitating with dogs for longer than we've actually been human.

Vilà dates the emergence of human-canid cohabitation to the end of the last ice age, more than a hundred thousand years ago. This was the period when climate change drove our small-brained, low-browed predecessors out of the African veldt and onto the Eurasian steppe. And what they found there were wolves. A lot of wolves.

Wolves were the top predator in Eurasia, able to keep pace with giant herds of ungulates, able to become what University of Vienna zoologist Wolfgang Schleidt calls the first "mammalian pastoralists"—meaning the first species to herd another species—and our ancestors quickly adopted their methods. They too started chasing large herds of ungulates across the wide-open terrain. That must have been a sight to see, and wolves, ever curious, came to watch the show. Pretty soon we had teamed up with those wolves, coordinating our hunting efforts, sharing our kills, forming the beginning of an alliance unlike any we'd made before.

For a long time, this alliance puzzled people. After all, we'd already lived alongside dozens of other primates—whom we are related to—yet never managed to find a way to cohabit with any of them. As Jane Goodall once pointed out:

> Chimpanzees are individualists. They are boisterous and volatile in the wild. They are always on the lookout for opportunities to get the better of each other. They are not pack animals. If you watch wolves within a pack, nuzzling each other, wagging their tails in greeting, licking and protecting the pups, you see all the characteristics we love in dogs, including loyalty. If you watch wild

chimps, you see the love between mother and offspring, and the bonds between siblings. Other relationships tend to be opportunistic . . . even after hundreds of years of selective breeding, it would be hard if not impossible to produce a chimpanzee who could live with humans and have anything like such a good relationship we have with our dogs.

In his paper "Co-evolution of Humans and Canids," Schleidt addresses this good relationship from a different angle: "There is something in the bond among wolves and between dogs and humans that goes beyond that between us and our closest primate relatives, the chimpanzees. Here *we are not talking about intelligence*, but about what we may poetically associate with *kindness of heart*." Why this bond is so strong becomes one obvious question, but how we learned to bond like this in the first place is the better place to start.

When early hominids first arrived on the Eurasian steppe, socially—which is to say emotionally—we were much more like primates, but we left more like wolves. Schleidt feels this happened not just because we liked the kindness we saw in wolves; rather, we liked it because we lacked it ourselves. What Schleidt is pointing out is that we are here, because we were first there, a fairly selfish animal confronting a hostile, new territory in the Eurasian steppe. Wolves were the steppe's top predator, and we wanted to share that spot. So we adopted wolflike strategies, and this decision not only changed the course of human history but also may have been the starting point for human history.

Scientists can trace intelligence, self-awareness, and long-term planning to our chimpanzee ancestry, but as Schleidt points out in "Apes, Wolves, and the Trek to Humanity," traits such as patience, loyalty, cooperation, and devotion both to one's immediate family and to a larger social group are not prevalent among primates. "The closest approximation to human morality we can find in nature is that of the gray wolf, *Canis lupus*," he writes. He then explains further in "Co-evolution of Humans and Canids": "Wolves' ability to cooperate in a variety of situations, not only in well coordinated drives in the context of attacking prey, carrying items too heavy for one individual, provisioning not only their own young but also other pack members, baby sitting, etc., is rivaled only by that of human societies."

So how did humans become more like wolves and less like primates? Researchers believe the first portion of the answer comes down to similarities. Unlike primates, both wolves and humans are nomadic, omnivorous, social species, which produces a certain sameness in our hierarchy of needs and, by extension, a shared commonality in behavior. Here was the common ground that allowed us to form our evolutionary partnership, but that didn't happen overnight.

In the beginning, before flight distances dropped, our partnership meant sharing the same camp without too much contact between species. This was the era when wolves were our garbage disposals—they ate our leftovers—and security guards—they barked at danger. Flight distances dropped next, and they became our hot-water bottles, keeping us warm when we slept (this is where the phrase "three-dog night" comes from: a night so cold it takes three dogs in the bed to stay warm). Then the real change: we started hunting together. Wolves had better hearing and smell, so they handled the tracking; we had opposable thumbs and bipedal stances, so we took over the killing. Finally, as we started noticing the attention they paid their young, we began trusting them with ours. The men went off hunting, the women gathering, leaving the elderly and the children behind with a bunch of wolves standing guard. And as each of these categories represent the fulfillment of basic needs—food, shelter, security—each of these stages exerted evolutionary pressure.

Then, like now, there were some people who were better with animals then others. Until we started hanging out with wolves, these folks probably helped track game, but otherwise didn't play too much of a role in community life. But once we began cohabitating with wolves, such skills were greatly in demand. Those who were better with animals—who felt deeper empathy, responded more to neoteny, and—considering this is wolves we're talking about—had a greater tolerance for risk had an advantage. Tribes who had these folks around had an advantage. Thus the moment we began cohabitating with wolves became the moment evolution began selecting for those traits that made us better wolf lovers.

And then it began selecting for other things. If we wanted to cohabit with wolves, we needed to learn to live with wolves. In simple terms, the size of our pack grew. A bigger pack is a stronger pack, but only if that pack is united toward a common goal. This type of unity requires more patience, wider loyalty, and better cooperation than existed in our primate past, so once we teamed up with wolves, evolution began selecting for these traits as well. What all this really means is that what we call our "humanity" is actually is a collection of traits borrowed from wolves.

This may also solve the mystery of cross-species altruism. The wolves not only taught us to expand the boundaries of community beyond kin—a lesson chimpanzees have yet to learn—but also taught us to expand beyond kind. And this may be the reason we still need ephemeral phrases such as "kindness of heart" to describe the bond between humans and dogs—because it was dogs who taught us how to bond like that in the first place.

This bond has had measurable effects, specifically on the size of our brains. A large brain is an expensive habit. Our version makes up two percent of our body weight but consumes twenty percent of

84

our energy. For this reason, the brain is always looking for ways to conserve resources. This is why domestication, essentially the process of outsourcing basic survival needs, affects brain size. When horses were tamed they no longer needed to know everything they needed to know to survive in the wild, so their brains shrunk by 16 percent. In pigs, the reduction was thirty-four percent; in dogs estimates fall between ten and thirty percent. Neuroscientists have recently discovered that human brains have also contracted by about ten percent—and this contraction happened not long after we began cohabitating with wolves.

The effect of the dog-human bond also explains what University of Maryland professor of nursing Erika Friedmann discovered in mid-1970s. Friedmann was the first to examine the rumored relationship between furry companionship and cardiovascular health. Her findings involved a group of patients who had undergone heart surgery: those patients who had dogs were much more likely to be alive one year after being discharged from the cardiac care unit than those without. Her results were independent of whether these patients had other people around to talk to, and independent of the severity of their condition. People who lived alone, had no friends, and had a terrible heart condition but who had a dog had better survival rates than those who were surrounded by friends and family, had a mild heart condition, but lacked a canine companion.

Friedmann's work was so startling that hundreds of similar studies have since been done for corroboration purposes. It turns out that dogs not only improve heart attack survival rates but also aid in prevention. Furthermore, canine companionship lowers blood pressure, cholesterol, triglycerides, and incidence of sleeping disorders; significantly increases survival rates after any serious illness; assists in childhood development; and enhances overall family life. A 2002 State University of New York at Buffalo study found that spending a few minutes alone with a dog can do more to reduce stress than talking with a spouse or best friend, while in 2006, in a St. Louis University School of Medicine study, nursing home residents reported that spending time alone with a dog was a far greater cure for loneliness than spending time with other people. A 2007 meta-analysis published in *Anthrozoos* summed up this work succinctly: "The company of animals provides considerable immunity from depression."

Many of the researchers involved in these studies found their own results so bewildering they tried to hedge their bets while presenting their data. "While the idea of pet as social support may appear to some as a peculiar notion," wrote lead researcher Karen Allen in the journal *Psychosomatic Medicine*, "our participants' responses . . . suggest to us that social support can indeed cross species." Despite Allen's hesitancy, with the new start date for human-dog cohabitation pushed back a hundred thousand years, what would be actually surprising is if these kinds of health benefits didn't show up. Humans evolved to share their lives with dogs, and our brains are no longer cut out to do this work alone. Scientists have been presenting this health data as if canine companionship were an evolutionary rarity rather than a near constant. Invert the equation and then there's nothing surprising about these finding. We have evolved to cohabit with dogs. Their presence is part of what makes us feel safe in the world. Remove them from our lives and—as I found out in LA—there's bound to be consequences.

There is a famous koan first uttered by the Zen master Chao-Chou Ts'ung-shen in the seventh century. Zen koans are stories, dialogues, questions, and the like wherein understanding requires not just intellectual prowess but an intuitive leap that often has little to do with the familiar. Chao-Chou's koan is known as "Mu," which was his answer to the question: "Does a dog have Buddha nature?" While "Mu" can be roughly translated as "none" or "without," Robert Pirsig, in his 1974 *Zen and the Art of Motorcycle*

Maintenance, defines it as "no thing," saying that it actually means "to unask the question."

What all of this Buddhist koan work is trying to root out is a myriad of formidable human assumptions, foremost among those a belief in the moral superiority of our species. This superiority, known philosophically as "human specialness" and biblically as our "dominion over every creeping thing that creepeth upon the earth," is often based on the purported highly evolved state of human nature. Among the many of things gleaned from all this recent research into human-canid coevolution is the straightforward realization that asking the question "Does a dog have Buddha nature" may, in fact, be no different from asking its inverse: "Does a human have Buddha nature?"

Then again, the answer is still *mu*.

PART FOUR

I don't do drugs. I am drugs.

—Salvador Dalí

18

By the end of July, our late afternoons were mayhem. Joy had taken to calling the mayhem "Chihuahua play hour." I had taken to calling the play-by-play: "There's Ahab sweeping across the left side of the lawn and Otis barreling up from the back fields. Leo barks twice, and—wow did you see that takedown? A pile of fur for sure. Otis is having a great season. He's just built for this game: low to the ground, good hips, great leverage. He smashes Ahab onto his back, which is all the opening Wookie needs—he dives in low for the neck grab. You've got to love his heart, but he's too small to play with the big dogs and has no defense for Ahab's spin move. So Wookie gets upended and goes sailing into Otis, and this clears a lane toward Leo—who's in a contract year and has great speed but no real lateral movement—and Ahab takes advantage." And that's about ten seconds of the fun; the games go on much longer.

Besides the wrestling matches on the lawn there's usually a marathon back on the porch. It's a charge that Dagmar likes to lead, her favorite route being two laps around the house followed by a dash to the fields and back again. Most days Bella, Farrah, Squirt, Lux, Damien, and Hugo run behind her and outside of a Disney movie very few people actually get to see five Chihuahuas chase a pit bull chase a dachshund, and—I can now say with some authority—it's a shame.

Occasionally Vinnie will join this parade, but at his age all he can usually do is totter, though lately he has begun to totter with some gusto. And he isn't the only one who has found country living supremely restorative. Dagmar is something like a hundred in human years but can now outrun the puppies. Farrah's mange has cleared up, Damien's arthritis as well. Gidget hasn't had a seizure in a month, and that's triple the last record. The real miracle might be Chow, though it didn't start out that way.

Chow started out without a backstory—the word rescuers use to describe an animal's past. Was she beaten? Ignored? Kept chained in a yard? A street dog used to roaming free? Without a backstory, all we got was a veterinary update and everybody's best guess. Rehabilitation is the difficult puzzle to solve. Some cases are easier than others. Dogs that have been abandoned need attention and affection. Dogs that have been abused need to know it won't happen again, which means they need to initiate all physical contact. When dogs have been both abused and abandoned, these treatments work at cross-purposes and how to fix that?

Or dogs that are afraid of doors—not their slamming, but their general presence—are often dogs that have never been allowed inside a house before. Sometimes this means picking them up and carrying them inside; sometimes they've been previously punished for similar transgressions and the sight of four walls is enough to set them trembling. This dilemma knots up quickly, since dogs never allowed inside are also dogs who have not been allowed to sleep near humans. Because dogs live in dens, they never willingly sleep alone. Since most people only have one dog, sleeping outside means sleeping alone, and learning to do so requires a difficult psychological adjustment on the dog's part that frequently leads to later difficulties in pack integration. Since dogs learn much faster by watching other dogs, the great advantage to doing rescue with a pack rather than a pet is that the pack does most of the work. This advantage disintegrates when dogs purposely keeps themselves apart. In those cases, different methods are required.

Chow was one of those cases. She was a white terrier with a host of problems: abused, abandoned, blind, deaf, gloriously fat, comically ugly, disliked humans, disliked other dogs, bit all species equally and with little provocation. Her heart was failing, most of her other organs not far behind. She took seven different medications daily but was a longshot to last the summer. Joy wanted for her dogs what she wanted for herself: for their last memories to be of love. How to pull this off with a dog like Chow is among the reasons rescuers dislike hospice care. Personally, I wanted a way to remember that she hated my guts. Most people pet their pets, hence the name, but the adjustment was taking some time. I was always forgetting and reaching for Chow, and she had a mouth like a piranha. Pretty soon I had sore need of a better plan.

Rescue can be a very intuitive process, and by intuitive I mean that one afternoon, possibly because some tequila was involved, my better plan was "Fuck it." I just reached down and picked Chow up. It was like trying to cuddle a tornado: spinning, shaking, snarling, biting, barking. I kept her at arm's length with my elbows locked and fingers firm until that first wave of panic subsided. In those moments of exhausted reprieve before the next round, I sat down in a chair and locked her waist between my legs. This was perhaps not the best maneuver. I had inadvertently exposed my genitals to her claws and my eyes to her teeth. Chow was already availing herself of the first target and working her way toward the second. I was all set to hurl her across the porch when intuition struck again and I shoved my perfectly healthy hand into her vigorously snapping maw.

I guess that's why they call it intuition. Chow's mouth turned out to be small enough that with my fist wedged inside she couldn't apply nearly as much pressure. She chomped and chomped and after about ten minutes the feeding frenzy vanished, suddenly replaced by profound befuddlement. Chow had finally noticed that my other hand had been stroking her back the whole while. This may have been the first time in her life that she'd felt affection, and where was it coming from? She glanced over her right shoulder, then looked left. Pretty soon she was whipping her head back and forth like a speed freak at a tennis match. It was fear of neck snapping that finally made me let her go. Then she leaped off my lap and shot across the porch, but froze at the edge, one paw lifted, the other legs bent. Whatever that next move, Chow never made it. Instead, she waddled back over, plopped down at my feet, and began licking my toes.

And in dog rescue, this is what a good day looks like.

Chow's good days began to add up. She became another of our backward-aging Benjamin Button cases. After that day on the porch, her fur stopped falling out, she dropped weight, and even her eyes cleared up. No longer blind, Chow discovered running. Her favorite gait a transverse gallop—a gallop without synchronized limbs—that's usually found in large ungulates and, well, dogs as chubby as Chow. She further augmented this traditional motion with a front paw hop that showed up every few feet and was usually accompanied by saucer-big eyes, a wide smile, and—not being the most coordinated of hoppers—a head-over-heels tumble that looked like an explosion at a marshmallow factory.

The only thing missing from her recovery was canine companionship. Chow had come to like the humans, but not other dogs. Even after three months in our care, she still fought any who came close. Most stayed away, or did until an afternoon in late July. I had been sitting in the rocking chair on the porch watching Chihuahua play hour, and Chow had been sitting beside me doing much of the same. Then she got thirsty, leaped off my lap, took three steps toward the water bowl, and *kaboom*. This was the moment the train of dogs that was always racing round the house came racing round the house. Dagmar caught her hind legs and Farrah caught her head. Hugo managed to miss entirely, but Lux clipped her hips and sent her spinning into Bella, whose front paws slid beneath her belly and—being a pit bull and three times Chow's size—shoveled her straight into the air.

In *Dogs Never Lie About Love*, Jeffrey Moussaieff Masson says: "Dogs do not appreciate time that is set by convention; they do not divide a day up into minutes or hours, nor do they think in terms of weeks or months or years. A dog does not tremble at the thought of his own mortality; I doubt if a dog ever thinks about a time when he will no longer be alive. So when we are with a dog, we, too, enter a kind of timeless realm, where the future becomes irrelevant." This was one of those moments—it stretched and stretched. Chow back-flipped over Bella and Bella rolled under Chow, and I could have knitted a sweater in the hours between dogs launching upward and dogs crashing down.

They landed in a tangled heap, faces inches apart, eyes locked, all hell about to break loose. I was already jumping out of my chair, but Chow had other plans. She leaned forward and licked Bella on the nose. I was staggered. Bella was dumbstruck. Her jaw dropped open and her tongue flopped out. Then she regained herself and barked once. Chow didn't need to be told twice. This was game on. She broke into a giant grin, jumped up, and ran off. Bella took off after her and all the other dogs fell in behind. The whole parade went galloping down the veranda and sometimes there's no better feeling in the world then watching a pack of happy dogs at play. Sometimes it's better than better.

Joy once told me of an exhilaration unlike any other she's ever known that comes from seeing a dog reborn. In the psychology of altruism, that rush is known as *helper's high*. The term was coined by Big Brothers Big Sisters executive director Allan Luks in the 1990s, after he interviewed more than three thousand Americans involved in volunteer service and found that their good deeds consistently produced a feeling of profound euphoria. "Many people were reporting," he wrote in his now classic *The Healing Power of Doing Good,* "that as a result of their helping they were experiencing a rush of physical pleasure and well-being, increased energy, warmth and actual relief from aches and pains."

Luks believes that helper's high is caused by endogenous—meaning internal to the body—opioids called *endorphins.* These chemicals help regulate parental bonding, social interaction, and physical contact. They kill pain and produce pleasure in the same way as exogenous—meaning external to the body—opiates such as opium and heroin. Since Luks's original work, researchers have further fingered serotonin, the "happy chemical" behind Prozac; anandamide, the body's natural version of THC—the psychoactive chemical found in marijuana; and, especially if risk taking is involved, the feel-good neurochemicals norepinephrine and dopamine.

Luks describes helper's high as a variation of what athletes call *being in the zone* or, as scientists now prefer, a *flow state.* Much of what we know about flow states comes from Claremont Graduate University psychologist, Mihaly Csikszentmihalyi, who has devoted his lifetime to the subject. Csikszentmihalyi defines this state as a joyous and complete merger of action and awareness, as "being so involved in an activity that nothing else seems to matter: the ego falls away. Time flies. Every action, movement and thought follows inevitably from the previous one, like playing jazz. Your whole being is involved, and you're using your skills to the utmost."

The depth and range of the experience vary considerably, but whatever the level, flow is considered among life's most exquisite ecstasies. The psychologist Abraham Maslow called flow states "peak experiences" and explains further: "During a peak experience, the individual experiences an expansion of self, a sense of unity and meaningfulness in life. The experience lingers in one's consciousness and gives a sense of purpose, integration, self-determination and empathy." Csikszentmihalyi notes this empathetic unity extends from one's immediate companions outward to "nature and contact with ultimate reality," which, as Luks points out, creates a feedback loop of motivations: "the sense of bondedness . . . can be both the inspiration for altruism and the result of the altruistic act." And for all these reasons University of Pennsylvania psychologist Martin Seligman calls flow *autotelic*—an end in itself.

It's an elusive end as well. While the zone is most frequently associated with sporting pursuits, California State University at Fullerton psychologist Ken Ravizza found peak experiences relatively rare in an athlete's career. Yet Luks discovered that charitable deeds produce flow states with almost clockwork regularity. Ninety-five percent of his original study group reported the rush, while eighty percent of those reported that it lasted for hours, occasionally days—which is exponentially longer than the average flow state. Why this is the case is not yet known, but there's one obvious explanation. Flow is the merger of action and awareness, and for that merger to take place one needs to be thoroughly engaged in the task at hand. This is exactly where do-gooders have an advantage. Flow might be relatively rare in athletics and relatively common in altruism because, as Leonard Koppett famously pointed out in *Sports Illusion, Sports Reality*, sport is fundamentally an illusion: "specifically, the illusion that the result of a game matters." Almost by definition, altruism is the opposite. The game always matters. Most of us don't need to be coached into keeping our eyes on the ball when actual lives are at stake.

Of course, I didn't yet realize actual lives were at stake, as I had been too busy enjoying myself. Watching Chow gallivant down the porch, I got my first taste of helper's high, and it came with the same deep time sensation I'd experienced at Wolf Mountain Sanctuary, only more intense and more intimate. It was a sense of cross-species connection that defied logic. I felt like I could speak dog. I felt, for the first time in my life, like part of the pack. How good did that feel? Two days later, I asked Joy to marry me—so go ahead, draw conclusions.

19

Joy agreed in July to marry me. For the wedding, we thought maybe next summer, we thought maybe small; we might have thought other things, but neither of us mentioned them, as we stopped talking about the idea not long after we started. Neither of us said another word until one morning late August when Joy woke up and rolled over and found me already awake. It seems we had both been having the same bad dream, specifically what our year would be like if we had to spend it planning a wedding. Neither of us had the stomach for it. Also, Joy had little family left and my parents were already planning a trip to Chimayo at the end of September. We couldn't think of a better way to welcome them than with a surprise wedding.

September was a good month for it. The long, hot days had grown cooler and shorter. The cottonwoods had begun to turn yellow, their bright torches igniting the desert. The coneflowers were in bloom, as were the sunflowers. The hollyhocks, which had risen to seven-, eight-, nine-foot giants over the summer, had died back, but fresh rains had brought new growth, and these second stalks were shorter, their flowers more vibrant. There was a dewy smell to the air, and the scent of sage and second chances as well.

Joy and I got married on our back porch. The catering was done by a guy who sold tacos on the side of the road. The ceremony performed by a rabbi found randomly in the phone book. Decorations were a couple of bonfires. Outside of my immediate family, our out-of-town guests included a rocket scientist, a television producer, and a jujitsu instructor. Our in-town guests, at least the ones we knew before they showed up for the wedding, were dog people, horse people, and one retired dominatrix who had left behind a thriving whips-and-chains business for a life raising chickens. What had started out as a small ceremony turned into a slightly larger festival as, in the days leading up to the ceremony, Joy and I kept inviting whomever we ran into. For reasons still unclear, a lot of those people showed up dressed as pirates.

Somehow, it was a perfect wedding. The phrase "over the moon" is not a phrase I'd ever paid much attention to, but in the days and weeks right after the ceremony that phrase was the only one that seemed to accurately describe my state of mind. It was right around then that I had another telephone conversation with Chris Malloy. We were talking about the satisfaction of married life, country living, and learning to build things with your hands when Chris said, "You'll be walking along one day thinking about all the things you can make and you'll glance down and think: 'Shoes—fuck ya, I can make shoes.'"

I had laughed with him then, laughed because I was over the moon, because I really believed I could make shoes, and mostly because it still felt like a game to me. I'd forgotten that choices have consequences. The Cherokee medicine man Rolling Thunder once said: "The teachings don't come like some people think. You can't just sit down and talk about the truth. It doesn't work that way. You have to live it, and be part of it, and you might get to know it. I say you might. And it's slow and gradual and doesn't come easy." I had set out to find a life that means something and was dumb enough to think I was well on my way. I did not yet understand how wrong this idea would prove to be and how right Rolling Thunder actually was—that the experience I wanted was not an experience that came easy.

20

Our neighbors have roosters, and being a light sleeper, those roosters often get me out of bed around 4:00 a.m. At that dark hour, the world works a little slowly. It's hard to remember key facts, like which dog had eaten something unusual the day before, like where that dog had slept, like turn on the lights before you walk through the living room. Cleaning dog shit out from between your toes before there's been time to drink a cup of coffee is the kind of thing that takes the shine off the search for the meaning of life right quick.

So frequent is this occurrence that dog rescuers have a term for it: "shit foot." Over the summer, on those mornings I got "shit-footed," I could treat the experience as part of the adventure, maybe not the best part, but rationalizable nonetheless. I knew that one of the main reasons older dogs get dumped at the pound is an inability to control their bowels. And few want to adopt a dog that craps all over the house. In the real world, shit foot is a terminal offense. So that first summer, there was a rebel pride here: I could take it—other people could not.

I started to change my mind a few weeks after our wedding. There had been a stretch of too many messy mornings in a row and pride was no longer cutting it. After six months of squish, the thrill was gone. This wasn't an adventure, this was a routine. And since Joy had committed her life to doing dog rescue and I had just committed my life to her, this was going to remain my routine for quite a while.

That was a mistake. You can't crack a door like that without further repercussions. I started to notice all the other times the dogs interfered with my life. Reading, for example, has long been one of my great pleasures. But these days, the moment I stretched out with a good book, five dogs would land atop me. As they all wanted to be petted, their goal was to put themselves directly between my hands—which is exactly where my book needed to go. I could ignore them, throw them to the floor, or lock them out of the room, but then guilt set in. We ran a dog rescue; our commitment was rehabilitation, and that required affection. Was I really going to be that selfish? I didn't want to be that selfish; I wanted to be that selfish; was this even selfishness at all? I was paying the bills and needed to read for work. So reading was critical, right? But was it more critical than a dog's recovery? Guilt became resentment, and resentment, as I would soon realize, often presages disaster.

There's not much margin for error in dog rescue. Oversights compound quickly. Take dog food. The good stuff costs sixty bucks a bag, the cheaper variations around twenty. One of the reasons I spent five hundred dollars a month on good food is because bad food often causes allergies in dogs. We had old dogs, sick dogs, and scared dogs—all with weakened immune systems—so either I spent the money up front on quality chow or I spent the money on the back end on medical bills. But with the still faltering economy and my savings account getting low, how to sort such priorities became another concern. Suddenly I was back where I started when I started with Ahab: surrounded by ethical questions with no easy answers.

Then a series of late fall thunderstorms washed away some of our driveway and left a hole beneath the front gate big enough for a dog to slip through. I noticed the gap when heading into town to buy—of all things—more dog food. I didn't want to be bothered, so decided to fix it when I got back. But buying dog food reminded me of all the other things I wasn't buying because I was buying dog food. The house was still half furnished, we hadn't been out to dinner in months, we couldn't afford to go on a honeymoon. By the time I made it back home I was definitely not going to fix that hole until I was good and ready. It was Monday night. Instead, I was going to sit down and watch football—just try to stop me.

Sometime in the first quarter, Otis discovered the hole. We found him not long after halftime, whimpering on the front stoop. He looked like he'd gotten up close and personal with the business end of an ice pick. There was blood on his paws and deep gashes over much of his body and Hugo, who went everywhere with Otis, was also missing. Bull terriers have incredible pain tolerances. It takes a certain kind of know-how to mess one up this bad. Hugo, on the other hand, was a Chihuahua.

Guilt got me out the door in an instant. It was pitch black and pouring rain, and I was underdressed and sprinting into canyon country. The Anasazi once made their home in the canyon country surrounding my house, and what happened to them remains anyone's guess. Six hundred and fifty years ago one of the earliest known North American civilization disassembled itself. Major religious centers were pulled apart. Doorways sealed with rock and mortar. Gigantic kivas—the central chapels of the Anasazi church—had their roofs peeled off and their interiors scorched by fire. Whole cities were abandoned. Then the Anasazi themselves vanished completely. But as I found out that night, disappearing into the desert of the Southwest is not nearly the trick many suspect.

I had never been back into those canyons during a thunderstorm before and probably won't be again. The high cliff walls were saturated with water and bleeding mud and rock and stone and shrubs and bushes and whatever else could be tugged free. Long-dry arroyos had turned into raging rivers. Being out there was dumb and dangerous and I should have gone home. But how could I go home? Instead, I tried hunting up one of those arroyos, a trail Hugo and I often hiked. Canyoneers use the term *slot* to describe canyons where the walls are close enough to touch with both hands. The canyon I was hiking started out wide, grew narrower, and then became a slot. I was somewhere between the narrows and the slot and the bottom was already a deep, churning muck. Not wanting to find out how deep, I was clinging to the bank and rounding a corner when I glanced up and saw a piñon tree riding a thick wave of water out of that slot and straight at my head.

I remember diving off the bank and into the muck. Something flipped me over and something shot up my nose. My shoulder smashed a rock, my body caught the current, and I'm pretty sure I was swept down five flights of stairs. I'm dead certain I landed on a prickly pear cactus. There were spines in my legs, arms, and back, but the new perch afforded a good view upriver. I couldn't see Hugo but could clearly make out the piñon tree wedged between rock walls, right about where I'd been standing only moments before.

It was a long trudge back to the house. I spent most of that slog trying to figure out how to tell Joy a dog was dead because I decided to watch a football game. As it turned out, I didn't have to. Hugo made it home alive, though he'd arrived in considerably worse shape than me. There was a long gash over his left eye, another down his back, and bite marks nearly everywhere else. Whatever he and Otis had encountered, it was bigger than a breadbox.

I fixed the driveway the next morning, then set out to source the source of their assault. Over the next few weeks, I discovered that farmers in Chimayo love to speculate about the weird shit that comes out of the night to maul the dog.

"It's a badger," said Raul.

"Wild boar," said Frank.

"Old man Caldron," said Pablo, "you know, when he's drunk."

Kerry thought extraterrestrials; Arturo suspected Chupacabra. I didn't know whom to believe.

After a while, Doc set us straight.

"Bobcat," she said, "big mama of a bobcat."

A bobcat? Who gets mauled by a bobcat? And in the face of that, seriously, it's hard to believe I was ever concerned about dog shit.

21

There's no real way to tell the truth about northern New Mexico without telling the truth about northern New Mexico. To be blunt: it's very weird here. To be clear: not in the way you think. I don't just mean the heroin dealers, outlaw bikers, UFO fanatics, conspiracy nuts, New Age astrologers, crystal healers, hippie communes, artist communes, alternative architects building recyclable castles out of straw and dung, and the large population of Catholic Penitentes who parade down the street Easter weekend, cat-o'-nine-tails in hand, flogging themselves as they go. I don't even mean my friend Matt, though Matt is a decent place to start.

I met Matt over the summer. I needed to run electricity to an outbuilding and that meant I needed to dig a trench—four feet deep and one foot wide and two hundred feet long—through dense clay and hard stone. Certainly there are machines for such madness. The machine is appropriately called a trencher and looks a lot like a six-foot chain saw strapped to a dishwasher. Running a trencher is akin to bronco busting and, after two days of it, despite the pair of sturdy work gloves I wore out along the way, I'd still managed to peel most of the flesh off both my hands. Worse, the trench was not yet complete. What was left was the delicate shovel work. By delicate I mean there were phone lines and gas pipes that needed to be avoided; by work I mean a good seventy feet of digging. With my flayed hands, there wasn't much I could do, so at the suggestion of a friend

I hired Matt, though I didn't yet know him as Matt. I was just given a phone number and a title.

"Call the number," my friend had said. "Ask for the Human Steam Shovel."

The Human Steam Shovel earned his nickname by being able to dig holes for days straight. If you've never dug a hole before, this may not seem like much of a talent, but there is very little in the way of work that is more difficult than punching a shovel through soil, and there are very few alive who can do this without pause for hours, let alone days on end. Matt did not tire. He dug and dug and dug—or that was the rumor. I was having a little trouble confirming the rumor because Matt was having a little trouble deciding if he wanted to work for me. The problem was not that he didn't need the work. The very first thing he said to me—after telling me that I could call him Matt instead of the Human Steam Shovel—was that he was completely broke and running out of food and thank God I called.

I told him I would both feed him and pay him and perhaps we could start on Thursday.

"You mean this Thursday?" said Matt, "two days from now?"

I told him that was what I meant, and he told me that was a bad day.

"So you can't work on Thursday?"

"No, I can't work, you can't work, no one can work on Thursday—it's a bad day."

"Well, um, bad how?"

Apparently, and the mythology got pretty confusing pretty quickly, Thursday was a bad day on the Sumerian calendar, which is technically known as the Umma calendar, which dates to the twenty-first century BCE. Anyway, as far as Thursday was concerned, the stars were misaligned and the timing inauspicious. The only thing I could think to say was: "You're starving, but you're turning down food and cash because of a calendar that's been out of date for four thousand years?"

"Dude," he said, "you need to understand how things work around here."

"Uh-huh," I said, "you betcha."

Matt went on to explain that there's a power here, in the land itself, some ancient juju to be respected but never understood. No one can quite explain it, but Matt said the closest he could come was "emotional amplifier."

"A what?"

"Like whatever you're feeling at the time, the landscape magnifies exponentially."

"Uh-huh," I said, "you betcha."

As it turns out, Friday was a fine day to dig trenches, so Matt came over then. As advertised, he dug for two days straight, and that was that. I probably wouldn't have given his warning another thought except for the plumber and what happened after the plumber and, well, you'll just have to judge for yourself.

I hired the plumber to help me fix my septic tank in the weeks right after the bobcat attack. He showed up and told us what most people tell us when they first show up at our house—that he had relatives who used to live in our house. This story is a little more straightforward: Chimayo is a small town and our house has a long history. It was built in the late nineteenth century, and just about everybody who lives in the area knows someone who used to live here. The father of the favorite aunt of the guy who sells us goat meat—a very special treat for the dogs. The sister of the cousin of our postman. And, of course, the plumber, who mentioned that his great-great-great-grandmother had given birth in the room that is now Joy's office. He also mentioned that the baby died at birth and they buried his body in "the old way."

I didn't know what the old way was, but had visions of Joy

heading into the backyard to plant cucumbers and accidentally digging up a corpse. He shook his head, then walked over to my living room wall and slapped a palm against it.

"The body's buried here," he said. "That's the old way."

The whole story is that back in the day, when a baby died and a house was under construction, the body was entombed in the foundation.

"It's to ward off bad luck," said the plumber.

"You sure? 'Cause it sounds like the kind of thing that might bring on bad luck."

"Don't say that."

"Huh?"

"Don't think about bad luck, don't mention bad luck. Don't you know there's a power here?"

Which is when I remembered Matt's warning.

"You mean the emotional amplifier? You think that's real?"

"Just wait," he said, "just wait."

As it turns out, we didn't have long to wait. Come late October, for the first time since we'd left California, the isolation of Chimayo was starting to get to me. Some of this may have been the coming of winter: the branches going bare, the thick clouds settling over the mountains, the desolation of a dying landscape. Most of it was that we'd been gone from Los Angeles about eight months, which was more than enough time for friendships to begin to fade. Most of the folks we knew in California had already stopped asking when we were coming back to California. By now they'd concluded that as rash as our move to Chimayo had appeared, our return was not imminent. Out of sight and out of mind and outside of my parents, by the end of October our phone had mostly stopped ringing. So I was feeling isolated and lonely, and something—something started to amplify that.

It started slowly. It started with the mail. After six months of perfect delivery service, our box stayed empty. No bills, no letters, not even a bundle of coupons for the grocery store. Either the post office was losing our mail or no one in California could forward it. Forms were filled out and phone calls made, but nothing seemed to help. Our cells never could get a signal in Chimayo, so those calls were made via our landline. But two days after our mail vanished, the city started repairing our road and—since the phone company had buried its cables directly beside that road—those workers started accidentally cutting our land line along the way. Every cut took a few days to repair and since cuts were a daily occurrence we lost our phones not long after we lost our mail.

Then our computers went on the fritz. Joy's went on Tuesday and mine went on Thursday. This shouldn't have been much of a bother, except we couldn't find a Mac repair shop within a hundred miles—so unless I wanted to drive to Albuquerque we had to ship our computers back to Apple for repairs. To make this happen, Apple needed to ship us a very specific box. Something about the warranty, but without that box they wouldn't fix the machines. Unfortunately, the only carrier Apple worked with at the time was DHL, and DHL wouldn't deliver to our area. So no DHL meant no repairs, and that meant no e-mail as well.

Our remaining lines of connection to the outside world became an old television set and a couple of carrier services. The TV sat in our living room, in the middle of a large table. The reception was poor in our area, so none of the standard channels came in. We didn't have cable, but the TV had a built-in DVD player and we used it to watch movies. Or we did until that Amityville night, when Joy pushed the power button and the set jumped straight up into the air, shot a foot forward, and crashed on the ground between her feet. I was standing two feet away at the time and saw the whole episode, and the only thing I can say is that with a dead baby in the walls, what the hell else would you expect?

This was followed by a freak heat wave, some global warming foreshock that only lasted five days but pushed temperatures into the nineties. In the middle of those days, Joy went into town to run errands and I decided to take a nap. As it was hot as hell in the house, I went to bed naked. Sometime not long afterward, the dogs started barking. As the dogs often bark while we sleep, I've learned which sounds to ignore. This bark was none of those. It was a tone used to signal real trouble. I heard their alarm, jumped out of bed, grabbed the closest available weapon, and dashed to the front door. I got two steps outside before I realized I was both brandishing an umbrella and not wearing any clothes. Until I bumped into our delivery woman at the supermarket a few months later and explained the situation, that was the last we saw of FedEx.

The next morning I asked Joy if she thought something was trying to sever our connections to the outside world.

"Well," she said, "there's still UPS."

Dog number thirteen was named Bella Chupacabra, with *Bella* being Italian for "pretty" and *Chupacabra* being Spanish for "the dreaded goat-sucker." Our pretty, dreaded goat-sucker was all muscle, all black, part heeler, part pit bull, and very protective—as our UPS driver soon found out the hard way. Bella bit him four days after I answered the door naked, and that was the end of that. I had started out lonely and ended up completely cut off. By early November, it was just us and the dogs and alone on the island—and that's when things got even stranger.

22

As we were accumulating dogs over the summer, Joy had mentioned that it could take five or six months for most of them to come out of their shell. "In November," she would say, "that's when we'll really get to know them." Well, it was November, and two things were clear: we had certainly accumulated a lot of dogs over the summer and all of those dogs had needed those months to come out of their shells. Those months had now passed and those personalities had now emerged. The easiest way to explain the difference was claustrophobia.

That autumn, our house just felt small. It felt like we'd lost a bedroom or added more dogs. I asked Joy. We hadn't lost a bedroom and, she seemed pretty sure, we hadn't added more dogs either. It was that the dogs we'd already added were suddenly starting to express themselves, and those expressions were taking up a lot of space. And after we got cut off from the outside world, this was my first lesson in island living: it's damn crowded.

The second lesson concerned the nature of that crowd. It wasn't just that we saw an expansion of personality, it was the particular personality we saw expand. He was a miniature Doberman who'd showed up in July. Joy called him Buddy, but by the time the shell shock wore off and his real self started to emerge I had taken to calling him Smashmouth Thunderfuck. Smashmouth had ended up at the Española shelter because he was a rambunctious adolescent who couldn't stop scent-marking. Dogs scent-mark out of instinct and trainers find erasing instinct among the hardest things to do. It only takes the right smell on a vertical surface to trigger leg lifting in some dogs. With Smash, even those things were optional. This guy pissed everywhere, but this was not why I called him that. He earned his moniker because he was missing half his face. Something had taken a bite out of him, and what grew back was not quite right. His jaw was offset, his mouth crooked. He had a tooth growing out of one nostril, and he only had one nostril. He also had the largest penis I've ever seen on a dog. The first time we saw it we thought tumescence emergency, the kind that requires surgery to repair. Then, as he came into his own, we saw it nonstop. Smash earned the second half of his name humping all of our male dogs.

He was a caricature of a Latin lover. His passion ran hot and fast. Smash burned through the men in our pack, then went back to the beginning and started over. And it was only the men. For a few days he'd be enamored with Hugo, then switch to Damien, then over to Leo. Whoever his hombre de desire, he would stare at him longingly, follow him around endlessly, groom him ceaselessly. He looked exactly like a lovelorn teenager with a crush. And like most lovelorn teenagers, he was also horny as hell.

Smash humped his paramour every chance he got. According to most researchers, male-on-male humping is always about dominance. Examples of this attitude are everywhere. Author and behavior modification expert Rena Murray, in her *Paw Persuasion Pointers* newsletter, says: "Dog humping, dog mounting, blocking and claiming are all serious and growing dog dominance issues, and most will lead to aggression if not handled." But Smash had no interest in aggression—he was a lothario, after all—just as he had no interest in dominance. In fact, a lot of the time, he didn't even mount his boyfriend. Just standing in the vicinity and thrusting into the air was enough to keep him smiling. And he would keep smiling until he had an orgasm. Being fixed, this could take a while. Two days of thrusting, three days of thrusting, that was what it took.

And Smash wasn't the only one who batted switch. We had gay dogs. A lot of gay dogs. Smash was in love with Misha, who was in love with Salty, and when I said there was less space in the house, I both mean psychologically and having to step around their bizarre hump triangle on my way to the bathroom. When Hugo wants to make a male friend, he licks anuses and testicles. He doesn't groom the whole body; he zeroes in on the erogenous zones. Squirt—how to put this—is a bull dyke. Same goes for Dagmar. Helgar only likes gay men, which makes her our resident fag hag. Damien, meanwhile, is a drag queen, a hunchbacked Chihuahua given to high-pitched operatic rampages and being extremely picky about his clothes. When Damien finds a winter sweater to his liking, he parades around the house and we are treated to the canine equivalent of a drag show. If our rescue was a television series, over the summer it was the canine equivalent of *Little House of the Prairie*, but by the time we were cut off from the outside world, we were clearly *The Real World: San Francisco*.

The arrival of the sexual revolution made me curious. Why did so much personality express itself as sexuality? Why was so much of that sexuality homosexuality? I figured the best place to start was with how psychologists assess personality. In a speech given to the American Psychological Association in 1933, Louis Leon Thurstone made first mention of the most comprehensive inquiry into human psychology yet undertaken. What researchers had done was identify, analyze, and categorize every word in the English language that could be used to describe disposition. When finished, they discovered that all our linguistic variety could be reduced to five personality traits, now known as "the Big Five," which—even though they were originally meant as theoretical categories—have since become so well validated that no one has yet to find a better model.

Openness, conscientiousness, extroversion, agreeableness, and emotional stability are those five, but it's helpful to see them for what they really are: strategies for survival. In his *The Five-Factor Model of Personality*, psychologist Jerry Wiggins explains that all cars have four wheels, a set of brakes and a steering device and that these components could loosely be described as "car nature." In the same way, all humans have two legs, an opposable thumb, and a relatively—compared to other primates—hairless body, and these could be similarly considered "human nature."

> When an engineer designs a car, both the "car nature" and differences in components must be considered in great detail. When choosing a car to purchase, however, the basic components of "car nature" become irrelevant because all cars possess them. Rather, the *differences* among cars become critical for selection—whether the car is large or small, powerful or weak, economical on gas or a guzzler . . . In the same manner, when we face social adaptive problems such as selecting a mate, it would be preposterous to use "having an opposable thumb" or "two-leggedness" as key selection criteria since, with rare exception, all potential mates have these attributes. Despite the fact that having an opposable thumb is a remarkably important part of human nature, a woman seeking a mate does not think: "Wow, I really find him attractive—he has an opposable thumb!" Constants do not count in decisions of selection. Just as in selecting a car, the differences among individuals loom large.

The differences he's referring to are all various combinations of the Big Five. The reason these differences show up as sexuality is because mate selection requires judging another's demeanor as a way of judging a potential partner's ability to provide for basic needs. Since reproduction is among those needs, sexual identity becomes a subcategory of personality. Take Smash. His Big Five breakdown looks something like this: he's open and agreeable (open and agreeable to lots of lovers) and extroverted (capable of charming those lovers), but not conscientious (he burns through his lovers) or emotionally stable (again, he burns through his lovers). Yet this balance works perfectly for Smash, because what he's really after is a strategy for survival known as *short-term mating*.

From a Darwinian perspective, the way to win the game of survival is to pass along one's genes. There are a number of routes available, with monogamy and polygamy being the most familiar. Scientists, wanting to understand the psychology behind both strategies, have done significant research into the personality traits associated with each. Across the boards, humans who score high on openness and extroversion and low on conscientiousness and emotional stability tend to have more lovers than others. Track a small child who scored this way into adulthood and you'll find a grown-up with lots of affairs and few long-term relationships. Moreover, the human data matches the animal data—as Smash bears out—because polygamy remains a viable option no matter the species. And, as Joy and I discovered, both strategies remain viable no matter one's sexual orientation.

And that orientation is not the anomaly some suggest. When the religious right calls homosexuality an "abomination against nature," they couldn't be more wrong. Homosexuality is everywhere in nature. Dogs, mallards, gulls, dolphins, bison, elephants, lions, sheep, lizards, dragonflies, and around four hundred other species display the preference. A couple of years ago a pair of male penguins living at the San Francisco Zoo fell so in love that they fostered an egg together. Giraffes have all-male orgies. Japanese macaques, on the other hand, are committed lesbians. Bonobos, our closest living relatives, go every which way they can whenever they can. But if Darwin is correct and evolution is competitive by design and the way to win the game is to pass along one's genes, then why is anything gay?

For a while the answer was genetic mutation. Then Stanford University evolutionary biologist Joan Roughgarden decided to march in the 1997 San Francisco Gay Pride Parade and was stunned by the number of gay people. "Even the most conservative estimates puts the number of gays at one out of twenty," she said, "but to see how that looked in the real world was another thing. It made me realize that Huntington's disease, the most common illness caused by genetic mutation, shows up in one out of every hundred thousand people. But there are just too many gay people in the world for that idea to be right. With this much frequency, there's no way the preference could be caused by an aberrant gene. Gayness has got to serve a purpose."

Roughgarden started with the idea that homosexuality has to be an adaptive trait because it's been adapted everywhere in nature. Rather than being edited out, gayness has been carefully preserved by natural selection for millions of years. Stranger still, the more "advanced" a species seems to be, the more prevalent its preference for same-sex coupling. Homosexuality, Roughgarden now thinks, is actually *the* telltale sign of advanced animal communities, writing in her book *Evolution's Rainbow*: "The more complex and sophisticated a social system is, the more likely it is to have homosexuality intermixed with heterosexuality."

This idea conflicts with one of the fundamental tenets of Darwinism. According to the theory of evolution, the relationship between males and females is governed by sexual selection—which is defined as anything that helps us reproduce better. Men compete for access to females, females compete by choosing the best males.

The poster child for sexual selection has always been the peacock. Why would a bird develop an ornament as detrimental to survival as a tail the size of Detroit? The answer, Darwin suspected, was female choice. Somewhere along the line, peahens decided big tails were sexy. So males with big tails got to have the most sex, and their offspring got bigger tails. Give it enough time and you end up where peacocks are today: stuck with useless bridal trains sticking out of their butts. Once we discovered genes, scientists went one better. They realized that the bridal train was an expensive costume requiring top-flight DNA to produce. It was those genes the peahens were after—it was why they developed this predilection in the first place.

Lately, a few problems have arisen, not the least of which was what University of Tokyo researcher Mariko Takahashi discovered after spending seven years observing a feral population of Indian peafowl. "We found no evidence that peahens expressed any preference for peacocks with more elaborate trains," she wrote in a 2008 article for *Animal Behavior*, before mentioning other related studies—some corroborating her results, others finding not enough variation between the size of male trains to make female choice even possible, while even more discovering no evidence that a large tail has anything to do with the quality of the male's genes—and concluded that it was time to face facts: sexual selection might not be the driver of natural selection we have long suspected.

Roughgarden believes that Darwin made a critical error in developing his criteria for success. Because paternity testing was not around in his time, sexual selection has been judged on *quality of mating* rather than *quantity of children*. "Obviously," she writes in *The Genial Gene*,

> offspring are impossible unless some mating takes place, but
> the quality of mating *per se* is only distantly related to the

quantity of offspring reared. Nonetheless, sexual-selection theory always refers to reproductive social behavior as comprising a "mating system." Within a mating system, evolutionary change then arises from differences in "mating success," and particular behaviors are understood by how they contribute to controlling and maximizing the frequency of mating. Male/female social dynamics are then seen to revolve around females as a "limiting resource" for males. Hence males must compete with each other for access to mating opportunities with females, or for control of the females themselves, and females choose males to maximize the genetic quality of their offspring. Sexual selection errs by elevating a component of reproduction, namely mating, into an end in itself.

So Roughgarden threw out sexual selection and replaced it with *social selection*, which views all "reproductive social behavior"—that's flirting to fondling to fucking—as part of an "offspring-producing system." In this system, the basis for evolution is cooperative teamwork, not individual competition, as the entire community tries to produce the most offspring. "The advantage of Roughgarden's new theory," says Jonah Lehrer in *Seed* magazine, "is that it can explain a wider spectrum of sexual behaviors than Darwinian sexual selection. Lesbian oystercatchers and gay mountain sheep? Their homosexuality is just a prelude to social cooperation, a pleasurable way of avoiding wanton conflict."

Under this model, same-sex sexuality becomes an important form of communication, like another version of grooming: a tactile behavior that feels good and establishes cooperative bonds. And those bonds are the point. "That's why," says Roughgarden, "you're much more likely to see two chimps working together than one clobbering the other over the head with a rock." It's also why we see so much homosexuality in our pack. None of our crew is related, so kinship-based altruism isn't an option. But if homosexuality is viewed as a form of tactile communication that abets social cooperation, then it's a viable survival strategy, especially in a pack as diverse as ours.

And this was my third lesson in island living—sometimes it's a tropical paradise, other times a Boys Town disco on a Friday night.

23

Gay dogs were a curiosity. Altruistic dogs were a curiosity. Being cut off from the outside world was a curiosity. Being cut off from the outside world with a pack of gay altruistic dogs was edging toward downright strange. But none of this, truthfully, was as odd as the fact that the majority of gay altruistic dogs in our pack were Chihuahuas. Chihuahuas, now, they're truly odd. But even this—with all its idiosyncratic glory—paled on the peculiarity scale compared to the fact that somewhere, sometime, somehow, during our first winter in Chimayo, I decided that I really liked our Chihuahuas.

Yeah, I know, pretty freakin' unbelievable.

Anyway, it helps to start at the beginning: The world's smallest dogs take their name from Mexico's largest state. The state of Chihuahua is roughly the size of Great Britain, and the dogs of the same name were discovered there in 1850, in the ruins of an old palace. The palace was built by the Aztec ruler Montezuma I, though historians believe the breed antedates his reign by almost a thousand years. There are Mayan sculptures of similar small dogs dating back to the fifth century AD. The Mayan called these dogs *techichi*, and when the Toltecs conquered the Mayans they took a serious liking to the *techichi*. They brought them into their homes as pets and began using them in religious ceremonies. It was the Aztecs who came calling next. After conquering the Toltec, they further elevated the *techichi's* sacred status, believing these dogs had the ability to guide the souls of the dead to the world of the hereafter. Thus when the Aztecs buried a warrior, they often buried a live *techichi* with him.

As these things go, it was mostly the ruling-class Aztec who thought the *techichi* possessed magical powers. The lower classes kept them around for more pedestrian reasons: the dogs were bedwarmers at night and meals the following day. To this end, the *techichi* were further crossbred with the Chinese crested, a breed that had already been introduced into South America by the Spanish. This mix served a purpose. *Techichi* were a medium-sized, long-haired dog, the Chinese crested smaller and hairless, so the hybrid was easier to control (smaller) and easier to prepare for cooking (hairless). And it's the descendants of that hybrid that we know today as Chihuahuas.

As mentioned, when I first met Joy, I had little interest in Chihuahuas. I had the familiar machismo—real men don't like small dogs—augmented by a near decade in Los Angeles—small dogs as fashion accessories—confounded by a professional problem: small dogs tend to be yappy, and it's darn difficult to write with a dozen yappy dogs around. To get around this, over the summer I had turned what was originally a dilapidated barn into an office of sorts. My new office, which we appropriately called the goat shack, sat about three hundred yards away from the house. The house, being an adobe, had two-foot-thick walls. The combination of those walls and that distance was enough to protect me from their ruckus.

As the pack continued to grow, my preference for quietude also meant that Joy and I began to split up the rescue work along size lines. I got the big dogs, and she got everyone else. During the day, the big dogs were with me down at the goat shack; the rest of the pack were up at the house with Joy. We went for separate walks and ate at separate times and—because Chihuahuas get skittish around big dogs they don't know—became much more of a divided household then a united clan. This started to change once winter arrived and the coyotes in the neighborhood got hungrier and more aggressive. We started noticing their paw prints in the neighbor's fields and hearing their hunting howls early in the morning. A couple of times when Joy was walking the Chihuahuas through the badlands, she'd been stalked by coyotes. We didn't want to lose a dog this way, but Chihuahuas are just too high-strung to be denied their exercise. The only way to solve this problem was for us to begin walking everyone together, hoping the big dogs would learn to take care of the small dogs.

It was Bella who learned first. She was part pit bull and part heeler—the perfect combination. Pit bulls are protective in general, and heelers are herding dogs and protective of their flock. Instinct is instinct. Bella didn't care if she was herding sheep or Chihuahuas; she took her responsibility seriously all the same. We'd hit the trail and the dogs would spread out in a very long line. Smash, being the fastest, always took point. Squirt, being the fattest, always lagged behind. The other dogs would mostly romp around in between. But by our third hike together, Bella had taken to patrolling the perimeter, running circles around the Chihuahuas, ensuring that nobody got lost or left behind or turned into lunch.

Perhaps the other big dogs just wanted some of the attention we were now lavishing on Bella or perhaps they too were starting to understand their roles, but it didn't take long for this protective behavior to spread. Pretty soon, Ahab and Leo were guarding the Chihuahuas' flanks, while Otis policed from the middle of the pack. All of which produced comedic results.

The *techichi* started out as pack hunting dogs, and Chihuahuas inherited this trait. One of the reasons I disliked these dogs so much was their skittishness. But this turns out to vanish when you have a pack of them. In a group, Chihuahuas are considerably more courageous than they are on their own. Then add in a few bigger dogs to serve as bodyguards and their bravery verges on insanity. Any hole in the ground becomes fair game for Chihuahua exploration—despite the fact that bobcats and bears live in some of those holes. Occasionally, ranchers let their cattle wander free in the badlands. When they're on their own, the sight of a cow is enough to send small dogs running for cover, but with the big dogs backing them up, the Chihuahuas began charging at the cows, rushing in between their legs, biting their ankles, barking them off to other pastures.

Of course, all of this newfound courage made Joy a bit nervous, but I found it inspiring. With every new foray into the badlands, the Chihuahuas got braver and braver. It felt like I was watching my kids grow up and come into their own. After a month in the backcountry, never mind the cows, the Chihuahuas had completely lost their fear of the bigger dogs. This was when the real fun began. It didn't take long until our hikes became less about getting from point A to point B and more about the game of rugby along the way.

Over the summer, even during the madness of Chihuahua play hour, wrestling matches were mainly separated along size lines. But after the group hikes began, it became anything goes and all the time. Small dogs would gang up on big dogs; big dogs would bum-rush small dogs. Surprise attacks—when five Chihuahuas would disappear down a side arroyo and lie in wait until one of the pit bulls came to investigate their absence, only to pounce on them once they arrived—became common. We also started to see role reversals, where a stronger animal lets a smaller one win, and repeated incidents of self-handicapping, which is the technical term for what happens when our miniature Chihuahua decides to wrestle our bull terrier.

Otis outweighs Gidget by over sixty pounds, but to keep their matches even, he flops onto his back and fights with one paw. Rolling over and letting a smaller animal wrestle the "top" position is self-handicapping. Only using one paw is self-handicapping. But with Otis things go further. While he may fight only with one paw, Gidget fights with everything she's got—including her teeth. Occasionally she'll bite his face and not let go. When this happens, Otis likes to stand up and strut around, with Gidget dangling off him like a long furry earring.

Despite how common play fighting is among mammals, it has taken a surprisingly long time for scientists to understand this behavior. For most of the last century, researchers had a red-in-tooth-and-claw view of nature and a survival-of-the-fittest view of nurture, so assumed play fighting between kids was practice for real fighting among adults. About twenty years ago, University of Colorado biologist Marc Bekoff and University of Idaho animal behaviorist John Byers began to rethink these assumptions. Since play fighting was supposed to be training for real fighting, what they wanted to know was if there was any correlation between rough-housing in juveniles and brawling among adults. Did the kids who won the most fights grow up to become the most dominant adults? Did less aggressive children become subordinate adults? Most important, was play actually combat practice or was something else going on?

To find their answers they reexamined forty years of research on play fighting in squirrel monkeys. Almost immediately, they noticed what should have been long obvious: during actual combat squirrel monkeys bite each other, but this rarely happens during play. This is a problem because only the repetition of exact patterns of movement can produce muscle memory and only with muscle memory does practice make perfect. There were other problems as well. The monkeys who played the most as children didn't win the most fights as adults, and the monkeys who won the most play fights when they were younger didn't win the most real fights when they were grown up. In fact, everywhere they looked, they found almost no correlation between play fighting and real fighting.

Next they expanded their inquiry and examined the data on other species. The results were the same. Then Washington State University neurobiologist Jaak Panksepp discovered that the neuronal circuitry behind aggression and the neuronal circuitry behind play were completely different. When people tried administering testosterone to research animals—known to increase acts of aggressive dominance—they found it actually inhibited play, while drugs that curbed aggression did nothing to diminish it. All of this caused Bekoff and Byers to back up and ask a different question: if play fighting wasn't training for real fighting, then what purpose could it possibly serve?

Turns out the purpose is moral. Take Otis and Gidget. Otis is our pack's resident silverback. So why would an alpha male self-handicap—essentially go out of his way to display weakness? What the research shows is this isn't a display of weakness; it's a display of a willingness to lose. "The fact that all animals self-handicap," writes Colorado State University ethologist Temple Grandin in *Animals in Translation,* "might mean that the purpose of play fighting isn't to teach animals how to win, but to teach them how to win *and* lose. All animals probably need to know both the dominant and the subordinate role, because no animal starts out on top, and no animal who lives to old age ends up on top, either."

And perhaps this is even more critical in a pack such as ours. There are dogs both bigger and smaller than Otis, and by parading around with Gidget hanging off his cheek, he's letting everyone know that around here might does not make right. By displaying subordination, he's telling the others that they're safe, part of a community, and no matter their size or strength or stamina, their needs will still be met. Essentially, Otis is doing the same thing politicians do when they kiss babies: he's advertising morality. Bekoff believes this is the primary function of these bouts, writing in his *Animals at Play*: "In their games, young animals learn the rules of living in a group—how to communicate or 'talk' with each other. They learn to cooperate and play fair. Life in the wild can be tough. It's even tougher when you're alone, so play helps create bonds and a sense of community."

And this is exactly what happened to us. The hikes, the danger of the hikes, the cooperative behavior that resulted from the danger, the play fighting that resulted from the cooperation, the agreed-upon standards of behavior that emerged from the play fighting, the community that emerged from these standards—all of it knitted us together that much tighter. It was like the sexual revolution had let all the dogs know that they were safe being themselves, then the group hikes had let them know they were safe being together. And with the goofy results, it didn't take long for my old opinions to begin to fade away. Once I started hiking with the small dogs, I really started to enjoy the company of the small dogs. I know how it sounds, but just so there's no misunderstanding, let me spell it out: I, Steven Kotler, being of sound mind and body, being heterosexual, fond of football and whiskey and flannel shirts, able to drive a stick shift and operate heavy machinery, having once flown a Mig-17 fighter jet, with some experience climbing mountains and surviving in rain forests, not scared of snakes or spiders or such, hereby do admit, out loud and in public, that I have become extremely enamored of Chihuahuas.

And here's why: with a dozen of them around, it's just pretty damn hard to be in a bad mood.

PART FIVE

O Lord, despite a great many prayers to you, we are continually losing our wars. Tomorrow we shall again be fighting a battle that is truly great. With all our might we need your help and that is why I must tell you something: this battle tomorrow is going to be a serious affair. There will be no place for children. Therefore I must ask you not to send your son to help us. Come yourself.

—The prayer of Koq, leader of the Griqua nation, before a battle with the Afrikaners in 1876

24

Pony Girl was one of those small dogs whose company I had really started to enjoy. Her name was a tip of the hat to S. E. Hinton's *The Outsiders*, her character Ponyboy, and lines like "Things were rough all over, but it was better that way. That way you could tell the other guy was human too." In this case, the other guy was a girl and canine, though it still made sense to us.

Pony was a late summer arrival, a half-Greyhound, half-Chihuahua mix that added up to a total mess. She'd been beaten and broken so badly that Joy's long-stated goal with severely mistreated dogs—giving them a few memories of the human species that don't involve pain and fear—was a tall mountain to climb. For her first three months with us, Pony's memories were of the back of Joy's closet. She hid beside the shoes, beneath the jeans, only her doe eyes still visible. There was no disguising those eyes. How to comfort a terrified dog at the back of a closet is the kind of question rescuers love to answer. Joy talked to experts, to other rescuers, to anyone with an idea. The discussions covered canine ethology, pet psychology, cognitive neuroscience, folk remedies, and best guesses. Joy's best guess turned out to be conversation. She devoted forty minutes a day to sitting at the front of the closet and talking to Pony—the weather, the world, how the Lakers were doing.

Around Christmastime, possibly because the Lakers were doing well, Pony came out of the closet, across the living room, up onto the couch, and into Joy's lap, and we drank plenty of champagne that evening. Our celebration didn't last. Less than three weeks later, Pony stopped eating. Then she stopped walking. Joy took her to Doc and Doc found cancer. Pony's pain was considerable, problematic because another of our main rescue goals was to relieve suffering, not prolong life. That meant immediate surgery or immediate euthanasia. The surgery was expensive, as was the dilemma.

Economics was the problem. No one was hiring freelancers. Back in LA, if things got tricky, someone was always looking for a word slut. Movie studios, advertising agencies, and PR firms all needed help. But the farmers who lived near me needed nothing more than what John Deere could provide. We had enough in the bank to cover two months of mortgage payments and maybe some bills. The surgery would cost all that and then some, so saving Pony's life meant risking our rescue. This might be the kind of crisis they made after-school specials about, but it was nothing I'd ever dealt with before.

The night Joy broke the news I got so frustrated I picked a fight with her just to buy myself some time to make a decision. Our phone was working again, so I used that time to call a bunch of people I hadn't talked to in a long while to ask for advice. That advice was unanimous. Everyone thought putting Pony down was the best thing, the right thing; some couldn't even believe it was a real question. During all those conversations, I kept finding myself getting wildly angry. Friends would talk softly and suggest euthanasia, and I would talk loudly and suggest they go fuck themselves— which is how I discovered I was going to pay for the surgery.

Ever since Joy had first suggested I go visit a shelter, I'd been trying to keep some emotional separation from the dogs, just enough distance to stop me from making exactly this kind of fool decision. But between Leo and Chow and Gidget and Otis and the gay dogs and the altruistic dogs and the island living and the infinite games and whatever, I had crossed that line. Truth be told, we didn't even feel like a pack anymore. We felt like family. And if I had to risk my house to save my family, apparently I was willing to risk my house.

In the end, I didn't have to risk the house. Joy called Elise, and Elise got on the fund-raising path and found a medical sponsor willing to cover the procedure. The surgery was a success, but the cancer was worse than expected. Doc told us it was only a matter of time until it came back. "You've got a lot of old dogs," she said. "This is what happens with old dogs."

And that's when it hit me: we were playing for keeps. I had managed to avoid this particular realization for quite some time. But hearing it from Doc, well, what I took away from the entire encounter was not the wonderful fact that Pony had lived, rather the absolute certainty that sooner or later one of our dogs would not. Right about then I realized that dog rescue is actually a game of death. And right about then I began to wonder if this was a game I was cut out to play.

25

State Road 76 is an exigent twist of blacktop that runs east from
city of Espanola through the town of Chimayo before threading
deeper into the Sangre de Cristo Mountains. The road is lousy
with blind corners and tight dips and drunk drivers. At least once a
week, it's possible to hear the screech of tires and the crunch of
metal that results from heavy machinery encountering blood
alcohol levels at high speeds. Rio Arriba County, where all of this
takes places, usually ranks first or second in the state tally of DWI-
related deaths and, because of the amount of heroin trafficking that
also takes place around here, usually two to three times above the
state average for murder. Back in the late 1990s, when the Chimayo drug wars were national news, the papers would report dead
bodies dumped by the side of the road—and 76 was usually the road.

In Mexico, as in New Mexico, tradition holds that the souls
of the dead linger in the spot of their death until proper tribute
has been paid, with proper tribute usually being an assortment of
flowers, candles, and Virgin Mary paraphernalia set in a bowl beneath a larger cross. Which is why local directions often involve
taking a left at "the fourth—no, wait, the fifth crucifix on the left."
Beside the crosses, the other thing that litters 76 are dead dogs.
Some began as erring pets, some as strays; a lot get turned loose
because their owners suddenly find themselves unable to afford the
cost of both drugs and dog food. Drunk drivers do the rest. It's

hard for animal rescuers to ignore any kind of cruelty, but when that cruelty involve entrails spread across tarmac, it becomes even harder to overlook.

But overlook them we had—at least until that first winter arrived. Unlike most of New Mexico, Chimayo is not a desert. The Española Valley serves as the main drainage for the southern flank of the Rockies and the eastern flank of the Jemez, so the influx of snowmelt keeps things lush and green during the summer months. But come winter, after the trees drop their leaves, the valley loses its charm and the once hidden became visible. Without the foliage to hide the carnage, we began to realize just how many dead dogs were piled along the side of the road. Too many to even count. Before I left California to hunt houses in New Mexico, Joy had asked for only one thing: a place where the dogs would be safe. When the trees dropped their leaves, I started to wonder if I'd broken that promise.

The other thing those leaves were hiding was poverty. With the trees bare, we could suddenly see into other people's yards, and really, there wasn't much to see. In her book *Chiva: A Village Takes on the Global Heroin Trade*, local author Chellis Glendinning describes the neighborhood this way:

> I will begin by telling you that Río Arriba is "Third World" rural. According to the 2000 US Census, only 34,000 people inhabit a county the size of the state of Massachusetts; 73 percent are Spanishs or Mexican-American, 14 percent have Native American roots, and 12 percent are European American, while three-quarters of the people speak Spanish or native tongues like Tewa, Diné, or Apache. The county is also "Third World" poor. During the 1990s the average household income was $14,263—in many villages per-capita income was under $5000—and each year

at the time snow dusted the valley between the Sangre de Cristo and Jemez mountains, unemployment swelled to 20 percent.

Alongside unemployment, the other thing that swells in the winter is violence. The *Rio Grande Sun* was chockablock with horror stories. A local gang war broke out, kicked off by a series of firebombings. The Box-and-Mail was burned down because the owners were the wrong color. Then a couple of trailers went up in smoke; the residents escaped, but their dogs didn't get so lucky. I tried telling myself that this was accidental, that people didn't take grudges out on animals here. Then some kids doused a cow in gasoline and lit it on fire. A poisoning competition erupted next. Tainted meat was being thrown over fences and more pets were dying. A place where the dogs would be safe was all Joy had asked for. Uh-huh. Absolutely, I'd managed to keep that promise.

The neighborhood now scared us enough that leaving town became a topic for discussion. It was a short discussion. With the economy in tatters, our house was worth less than we owed the bank. So selling wasn't an option and moving wasn't an option. The heavy snows that fell in early January didn't help much. By late January, temperatures were near zero, and for a couple of ninnies from California no amount of clothes could keep us warm. We were sleeping with ten dogs in the bed and three down comforters by early February. By middle February, because neither of us had worked in months, there wasn't enough money to heat the whole house. We both knew there was only one way to save money: we had to shed dogs.

Up to now, this had been difficult. Dog rescue is a networking game. If you want to find homes for dogs, it helps to know lots of people who know lots of people who know lots of people. Being new in town, we didn't know lots of people. And New Mexico rescuers aren't as organized as California rescuers, so there wasn't a previously existing network we could plug into. But desperate times call for desperate measures, and we both started talking up our dogs to everyone we met.

In February, Joy met a woman at the gym who had just lost her dog to old age, and while the woman didn't know if she was ready for another, she heard tell of Leo and agreed to meet him. As much as we needed to shed dogs, I hated the idea. Why couldn't we get rid of a dog that I hadn't spent a month sleeping beside on the porch? Why not, um, a Chihuahua? I understood that Leo ate as much as six Chihuahuas and we were trying to save money, but I had become really attached.

Joy set the meeting for the coming Saturday and thought maybe I wanted to tag along. Not a chance. Instead of tagging along, I spent money we didn't have to spend and left town, hoping her matchmaking efforts would fail before I returned. They didn't fail. Leo got a new home while I was gone. Joy was thrilled. After eight months of trying, she'd finally managed to place a dog. I was not nearly as happy. I missed Leo. Then I really missed Leo. Then I couldn't believe how much I really missed Leo.

Then Wookie went. He was a shih tzu who'd showed up at the Española shelter in October. Normally, we would never have considered taking him on. Joy likes the "worst of the worst"—the dogs that wouldn't stand a chance otherwise—but there was nothing wrong with Wookie. Plus he was a purebred, and purebreds are always in demand. But it had been so long since Joy had actually found a home for a dog that I told her to adopt him anyway, just so she could have an easy victory. But the economy was a mess, and even with a purebred like Wookie, there were no easy victories to be had.

So he stuck around and I grew attached. He was furry and friendly and just my type. After a couple of months the fact that we couldn't find him a home was just fine with me. But purebreds are purebreds, and Joy had posted his picture on a couple of California rescue websites. A few days after Leo left, a woman called from San Diego. She was a shih tzu fanatic, willing to drive across the Southwest to adopt Wookie.

"That bitch," is all I had to say about that.

And once he was gone, I missed Wookie almost as much as I missed Leo. I was petulant. I walked around the house muttering "Dog rescue sucks" for days straight. It was the truth. Both of these dogs had abandonment issues. I had spent months convincing them they wouldn't be abandoned again—only to abandon them again. Certainly they were going to great homes, but they didn't know that, and the look on Wookie's face when he left was the saddest I had ever seen. I felt like I had betrayed him, to say nothing of how badly I missed him. From my end, placing a dog felt like falling in love and getting dumped and falling in love and getting dumped, over and over again. As I said, dog rescue sucks.

About a week after Wookie left, I was still so down and out that I asked Joy to stop finding homes for our dogs.

"Just for a little while," I said. "Just until I feel normal again."

That conversation took place on a Sunday. The next day I felt a little better. Just the knowledge of temporary reprieve was enough to lift a weight from my chest. By Tuesday, I was almost happy, which turned out to be just another way of saying I hadn't a clue what was coming next. Next was Wednesday, the day that Ahab's legs gave out. He was doubled over by Thursday, diagnosed on Friday, not that it mattered by Sunday. His insides had rotted out, a blockage backed up, and his intestines had gone south. On Monday, not even Doc could save him. Ahab was dead before he left the operating table. By then it was clear. It was gonna be a long, long time until I felt normal again.

26

Freud said that the process of grieving "involve[s] grave departures from the normal attitude to life." Well, chalk one up for the old master. In the weeks after Ahab's death, I found myself unable to complete the most mundane tasks. My memory was shot, my mind not far behind. I lost my ability to sleep, write, exercise, talk on the phone, or visit with friends and instead spent my time sitting in a old rocking chair on our porch, wrapped in blankets, staring at bare trees and a winter that would not end.

Despite the plenitude of such stories, for much of last century most psychologists thought the grief that resulted from pet loss too silly to treat, while those who disagreed could get no funding for research. But anecdotes continued to accrue and after a while so did a few hypotheses. Researchers tried anthropomorphism and emotional transference and various surrogate offspring theories and nothing quite stuck. In the early 1980s, they got serious. Psychometric instruments such as the Pet Loss Questionnaire, the Pet Attachment Worksheet, and the Lexington Attachment to Pet Scale were developed specifically to examine this form of bereavement. Hundreds of studies have now been done, the conclusions well summarized in a recent paper by Canadian psychologist Annique Lavergne: "An overview of these results clearly demonstrates that grief following the loss of a companion animal is an undeniable and omnipresent reality."

Well, no shit, Sherlock.

Along the way, older notions, such as those who suffer worst from the loss of a pet are women, the elderly, and individuals living alone or without children, have been called into question, with the newer thinking being that pet death affects everyone equally, regardless of background. And those effects are significant. Psychologists use the terms *uncomplicated grief* and *complicated grief* to differentiate between the most common bereavement states. Uncomplicated grief is the kind you get over quickly, while complicated grief is the technical name for not being able to move from a rocking chair on the porch. One of the things now known is that pet loss triggers complicated much more than uncomplicated grief. In fact, grief resulting from pet loss often exceeds grief resulting from the loss of a human companion, including close family members.

In 2008, UCLA psychiatrist Mary-Frances O'Connor shed some light on why this happens. O'Connor used functional magnetic resonance imaging to examine the brain-firing patterns associated with complicated and uncomplicated grief. She did this by recruiting test subjects grieving the loss of a loved one and showing them photos of their deceased while snapping pictures of their brains. Photos of strangers' brains—who had not suffered a loss— were used to establish a baseline. What O'Connor found is that the photos of loved ones produced activity in the brain's pain centers, but those suffering from complicated grief also had action in their nucleus accumbens—a group of neurons in the forebrain that play a central role in the brain's reward system.

The reward system is a group of neuronal circuits that let us know when we've done something right by giving us a squirt of the feel-good neurochemical dopamine. To give you an idea of how good that feels, we need only turn to cocaine. Bolivian marching powder causes dopamine to be released into the brain and then blocks the receptor sites that allow for its reuptake, much in the way

Prozac blocks the reuptake of serotonin. Fifty years ago, when neurobiologist James Olds put an electrode in the nucleus accumbens of a rat's brain, he found the animals would pull a level to stimulate it without pause. They would neglect all other activities, including eating and drinking, for the pleasure. Rats would rather starve to death then walk away from dopamine. And humans aren't much different.

Humans learn by association. Every time we associate a new fact with an old idea we get a dopamine reward. This is the brain's pattern recognition system at work, and O'Connor discovered that it backfires during complicated grief. "The idea is that when our loved ones are alive, we get a rewarding cue from seeing them or things that remind us of them. After a loved one dies, those who adapt to the loss stop getting the neural reward. But those who don't adapt continue to crave it, because each time they see a cue, they still get a neural reward." And this is what makes complicated grief complicated—it's like a forced detox from a bad coke habit.

O'Connor's work also explains why the grief associated with companion animal loss can exceed the grief triggered by the death of another human. This happens because many of us spend more time with our pets than we do with other humans. Ahab was with me most of the day, thoroughly embedded in my pattern recognition system, linked to just about every environment I passed through. And every time something in those environments reminded me of him, since my brain was unable to stop craving the "reward" of his company, I was instead reminded of his absence.

And I was not taking these reminders well. When it become clear the "tears in my beer" had moved from hillbilly cliché to morning, noon, and night, I decided there was strength in numbers, and since my numbers were disappearing, it was time to bring in some help. I started, like most grown men would, by calling my mother. As these things go, my mother is a lovely woman, sweet and supportive and unable, for the life of her, to understand what her son is doing with so many dogs.

"They're making you miserable. Joy says you haven't gotten out of that rocking chair in weeks."

"What kind of reasonable mother believes her daughter-in-law?"

"You can barely work."

"You don't think this is work?"

"I think you can't pay your mortgage, but you spend five hundred dollars a month on dog food."

She had a point there, but I wasn't giving in so easily.

"And don't forget I start most days by stepping in dog shit."

"For the love of God," she said.

So I moved on to calling my father, my friends, and just about anyone else I could think of. While everyone agreed that finding a life that meant something was a noble cause, none thought it was worth losing my mind over.

"This is just dogs you're helping, right?" said Joshua.

"It's not like you're saving refugees," said Michael.

"It's not like you're saving orphans," said Micah.

"You're upsetting your mother," said my father.

Which is about the time I realized that if I was going to solve my animal problems, it might help to talk to people who worked with animals. I had an ex-girlfriend who was a zookeeper in Texas, and an old roommate who once saved whales with the Sea Shepherd Conservation Society. The ex-girlfriend wasn't speaking to me, I couldn't find the roommate, and anyway, my mother wasn't wrong. I was miserable. It was time to bring in the big guns.

Patricia Wright was a big gun. Currently a professor in the department of anthropology at Stony Brook University of New York, a member of the National Geographic Society's Conservation Trust, and executive director of the Institute for the Conservation of

142

Tropical Environments, Patricia Wright is one of the world's leading conservationists and primatologists, recipient of a MacArthur Foundation "genius award," and most famous for discovering two new species of lemurs on the island of Madagascar and then devoting her life to the creation of Ranomafana National Park, which now spans 161 square miles and became a World Heritage Site in 2007, to protect them. Which is to say that in the world of animal rescue, where status is measured by devotion to the cause, Patricia Wright is flat out royalty.

Over the course of my career, I've written a couple of articles about Wright and we've become friendly enough that I can still call her up with the occasional question—though my new question was something else entirely. I started by mentioning the recent stories about "Leakey's Angels," Dian Fossey, Jane Goodall, and Biruté Galdikas, the trio of women sent by the anthropologist Louis Leakey to study primates in their natural environments. In the past few years, we learned that Dian Fossey had lost not only her life trying to save mountain gorillas, but most of her mind as well. Then Linda Spalding's *A Dark Place in the Jungle* alerted us to Galdikas's plight: that she had gone to Borneo to save orangutans and found that the only way to do so was to keep eighty of them trapped in her house under a kind of last-chance martial law. And, apparently, Jane Goodall was now throwing her weight entirely behind educational programs for children because she had lost faith in the world of adults. Wright's accomplishments are often listed as parallel to these women's, yet somehow she's managed to both save animals and stay sane, while these other women had not. It now seemed important to find out why.

I reached Wright at her office in New York. It didn't take her long to answer my question.

"That's any easy one," she said.

"What do you mean?"

"It worked. If it didn't, I'd be a lunatic for sure."

"What worked?"

"Ranomafana, all the rest."

I asked if that was the extent of her advice. She thought about it for a moment, then said: "Work with animals and there's going to be heartbreak."

"Uh-huh."

"You take it, that's what you do. You just take it."

27

In March I found a little work and Joy found a little work, and in the way these things can go, her work turned out to be harder than mine. She got an internship with Doc at the Cottonwood Clinic. The clinic is a couple of ramshackle buildings and a gravel parking lot tucked beneath a band of tall cottonwood trees, on the appropriately named Shady Lane. Inside is a waiting room, two examination rooms, a surgical theater, some storage spaces, a couple of offices, and a series of cages. Outside is a leaky roof and a clear view of Sikh Dharma, a religious compound home to men and women in white robes and white turbans who believe they are the spiritual descendents of an ancient warrior tradition and try to act accordingly. They also drive a lot of minivans, but this may be neither here nor there.

This being March, the season most animals give birth, the majority of the dogs at Cottonwood were puppies and the majority of those puppies had parvo—the results of more people unwilling to spend seven bucks on a vaccination. As Doc once pointed out, in Chimayo euthanasia has a season. Those euthanasias were frequent, five, six, seven a morning, and they were better than some of the other things that passed through the clinic.

Julia passed through the clinic at the start of Joy's fourth week. She was once a standard poodle, but street living and starvation had stunted her growth and matted her coat, leaving behind a dreadlocked mess. She had been found hiding behind the Jumbo

Burger in downtown Española, trying to evade the group of ten-year-olds who were stoning her to death while waiting for the morning school bus. Stoning her to death? Ten-year-olds? Seriously, it's no wonder the problem of evil is considered central to philosophy, theology, and dog rescue.

This problem dates back to the Egyptians at least, but the Greek thinker Epicurus is traditionally credited with its first elegant summation: "Either God wants to abolish evil, and cannot; or he can, but does not want to. If he wants to, but cannot, he is impotent. If he can, but does not want to, he is wicked. If God can abolish evil, and God really wants to do it, why is there evil in the world?" Since then just about every major religion has since tried to solve Epicurus' paradox, as have most major philosophers. About this, the cultural critic Roger Kimball once wrote:

> I do not propose to add to the oceans of ink that have been spilled over the centuries in the effort to answer that question. I merely wish to note that oceans of ink *have* been spilled in the pursuit of an answer. Whatever satisfactions we might take in the clever lucubrations of an Augustine or Thomas Aquinas to answer the question, we find in the end that the question is, if not unanswerable, exactly, at least it is perpetually renewed. The question of suffering, that is to say, is not susceptible of being "solved." At bottom, it is not an intellectual puzzle (though thinking about it involves intellectual puzzles) but an existential reality inseparable from the adventure of human life. . . . In the end, the meaning of suffering must wait upon one's answer to the question: What is the meaning of life?

I left Los Angeles and moved to New Mexico because I loved Joy and Joy loved dogs and nothing else made much sense. I knew that dog rescue was going to involve getting up close and personal with Epicurus' paradox, but Aeschylus believed "wisdom comes alone through suffering" and I had Joy backing me up. What I hadn't counted on was how much suffering that would actually involve. What it would do to Joy. What it would do to me. Mostly, what I hadn't counted on was Elton.

Because there are so many dogs in need, rescuers tend to be very protective of their phone numbers. Not being protective means getting inundated with requests for help and, since space and time and money are supremely limiting factors, being inundated with the guilt that results from not being able to help. Which explains why, in early April, Joy got a phone call from a woman who refused to tell us where she got our number, but would say that she'd gotten an e-mail from a rescue organization in Albuquerque who was working with one in Roswell that heard from a vet clinic in Los Alamos of a woman in Chimayo who was excellent with small dogs with big problems. Joy was that woman and Elton was that dog, and things spiraled from there.

Hypothetically, Elton was some kind of Chihuahua with epilepsy. The current owners were too poor to be able to afford the twenty-five bucks a month in treatment, so Joy took the call and requested a picture. What showed up was young and brown and cute and cuddly. We were still short on money and short on time and I thought it was a bad idea. But Joy thought epilepsy treatable and Elton adoptable and anyway, she said, "this is what we do."

So the meeting was set for the parking lot of Trader Joe's in Santa Fe on Thursday afternoon. We were told to look for a blue truck. Since Elton's owners had pled poverty, I'd expected a beat-up pickup. They were driving a brand-new Dodge Ram with after-market hubcaps and tinted windows. Nor was the dog quite what we had anticipated. In my experience, epilepsy was a disease that causes seizures, not paralysis, and Elton had no use of his hind legs.

147

In Joy's experience Elton had distemper. Complicating matters, the owners believed that in rescuing him, we were agreeing to pay them for him. When they found out this wasn't the case, they still tried to get us to spring for gas money.

"But we drove all the way from Roswell," they said.

Distemper, like parvo, is another incredibly painful, usually fatal, and completely preventable disease—that is, if the owners are willing to spend ten bucks on a vaccination.

"Yup," I replied, "you sure did—in your brand-new truck."

By Friday, the paralysis had spread from Elton's back legs to his torso; by Saturday his front legs were starting to freeze. The next day was Sunday, and our fear was the paralysis would reach his throat before his brain and he was going to starve to death or choke to death trying not to starve to death. Since we believe suffering is worse than death, on Sunday Elton went to the emergency vet clinic in Santa Fe and we spent next month's grocery money putting him to sleep. On Monday, when Joy went back to work at Cottonwood, she helped euthanize another half dozen dogs with parvo, and a few more with distemper. No one needed money this badly. By Tuesday I was begging her to quit, thinking that would solve the problem, just like Jonah thought he could hide from God. In such situations, it's helpful to remember there's often a whale around the next corner.

28

Pierre and Claudia were among the first friends we made in New Mexico. Connie was Claudia's close friend. Most of the time she lives in Florida, but she'd decided to spend the summer in a guest house at the tail end of their property. The guest house sits in the middle of an apple orchard, and Connie's dog, Rio, had big plans for that orchard: trees to mark, ball to play. Rio had been Connie's constant companion for the past eight years and would have been her constant companion for the next eight, except one afternoon the phone began to ring and she left Rio alone in the orchard for less than five minutes. Really, it takes almost no time at all for an anonymous stranger to sight a high-powered rifle over a small fence and kill a golden retriever for no particular reason whatsoever.

Connie cried for days. Claudia cried, and Joy too. Pierre had to be talked out of a killing spree. I had to be talked out of joining him. "It happens around here," the police said, "happens far more than you can imagine." But no, actually, I think this one's my limit, I think this is the thing I can't imagine.

As it turned out, there were a few other things I couldn't imagine as well.

At most puppy mills, they pack the dogs into wire cages, usually for the entirety of their lives, often in pitch-black conditions. There are waste collection trays beneath these cages, but they're rarely emptied. Flies are a constant. With no air-conditioning in the summer and no heat in the winter, dogs freeze to death or die from heatstroke with regularity. During the hottest months, when the cage metal heats up, puppies have been known to cook on the wires. The food is poor and veterinary care infrequent. Open sores, tissue damage, blindness, deafness, ulcers, tooth decay—even rotting jaws because the tooth decay has gotten so bad—are more the rule than the exception. The animals are often fed mechanically, so their only human contact comes, and this is only in the case of breeder dogs, in the form of artificial insemination and, nine weeks later, a pair of hands snatching babies away. If Dante Alighieri were adding a maternity ward to his inferno, puppy mills seem to strike the right note.

Maus was a Chihuahua, a breeder dog, rescued from a puppy mill. For two years, Joy worked with her on a daily basis, though *work* is something of an euphemism. By the time we got her, Maus was mostly deaf, completely blind, and seriously damaged. Open spaces were too much for her to bear, as were the company of people, especially men, other dogs, sunshine, loud noises, and any sort of affection. To get around these things, Maus lived at the back of a closet. The door was always left open, but she never left. Her world was a bed, a water dish, and a couple of pee pads.

Doc thought Maus had the worst case of post-traumatic stress disorder she'd ever seen, and it was hard to disagree. To work with her, since holding her was an impossibility, Joy would scrunch under a shelf that ran along one side of the closet and stay still. After six months, she got Maus to accept a scratch on the neck. It took nine for her to allow her head to be rubbed. That was as far as things went. Anything else and Maus would begin screaming and shaking and not stop. We tried every drug on the market and a good dozen other therapies—nothing did the trick. In the end we decided that prolonging her suffering was the worst of our available options.

Dagmar looking dapper.

Bucket and Poppycock kissing in the backyard.
That's the goat shack over toward the left.

Nap time at the zoo.

Strolling around the neighborhood. That's Joy and Damien up front, Steven and Blue in the back, and Apple in the middle. (Thaddeus Kostrubala)

Doc releasing the
mountain lion.

Still life with tractor and dogs.

Gidget.

Moving from left to right and back to front: Steven, Bella, Blue, Bucket, Damien, Turtle, Helgar, and Apple.

Hiking the crew. The snow capped mountain in the background is Truchas Peak. (Thaddeus Kostrubala)

That's Joy reading the paper on the porch of the goat shack. Flower is in the upper right corner with the red collar and Dagmar, in purple, is below her. Then going right to left: Squirt, Lux, Apple, and Gidget. Farrah is the blonde in the front, Damien is behind her, and Marco is on the far left. (Thaddeus Kostrubala)

Steven and Blue. (© Gabriella Marks/Triggerfinger.com)

The Thumb. (© Gabriella Marks/Triggerfinger.com)

Not only was Maus my first experience with an incurable case, but the timing of our decision to put her down couldn't have been worse. Three days before Rio was shot, Maus was euthanized, Vinnie alongside her. Vinnie was an old schnauzer from Los Angeles whose owner had died of AIDS. Someone heard the story and stepped in, and Vinnie ended up on the rescue circuit. At the time, we were babysitting a couple of young Chihuahuas for the Española Humane Society. Since finding young Chihuahuas homes in Los Angeles is significantly easier than finding an old schnauzer a home just about anywhere, a trade was engineered. The Chihuahuas went to Beverly Hills, Vinnie came to New Mexico.

Vinnie seemed to quite like life in Chimayo. He had a stump for a tail, but that didn't stop his self-expression. In most cases, tail wagging is an innate display of happiness for dogs. The case not to be trusted is when the tail is held high and the wag tight and rapid. Otherwise, according to Steven Lindsay's *Handbook of Applied Dog Behavior and Training*: "The friendly, confident tail wag is a loose sweeping motion from side to side with various undulations and shifts of direction." Lindsay also says that a proper wag involves motion of the rump, an inclusion that's important since the portion of the tail wag lost on most humans is the "transmission of various cues emanating from the anal and supracaudal glands." Every morning, never mind that he was over eighty in dog years, when Vinnie first went outside, he would glance up and see wide sky and open fields and run big laps around the property before flying back to the porch to wag that stump. The wag started at his head and ended at his butt and looked not unlike a freight train trying to break-dance. Thus the phrase "schnauze that ass" came into heavy usage around our house.

About the time we decided to euthanize Maus, Vinnie's heart started to fail. His liver as well. So we made another tough decision and forty-eight hours later both Vinnie and Maus were put to sleep on our back porch. Maus died in Joy's arms and Vinnie in mine. He was the first living thing to die in my arms—but not the last. A few days later, Chow started coughing around six in the morning; by seven her lungs had filled with fluid; by eight she became the second creature to die in my arms. The following week we lost Jerry, for reasons still unclear. Then Otis, our beloved bull terrier, went by stroke three days after that. By now, the count was eight dead in two months.

Move to New Mexico to save dogs had been the plan—who was going to save me became the problem.

PART SIX

Nothing
could put
Humpty Dumpty
together again.
But there was a war on
so they had to try
all those other things.

—Richard Fariña

29

Webley Edwards was an Oregon State University graduate who moved to Hawaii to become an auto salesman, instead developed an interest in local music, and created the *Hawaii Calls* radio program. It ran worldwide for forty years on more than seven hundred stations and always opened with the sound of the waves breaking on the beach in Waikiki and Edwards proclaiming: "The sound of the waves breaking on the beach in Waikiki." Edwards was also on the air when the bombs began falling on Pearl Harbor, though what he proclaimed that December morning carried a different message. "This is an air raid," he repeated over and over. "This is an air raid, take cover, this is the *real McCoy*."

By most accounts, the real McCoy was a Prohibition-era rum runner named William McCoy known for a high level of craftsmanship in his wares, but this may be beside the point. Perhaps the boxer Norman Selby, dubbed "Kid McCoy," who invented the rope-a-dope and once—after taking a heavy beating before bouncing back to TKO his opponent—caused the announcer to ask: "Which is the real McCoy?" This too may be beside the point. The point is that when I was living in Los Angeles the phrase "I have measured out my life in coffee spoons" stayed with me, but after those dogs died, around the time I found it impossible to move from the rocking chair on the back porch, "This is the real McCoy" were the five words that replaced it.

These words became my mantra, a way of reminding myself that despite all evidence to the contrary, this was in fact my life. The problem, beyond the obvious—well, there was no getting beyond the obvious. Too many dogs had died and they'd taken too much of me with them. Of depression, in his classic work on the subject, *Darkness Visible,* William Styron once wrote: "The pain is unrelenting, and what makes the condition intolerable is the foreknowledge that no remedy will come—not in a day, an hour, a month, or a minute. . . . It is hopelessness even more than pain that crushes the soul." I'd say that about covers it.

As it happens, the view from that chair is South Truchas Peak, both the second-highest mountain in New Mexico and what my friend Tadz—pronounced "Taj," short for Thaddeus—wanted to climb. He called in the late spring to find out if I was interested. "It's mostly a walk up" was the extent of his sales pitch. Since Tadz had spent a decade working for Outward Bound, his definition of a walk up is a little different from that of a guy who spent his winter wallowing in a chair, but I had to do something, and maybe this something would do some good.

At thirteen thousand feet, Truchas Peak is a bit of a haul. You can do it in a single shot; most don't. The only guidebook I've seen recommends three days for the trip. That seems excessive, but even that book didn't account for the storm that washed out the fire road that added five more miles to our circuit. Tadz saw the destruction, realized our long day had just gotten significantly longer, and wanted to know if I was still up for it.

"After the past few months," I said, "what's a few more miles?"

Not much in the beginning. We parked and let out the dogs. Tadz had brought along a pair of big, tough mutts. I'd only brought Bella. Together, we chewed up that fire road and plunged into the forest. Around us were stands of conifer and clusters of columbine and dogs happy to play among them. Bella, who had filled out over the winter, adding weight to her frame and broadness to her shoulders and now looking mostly like the kind of all-black, thick-necked, iron-jawed pit bull that makes people cross the street when they see her coming, had some kind of primordial respect for these flowers. She would crash through whatever was in her path, but those columbines were off-limits—which was how we found the stream.

Bella was chasing one of Tadz's dogs through a meadow, jumped sideways to avoid some flowers, and ended up splashing into it. The water was clear and cold. There were trout in there, flashing silver and brown in early morning light. In Japan, the mountaineering sport of *sawanabori* is played by tracking streams back to their origins. The writer Tsunemi-chi Ikeda believes it originated in hunter-gather days, possibly as a way of remembering short cuts on game trails, but the urge is still with us. All it took was one glance and immediately we knew which way we were going. The dogs knew as well. *Truchas* is Spanish for "trout" and slang for "dagger," and we were all in for the New Mexican version of *sawanabori*: follow the flash of trout up the dagger of the mountain.

A few hours later, we were somewhere between the end of the dagger's hilt and the start of its blade when the route got steep. Deep pillows of snow started to appear, white dots in a green world, turning into thicker blankets the higher we climbed. The snow was melting into our stream, and our stream was turning into a torrent. We switchbacked up a small cliff and heard the telltale sound of thunder, rounding another bend to find several hundred feet of waterfall roaring toward us. Past the waterfall and through an amazing high meadow and over another ridge, and finally the summit in sight. Normally, the way up there was over a high saddle and across a knife-edged ridge, except both were covered in snow. We decided to scramble up a small cliff, traverse onto the saddle at its halfway point, then dash for the top. A couple hundred feet up the snow turned to ice and I couldn't keep my footing. Tadz wasn't slipping, the dogs weren't slipping, but I'd sat in a chair for two months and, well, I needed a new plan.

I decided to head diagonally across the saddle to a large rock wall. The wall looked like easier climbing, and was, for about eighty feet. Then the rock turned crumbly and the angles treacherous and one bad idea led to another, and pretty soon I was rammed into a crevice on the underside of a boulder, not really sure how to move. There were two hundred feet of nothing between me and the ground. My left hand was hanging on a thin shard, my right trying for a firmer purchase. I couldn't find firmer purchase, so instead tried to hook my left foot on a rock. My shoe hit a pocket of snow and started to slip. "Have fun, don't die" was all Joy had asked. It seemed this was yet another promise I was about to break.

I was seconds away from falling when scree started raining onto my head. All I need now, is what I thought, and looked up to see Bella seventy feet above me, charging down at full gallop. A few months after this happened, I saw David Attenborough's documentary *Planet Earth* and the rare footage of a snow leopard hunting a mountain goat in the mountains of Pakistan. It remains the only comparison I have for Bella's gymnastics. She was bounding from rock to rock, dropping ten feet at a stretch, realigning herself midair, changing direction by dragging a paw against a boulder here, a tree trunk there. And just as she looked sure to drop clear past me, to keep falling straight to her death, she skidded sideways and stopped, her body wedged below my slipping foot, her paws dug deep. She gave me a look that said, "You're not going anywhere," and then clamped her teeth around my pant leg for good measure.

According to psychologist Carl Jung, the dog is the archetype of unquestioning loyalty, but it's one thing to read this in a book and quite another to encounter it in the raw. It was potent, all right. Everything I had poured into the dogs, and here, finally, was a bit of reciprocity. I was grateful, both dumbstruck and awestruck. Immediately I felt better. You want proof? My curiosity returned. It was almost silly. Even before I was back on terra firma, questions began forming in my mind. Joy has long believed that our animals know what's happened to them, that they understand they've been rescued and have a pretty good idea of why. I was never so sure. While it's true that when we get a new dog, once they figure out it's not a hallucination—they really do get to romp with the others and sleep on the couch and these humans keep on feeding them— the reaction is a long bout of puppy love. So whether dogs feel gratitude is not my question—how long that feeling lasts is another question. Does this experience stay in their memory in the same way it would stay in ours? In their dotage, do they sit around and bark about how they got sprung from prison, in the way that my grandparents used to talk about their flight from Russia? In other words, when Bella saved my butt, was she saying thank you?

To explain canine memory, Stanley Coren, director of the Human Neuropsychology and Perception Lab at the University of British Columbia, tells a story about a terrier named Kraus who lived in Vienna. Kraus was trained to take a quarter in his mouth, trot down to the local store, trade the money for a small pouch of pipe tobacco, and trot back home. Then the dog and his owner moved to Prague. After a few weeks there, the owner found another tobacco shop, told them about Kraus's abilities, and set up the same kind of exchange. He spent a few days training Kraus on the route and then gave it a try. The dog took the quarter and went out the door, but didn't come back for four days. When he finally did, his paws were bleeding, his coat a mess, but he had a pouch of tobacco in his mouth. Only it was from the shop in Vienna, 120 miles away.

Is this a true tale? It's certainly not out of line with thousands of others. Coren heard it from a woman in Belgium and doesn't know for sure. "I'm certain the woman who told it to me believed it, but I don't have any evidence one way or the other." However, he also says that dogs are extremely social creatures and there's a lot of evidence they remember people they've associated with, including those who abused them and those who loved them. "Those memories are very strong and enduring," he continues. "I don't know if the dogs remember the specific situations they were in when they were with various people, but through the process of classical conditioning it is clear that each person is associated with, and can trigger in the dog, specific emotional responses."

When we got back down to solid ground there was no proof either way. My heart was pounding, my clothes soaked with sweat. Bella was the opposite. She just wagged her tail a few times and lay down on her belly to eat some snow. She was acting as if nothing had happened. I'm sure something had happened. And whatever else was true, that something, it was the real McCoy.

30

Ever since Otis had died, Joy had been pining for another bull terrier. I had been holding her off. We were still broke, and big dogs are never a minor expense, and this was perhaps the truth—at least some of it. The rest was that I knew that as long as we continued doing dog rescue, by din of nothing more than the limits of life span, dogs would continue to die. I wasn't sure that was something I wanted to go through again and I wasn't sure how to solve this problem. Until I figured it out, I didn't want to add more animals to our pack. But then I came home from Truchas Peak feeling grateful and hopeful, and one thing led to another, and by another I mean Igor.

Igor was a bull terrier puppy with epilepsy. He'd been born in a puppy mill and shipped to a pet store. Then the economy faltered and the pet store went out of business. The breeder didn't want him back, so Igor ended up living with the pet store's now jobless groomer. But the groomer couldn't pay her mortgage and lost her house, and Igor got trucked to Southern California Bull Terrier Rescue, where things didn't go much better. Under normal conditions, Southern California Bull Terrier Rescue handles about five dogs at any one time. Most find homes within a few months. But over the summer of 2008, with the housing crisis in full swing, they had more than fifty. And few takers—especially for one with epilepsy. For three months no one so much as looked at Igor, but the rescue community is small and tight and news of his plight had spread. Elise heard about him and told Joy and she told me, and that was how it began.

The plan was for Elise to hop on a plane and bring Igor with her. Theoretically, she was supposed to arrive sometime the next afternoon, but ended up missing that flight. On the way to the airport, Elise had been driving by an industrial park in West LA when she spotted a cardboard box sitting beneath an old cargo container. The container was jacked up on blocks and the box was tucked deep beneath. She only saw it for a second, "but, you know," said Elise, "being me, I was worried that there were puppies inside."

Some rescuers are magnets. Elise cannot go to the store for milk without finding a stray. Joy often points out that a lot of rescuers have abandonment issues and overcompensate by developing a sixth sense for the abandoned. But even if you don't go in for the paranormal explanations, there's plenty of old-fashioned paranoia to be found—Elise once discovered a box of puppies stuffed inside a dumpster, which is also why she made it two blocks past that warehouse before turning around.

Every animal rescuer I've met considers their mission a sacred task. I once asked Joy about this and to her it wasn't much of a question. "Dog rescue is speaking for those who have no voices. Defending the meek. According to Jesus, that is *the* sacred task." And like many other people involved in holy work, rescuers answer to a higher authority—which is to say, when Elise found a six-foot-high fence surrounding that industrial park, she just scaled it.

Of course, she found kittens in that box, a couple of them, well on their way to starving to death. But this presented something of a bigger problem: how do you scale a six-foot fence with a box of kittens? Well, if you're trespassing on private property and short on time, never mind that you're on a busy street, you take off your shirt and roll one of the cats inside of it, tie the sleeves around your shoulders like a sling, climb the fence, deposit it in your car, and go back for the second. Which is right about the time the security guards found her—standing in her bra, covered in grime, with a kitten in her arms.

"Clearly," said Elise, "I'm not having the best day."

It turned around pretty quick. The security guards didn't arrest her. Instead, they helped her get dressed and helped her get the other cat in the car. After a blizzard of phone calls and a lot of drive time, both animals got lucky and both got homes. Elise and Igor got back on the road.

Which is about when her troubles ended—and ours began.

Mostly, a bull terrier puppy is an exercise in collateral damage. They're a lot like a steam shovel on PCP. With the jaws and the teeth and the disposition, they can draw and quarter a new pair of jeans in twenty seconds. Table legs survive about five minutes. Couches can last a half hour; most don't. Making matters more complicated, Igor didn't like small dogs. This wasn't a prey drive issue—he knew they were his own species and not supposed to be dinner—but the Chihuahuas just bugged him. It's not that uncommon a reaction, but when housing a dozen of them it can be cause for alarm.

The only way to ensure peace was to exhaust Igor. In the beginning, because he wasn't used to the altitude, a good walk did the trick. Pretty soon the walks weren't working. Runs were required. And not just for Igor. On the Fourth of July some shithead wrapped a dog in firecrackers and lit the fuse. They found him screaming down the highway with a skunk stripe of singed fur and melted flesh. We got the call because the burns were going to take a while to heal and in dog rescue time requires space and the Española Humane Society didn't have any. We didn't have any either, but our friends at the Humane Society knew exactly what kind of sucker my wife was for injured Chihuahuas, so that's how they described him to her.

He is not a Chihuahua. He is maybe part pit bull and maybe part hellhound and shaped like a blacksmith's anvil, with a face that's unmistakable Calvin Coolidge. I don't remember what his name was originally, but he had to wear a cone until the burns healed and, being a puppy, quickly destroyed six of those. We next cut a hole in the bottom of an old bucket, and Bucket was the name that stuck. And if Igor was an eight on the Richter scale, Bucket was a ten. By the middle of summer, exhausting these two went from crisis management to the only prayer we had left.

Thus began what soon became the Five-Dog Workout, but this isn't entirely accurate. Sometimes there were five dogs, sometimes there were ten. At the start, the workout was a trail run up a fire road. The local fire roads are perched atop high berms and come with better views. Sometimes the dogs were game for the run; other times they got lost or tired or hot or bored, and that's when the better view came in handy. That said, on the days Igor preferred chasing rabbits to following the pack, even the view didn't help much. He was too fast and too dumb, and this was canyon country, after all. Those days, the only thing that got any real exercise was my temper.

After one particularly long disappearance, I decided to switch from running fire roads to running canyon bottoms. The sides of these were steep enough to keep the dogs penned in. Since the heavy rains tend to pile up debris at various points, running the ar- royos required stopping to climb over tree limbs, rusted car parts, and everything else that washes downstream. Or it did until about a month into this experiment, down near one of those debris piles, when Igor spotted a jackrabbit and bolted. Rather than climb over the pile, he shot up the canyon wall, took a half dozen steps forward, and came down on the other side. He looked like a skater on a ramp or a snowboarder in a half-pipe. And before I had time to think about it, I went right up after him.

The dirt was soft and my feet stuck firm and momentum did the rest. I tore up the wall, banked a turn, came back down, tore up the other side and so on down the arroyo. It did, in fact, feel like being a skater on a ramp. Or a snowboarder in a half-pipe. It felt like I was eight years old. It was so ridiculously fun that I forgot what I was doing and just kept going. There were seven other dogs with me that day, and it was about three hundred yards later that I caught sight of them. They were right behind us, running up and down the walls of the arroyo, looking like a bobsled team on a course, except this team seemed to be laughing.

This was another surprising discovery. For a long time laughter was considered impossible for dogs because laughter requires a level of conscious awareness no one believed dogs actually had. But in the early 1970s, a neuroscientist named Jaak Panksepp became interested in the foundations of human behavior. This was around the same time that Georgetown University molecular biologist Candace Pert discovered the opiate receptor. The most common endogenous endorphin has a potency a hundred times as powerful as morphine. When scientists figured this out they started wondering how much of what we call human behavior is actually a direct response to addictive neurochemistry. Panksepp realized that if he really wanted to know why humans did the things they did, he would have to understand these addictive roots. And the easiest way to understand those was to start looking for them in animals.

In the beginning, Panksepp gave rats opiates and recorded the impact they had on basic emotions such as fear and rage. There was plenty to observe, but pretty soon he got curious about more complicated emotions. He decided to study the separation response, a subset of attachment theory, which was the end result of British psychiatrist John Bowlby spending his career trying to understand patterns of familial interaction. Bowlby realized that attachment, defined as the feeling of devotion that binds one living creature to another, is the direct result of an infant's reaction to alarming situations. Essentially, early bonds form when a newborn encounters distress for the first time. The nearest "identified attachment figure" to respond to the crisis becomes the primary caregiver. Over time, this primary caregiver becomes what's called a "secure base" from which the newborn learns to explore the world. University of Virginia developmental psychologist Mary Ainsworth soon extended the idea of the secure base, adding in the notions of "stranger wariness" and "reunion behaviors" and developing the now ubiquitous strange situation procedure for classifying different attachment styles.

Out of this emerged the realization that in mammals, attachment to a secure base—usually the mother—is the foundation upon which most emotion rests. For this reason, when Panksepp took five-week-old puppies away from their mothers, they went into puppy hysterics. Then he gave them opiates and the crying ceased. Opiates, he discovered, turns the separation response on or off like a switch. He soon found that just about all of the social emotions— from the need for interaction with others to a mother's love—worked the same way. And since the same is true for humans, Panksepp started to wonder about a different question: could it be that animals had the same range of emotions as humans?

There was only one way to find out. Relying on the same neurochemicals that humans depended upon for emotions wasn't enough, what Panksepp had to figure out was where in their brains these emotions were taking place. If humans and animals shared the same neurochemistry and the same neuronal architecture, then he had a pretty strong argument they also shared the same emotions. This led to a multidecade adventure in electrical stimulation.

Panksepp literally worked his way through the brains of animals, stimulating different parts with mild electrical currents and recording the resultant behaviors. After years of this, he found that these emotional signals emerge from the periaqueductal gray (PAG), a near-ancient portion of the midbrain present in all mammals. And he didn't just find fear, rage, lust, and separation anxiety in there; he found the need for nurturance, the desire to care for another, and the urge to play.

The urge to play caught his attention, so Panksepp began observing it in rats. He figured out that what's called rough-and-tumble play emerges at seventeen days of age, regardless of whether or not newborns have been exposed to other rats at play. Fear and hunger can inhibit the full expression of this response, and a strong, secure base can boost it. He also noticed that certain neurochemical combinations (acetylcholine, glutamate, and opioids) enhance the behavior and certain combinations (serotonin, norepinephrine, and GABA) reduce it. And, contrary to popular wisdom, the rough-and-tumble impulse is just as strong in females as males. Which is when he began to wonder about laughter.

"The hallmark of PLAY circuitry in action for humans is laughter," wrote Panksepp in his *Affective Neuroscience: The Foundations of Human and Animal Emotions*, "a projectile respiratory movement with no apparent function, except perhaps to signal to others one's social mood and sense of carefree camaraderie. Some believe laughter is uniquely human, but we would doubt this proposition." Panksepp doubts this because he discovered that rats make a chirping sound while playing. Because the noise occurs at fifty kilohertz, the same ultrasonic frequency rats use to communicate and one that requires special equipment to hear, he didn't notice for a while. But after he did, he noticed these chirps showed up every time the animals played.

Was this chirping really laughter? It seemed a stretch, so

Panksepp decided to probe further. In human children, tickling is the easiest way to provoke laughter, so he started tickling rats. He found that tickling the neck, which is normally how rats solicit play, produced more chirping then tickling their rumps. He found full-body tickling more effective than neck petting. And when he stimulated a portion of the PAG with electricity or just flat out administered dopamine to the rats, he got the same response. And the rats liked it too. They started seeking out their human caretakers for more tickling.

When news of this spread, other researchers discovered similar behavior in other species. Chimpanzees, for example, have a "play pant" that resembles laughter and shows up as a response to tickling. Cognitive ethologist Patricia Simonet recently recorded the sounds of dogs wrestling and discovered a pant she also believes is laughter. When Simonet played the sound over loudspeakers in an animal shelter near her home in Seattle, the dogs inside stopped barking within a minute—which is something that rarely happens. And this result has been duplicated by other researchers in other shelters across America. You can hear a tape on the Internet. I did. That's how I figured out what I heard was actually laughter.

I don't know how far we all ran that day, but much of that canyon for sure. What finally drew us to a halt was a six-foot drop where the riverbed should have been. I bailed off to the side, and five silly dogs landed on top of me. By then, we were all laughing. It was an experience unlike any I'd previously had with animals, which meant it was like just about every experience I had with animals. Which also explains illustrator Brad Holland's famous definition of surrealism: "An archaic term. Formerly an art movement. No longer distinguishable from everyday life."

31

By the time that second summer was in full swing, our network had grown large enough that I actually got to see what it took to run a real rescue. And *see* is the operative word. While I was down in the goat shack writing, Joy was in charge of the vast understatement I called "daily living."

We had about twenty dogs by now; many were older, many without teeth. Each of these older dogs needed to be fed individually, some hand-fed with a spoon. All told, about a half hour's work. The dogs' diets varied depending on health status and nutritional requirements, and there was some home cooking involved, so food prep took her another half hour. The dogs get their big meal in the morning, and two smaller snacks in the afternoon, and that's one more hour's work. The distribution of medicine requires two twenty-minute installments, the washing of dog towels and pee pads and other rescue paraphernalia about the same. Dog walks last around seventy-five minutes. And then there's the work of rescue, which doesn't look like much from the outside, but it's most of the secret. What it looks like is a woman sitting in a chair petting a dog. Joy tries for twenty minutes a day for each of ours. I've tried it as well. It took three hours and my hand went numb. What I called "daily living," Joy called a solid eight hours.

What I called public relations was another part of the job I finally got to see. PR was split into administration, admissions, and anomalies. Administration is the standard pile of non-profit paper-work plus a three-stage adoption process. The first stage is a tele-phone interview with a potential adopter. A lot of our dogs have been too traumatized to handle much roughhousing, so placing dogs in homes with small children is something we try to avoid. For this rea-son, during those phone calls, "Do you have kids?" is where Joy often starts. She goes on from there. "Do you work from home? How much time will the dog spend alone all day? Will the dog be walked? Sleep inside? Is the yard fenced?" As most of our dogs have chronic health problems, "Can you handle the medical responsibilities?" is important. Mostly, though, it's a vibe thing. If Joy likes their vibe, then it's on to stage two.

This is when the potential adopter meets the potential adoptee for the first time. This is also about vibe, but we're less interested in how much the person likes the dog than in how much the dog likes the person. After initial introductions, does the dog hang around, want to be petted, want to play? If the dog climbs into the potential adopter's lap and goes to sleep, this is among the better signs, because it means the dog feels safe. One story comes to mind: the potential adopter a woman named Janice, in her seventies, a little odd, huge breasts—more on that in a moment.

The elderly are a difficult conundrum for dog rescuers. On one hand, older folks tend to make fantastic dog owners, especially for special-needs dogs that require more time, patience, and tenderness than others. But a lot of rescues are nervous about placing a dog with a senior because the senior could die at any time. The long-term concern is having to start over and find the dog a new home, a process that is both time-consuming for the human and traumatic for the animal, but the short-term concern—the person dies and the dog is trapped with no food and no water until someone discovers the body—is the real problem. To get around this problem, Joy had started "Seniors for Seniors," a canine lending library of sorts. Instead of adopting out the dog, we leased, with the critical condition being that the leaser agrees to call in every other day to verify their status among the living.

Before we lease an older person a dog, safety concerns demand that we verify dementia hasn't set in, so we tend to conduct lengthy in-person interviews. In the middle of our interview with Janice, the phone rang and Joy went to answer it. A second later a barking riot broke out at the far end of our fields. I went to check on that. Janice stayed behind with Flower, her potential match, a teacup Chihuahua with special needs. Ever since celebrities started appearing in magazines with these tiny dogs, demand has gone up. Since breeders can charge six thousand dollars for one, supply went up as well. The hidden cost is the severe inbreeding needed to make a dog that small. The results are litters of sickly, often brain-damaged animals sent to shelters for every healthy one sold to a Paris Hilton fan. Dealing with these dogs takes a certain touch. Janice didn't have dementia; we were trying to decide if she had that touch.

The reason I mention her bust size is that Joy's phone call lasted a little while, as did the ruckus. Ten minutes passed by the time I returned from the field. I got back to find Janice beaming. When I asked what was up, she flashed me: lifting her blouse clear over her head. It wasn't her boobs she wanted me to see. It was Flower, dead asleep, tucked perfectly between them. What do we look for in a potential adopter? Janice had the right touch.

Stage three is a home check. Just as it sounds, one of us drives out to the adopter's house, makes sure the dog still likes the match, makes sure the person still likes the match, and makes sure the house is safe enough for the both of them. Some of this is preventive medicine. Joy likes to point out all the things that are likely to get broken by introducing a dog into the environment. She says it helps with the "bereavement process"—meaning it tempers how pissed off that adopter is going to be when a favorite rug becomes a jigsaw puzzle.

Admissions are the second component in public relations, and they're supposed to be straightforward: we get a call about a dog in need and help if we can, but there are too many dogs and not enough rescuers and never enough space. I have learned to fear those phone calls. I know of no other job save those in war zones where death is such a constant, and fewer still where just trying to help means making so many decisions of the who-should-live-and-who-should-die variety. Every rescuer agrees: admissions are the worst part of the gig.

The last part, anomalies, is mostly reputation. To date I have fielded calls from three countries and every state save Alaska, and I don't much answer the phone. Typically the person on the other end knows almost nothing more than Joy's name and the rumor that she has a way with small dogs with big problems. The first thing Joy always tells them is that her way is to let the dogs be dogs and love them for it—but no one thinks it's that easy and the conversations take much longer. What I call anomalies, Joy calls another two hours of her day.

Perros is the Spanish word for "dogs." Not long after returning from the Gila, a woman I'd never met stopped me at the grocery store to ask if I was married to the *angel de los perros*.

"I'm not sure," I said. "Is the angel smart, skinny, and smoking hot?"

Turns out we were talking about the same person.

"*Necesitamos más como ella*," is what this woman said to me. It means "We need more like her."

I couldn't agree more.

32

Back when my friend Joe first introduced me to his friend Joy, as I was immediately smitten, he followed that introduction with a warning.

"Great woman, amazing writer—but crazy."

"Crazy how?"

"Dog rescue," he had said. "It's not a cause, it's a cult."

This may not exactly be the case, but it's not entirely wrong. The British philosopher Stephen R. L. Clark once asked: "What are animals really like? How far can we trust our own unthinking recognition of their fear, fidelity or cleverness? How far should we accept the impulse to decree a strict division between us and them? Here then is the issue. How shall we decide?" Dog rescuers appear cultish because they have already decided and their decision is not a popular one. They reject, at least on some level, the division between "us" and "them." Quite simply, they don't see humans as special.

To understand all this it helps to start at the beginning. In 1637, the French philosopher René Descartes published his *Discourse on Method on Rightly Conducting the Reason and Seeking Truth in the Sciences* and laid out his four fundamental rules for doing philosophy: Accept as true only what is indubitable; divide every question into manageable parts; begin with the simplest issues and ascend to the more complex; review frequently enough to retain the whole argument at once. Out of this emerged a number of different ideas, including his legendary *Cogito*—"I think therefore I am"—and a bunch of downstream correlates upon which most of modern science was built. The anchor in Descartes's *cogito* was language. He knew he thought because he could describe his thoughts in language. What he didn't know was if animals thought. Descartes had already decided to doubt anything he could not prove, but lacking a common language, he had no way to prove animals could think. He concluded they couldn't. Animals, in his opinion, were machines with intricate parts. They were not a "special case" like humans; they had no thoughts and no feelings, and were guilty of that ultimate Funkadelic crime: having no soul.

During his lectures—as insane as it sounds—Descartes liked to nail this point home by nailing dogs to the wall. He told the audience that the screams they heard were not real, rather the product of complicated automa producing mechanistic noises, not unlike the squeak of a screw turning in a tight hole. When people say that animal rescuers are crazy, what they really mean is that animal rescuers share a number of fundamental beliefs that makes them easy to marginalize. Among those is the belief that René Descartes was a jackass.

There is a long line of thinkers who have fallen into this anti-Cartesian camp. Voltaire devoted much of his career to shouting down his ideas. Ralph Waldo Emerson once wrote, "You have just dined, and however scrupulously the slaughterhouse is concealed in the graceful distance of miles, there is complicity," and the rest of the Transcendentalists tended to agree. The English philosopher Jeremy Bentham upped that ante when he realized, "The question is not, 'Can they reason?' nor, 'Can they talk?' but rather, 'Can they suffer?'" But it was Princeton philosopher Peter Singer's extension of Bentham's principle that's become the most infamous counter-argument.

Singer is a pragmatist, a devotee of Bentham's school of utilitarian moral philosophy, concerned here with the foundations of equality. When Bentham wrote, "Each to count for one and none for more than one," he was expressing his fundamental basis for equality among people. In his 1975 *Animal Liberation*, Singer extended this argument to what he calls "nonhuman animals," and the resulting ruckus has never quite ceased.

In trying to separate Singer from that ruckus, I've found that history is helpful. In August 1969, the preeminent journal *Science* published a paper by Allen and Beatrice Gardner about a female chimpanzee named Washoe whom they'd taught to talk. Before Washoe, chimps couldn't string together a sentence. Their world record for words learned totaled at three. The Gardners' breakthrough was to recognize the limits of primate anatomy. Rather than attempting to teach Washoe to speak, they taught her to sign. Washoe got a little farther than *mama*, *papa*, and *cup*, developing a 250-word vocabulary and an ability to react to novel linguistic combinations.

The Gardners' method spread through the scientific community. Around the time Singer began writing his book, Stanford primatologist Francine Patterson had moved beyond chimps and taught a gorilla to sign. At Columbia, Herbert Terrace collected twenty thousand instances of a chimp named Nim Chimpsky—a direct challenge to Noam Chomsky, then Descartes's most ardent supporter—stringing together grammatically correct sentences. Not long after, Johnny Carson introduced Washoe to the nation. Carson was so impressed that upon his death he left a million dollars to the Carson Center for Chimps, established in his home state of Nebraska.

Despite the appeal of signing chimps as a counterargument to Descartes, Singer didn't hang his theory on them, but for the general public the connection was critical. Also critical was the equal rights movement of the early 1970s. Racism and sexism were hot topics, and when Singer began looking into the question of animal rights, it's there he started. He wanted to know what the ethical basis for equality was: "When we say that all human beings, whatever their race, creed, or sex, are equal, what is it that we are asserting?"

> Those who wish to defend hierarchical, inegalitarian societies have often pointed out that by whatever test we choose it simply is not true that all humans are created equal. Like it or not we must face the fact that humans come in different shapes and sizes; they come with different moral capacities, different intellectual abilities, different amounts of benevolent feeling and sensitivity to the needs of others, difference in the ability to communicate effectively, and different capacities to experience pleasure and pain. In short, if the demand for equality were based on the actual equality of all human beings, we would have to stop demanding equality.

Joining a long line of thinkers, Singer came to realize that equality is not a fact, instead considering it a "moral idea." As such, his basis for equality comes down to Bentham's key question: "Do they suffer?" If a being is sentient, and thus capable of suffering, it must receive the same "moral consideration" as any other regardless of race, sex, intelligence, creed, moral capacity, or—and this is the key point—species. "Racists," writes Singer, "violate the principle of equality by giving greater weight to the interests of members of their own race when there is a clash between their interests and the interests of those of another race. Sexists violate the principle of equality by favoring the interests of their own sex. Similarly, *speciesists* allow the interests of their own species to override the greater interests of members of other species. The pattern is identical in each case."

So what does equal consideration look like? When HBO's Bill Maher said, "To people who say, 'My father is alive because of animal experimentation,' I say, 'Yeah, well, good for you. This dog died so your father can live.' Sorry, but I am not behind that kind of trade-off," he was merely extending Singer's principles to real-world situations. Of course, sometimes that extension takes the form of firebombing three buildings and four chairlifts as the Earth Liberation Front did in Vail, Colorado, in 1998 on behalf of the lynx—but who said revolution was ever easy?

And this is another thing about dog rescuers: even though a great many abhor violence, the vast majority do believe they are fighting a revolution. Another is that many have misinterpreted Singer. The philosopher never departed from Bentham's basic ethical equation: "Do the greatest good for the greatest number." Singer's argument is that we cannot exclude animals from that number based on their species—though he does say that when he talks about those species deserving equal rights he really means all primates, most mammals, and even leaves the door cracked open for animal experimentation as long as the benefits outweigh the consequences and *all* non-animal alternatives have been ruled out. Animal experimentation, he feels, is never okay for testing makeup or cleaning products, but just may be acceptable for lifesaving research. In 2006, Singer told Oxford neuroscientist Tipu Aziz that his work with Parkinson's disease and primates was "justifiable" because a hundred monkeys had been sacrificed to save forty thousand people.

Nor is Singer the ardent supporter of vegetarianism some presume. While he does believe that not eating animals is the best practical solution to a thorny problem, he bases that not on individual suffering, rather on planetary suffering. He agrees with author Eric Schlosser's *Fast Food Nation* argument—meat might not be murder, but it's certainly murdering the planet—writing: "Concern for world hunger, for the land, and for energy conservation provides an ethical basis for a vegetarian diet, or at least one in which meat consumption is minimized."

But who needs logic when there's gut instinct? And that seems to be the real problem. Much of modern society depends on the subservience of animals, and this is as it should be, we are sure, because animals have never created anything like modern society. Philosophers call this a reflexive argument; the rest of us think of it as common sense.

And this was the exact wall I ran into. Before moving to Chimayo, I had never seriously considered Peter Singer. I had told myself I didn't need to consider his work, because my sense of common sense also told me humans were special. Even if Descartes's "humans are the only species to use language" example of our distinctiveness no longer held water, I knew it was only one out of many attributes that scientists used to make this case. But those attributes are either things such as emotion, personality, and the capacity for abstract thought—capabilities that have also been discovered in most animals—or compassion, cooperation, morality, and altruism, capabilities I'd already seen in my dogs. Laughter, as mentioned, was another item on that list. Seeing it in my dogs was something of the last straw. Afterward, the whole line of reasoning just fell apart.

I spent a bit more time thinking through Singer's argument. While I find "Do they suffer?" an incredibly important question, I also knew that creating a society where animals had rights equal to humans' was—at least for a while—going to create a whole lot of human suffering on its way to alleviating a whole lot of animal suffering. Ultimately, I decided a better approach might be to reframe the debate and just check the scorecard. For the past four thousand years, ever since the Bible gave us "dominion over the beasts," humankind has been acting like the superior species. If moral concerns are the topic on the table, it seems the only question worth asking is how this arrangement has worked out so far.

In 2002, according to a survey of four hundred top researchers conducted by the American Museum of Natural History, the planet is currently facing a "mass extinction" the likes of which has never been seen. Species are disappearing faster than ever before in history. In 2008, this time according to the International Union for the Conservation of Nature, seventeen hundred experts from 130 countries all agreed: one out of every two species on earth is in decline, and one in four is at risk for extinction.

Worse, as Richard Manning explains in "The Oil We Eat," we know exactly why this happened:

> Special as we humans are, we get no exemptions from the rules. All animals eat plants or eat animals that eat plants. This is the food chain, and pulling it is the unique ability of plants to turn sunlight into stored energy in the form of carbohydrates, the basic fuel of all animals. Solar-powered photosynthesis is the only way to make this fuel. There is no alternative to plant energy, just as there is no alternative to oxygen. The results of taking away our plant energy may not be as sudden as cutting off oxygen, but they are as sure.
>
> Scientists have a name for the total amount of plant mass created by Earth in a given year, the total budget for life. They call it the planet's "primary productivity." There have been two efforts to figure out how that productivity is spent, one by a group at Stanford University, the other an independent accounting by the biologist Stuart Pimm. Both conclude that we humans, a single species among millions, consume about 40 percent of Earth's primary productivity, 40 percent of all there is. This simple number may explain

why the current extinction rate is 1,000 times that which existed before human domination of the planet. We 6 billion have simply stolen the food, the rich among us a lot more than others.

These assessments are more math than morality. Plain old animal stewardship has been our charge, and by almost every metric available we've failed spectacularly at that charge. And while I was still not entirely sure what to make of Peter Singer, as Joan Didion once said: "However long we postpone it, we eventually lie down alone in that notoriously uncomfortable bed, the one we make ourselves." And, if for no other reasons than the scale of our error and the lumps in our mattress, isn't it time to reevaluate first principles? If we can't push past the morality of yesteryear to reshape the common sense of tomorrow, then we really should consider punishing football players for their crime of touching pigskin on the Sabbath.

PART SEVEN

Because how we spend our days is, of course, how we spend
our lives.

—Annie Dillard

33

It was Friday night and early August and as good a time as any to climb into a cage with a mountain lion. This particular mountain lion got hit by a car while trying to cross a busy freeway in the southern portion of New Mexico about ten months back. The police first got the call, and then the Department of Game and Fish, and Doc not long after that. There was some discussion about whether or not the cat would even make it through the night, let alone survive a complicated surgery, but Doc decided to try. She hitched a trailer to her truck, drove halfway across the state, loaded the cougar into a cage, and drove back across the state, this time to an emergency surgical theater in Albuquerque. Working with another doctor for six hours straight, they managed to put ten titanium screws and who knows how many pins in the lion's leg, and when that leg healed enough for transport, the cat ended up at the Wildlife Center's Large Mammal Facility outside of Española. Which is also where I ended up in that cage, trying to wrestle a 180-pound man-eater to the ground.

I guess there were two real reasons I ended up in that cage. The first was that I had reread Peter Singer, but this may require a little more explaining. As I was rethinking my ethical stance on animals, it wasn't lost on me that a great many of the so-called anomalous behaviors I was seeing—behaviors that weren't supposed to exist in nonhuman animals and behaviors whose absence was used to justify human specialness—I was seeing in dogs. But humans co-evolved to live with dogs. They are the species we know better than all others because they are the species we have been around since their very beginning. It made me wonder about all those other species we don't know as well as dogs. It made me wonder what else we've missed along the way.

The second reason was that dog rescuers are really just a subset of animal rescuers, and while I knew a little bit about the former, I had no real understanding of the latter. One thing I knew already: animal rescuers, especially wildlife rescuers, were a tougher lot than dog rescuers. There's just no way around one central fact: whatever the size of the sacrifice made in dog rescue, we at least get the "cuddle factor"—specifically, we get to cuddle our dogs. This was a hell of a payoff, but rescuers who work with wildlife never cuddle. They interact with the creatures in their care as little as possible. Their goal is to heal wounds and return the animals to their natural habitat. The last thing they want to do along the way is habituate these animals to the presence of humans, since there's a good chance those wounds originated with humans. With absolutely no reciprocity, wildlife rescue is the extreme end of the cross-species altruism spectrum. It's the purest form of altruism on the planet, and I wanted to see what that looked like up close.

As Doc had devoted her life to working with wildlife, I asked her if she minded playing tour guide. She didn't, and a plan was concocted. I was supposed to meet Doc and a New Mexico game and fish warden at the Large Mammal Facility to help them tranquilize that mountain lion so he could be put into a transport cage, loaded into a truck, and then driven back across the state for release back into the wild. That was still the plan, but along the way we'd seriously underestimated the weight of the cat and the amount of ketamine it would take to knock him out.

After we darted the lion, he went into a howling frenzy,

running laps around his cage, lunging at anyone who came near the bars. Then the drug started to work and he dropped to the ground, but didn't stop thrashing. Doc was worried he'd rebreak that leg. To prevent this, she decided to jump into the cage to try and pin him down, all ninety-five pounds of her. What was needed was another shot of ketamine, which was the warden's responsibility, but the warden was New Mexico country folk and would not be rushed. Since animal rescuers often operate on the edge of the law, shouting at the warden to pick up the pace wasn't going to help the larger cause. So I did what any other concerned moron would do under the circumstances: I jumped in the cage with her.

"You get the head," shouted Doc, "I'll hold the legs."

Sure, hold the head. The fucking thing is bigger than a bowling ball and those jaws work just fine. Absolutely, I'll hold the head. And afterward, so the party won't end, let's drink some hemlock.

Unfortunately, rescuers like Doc are needed because it's already the end of the party. Forty thousand years ago, when humans first crossed the land bridge from Asia, *Puma concolor* ranged freely from the Yukon in Canada to the southern tip of South America. That was the last time things went right for these animals. Despite the relevance wildlife has for most Indian cultures, a great many of them didn't know what to make of these big cats. In *Mountain Lion: An Unnatural History of People and Pumas*, Chris Bolgiano mentions a 1955 interview with a Nootka who said the lion was "the one animal the Indians didn't understand." But the Indian's mistrust of the cat was nothing compared to the antagonism felt by early European arrivals. By the turn of the twentieth century, mountain lions had been hunted to near extinction in the eastern portion of the United States and didn't fare better out west. In California alone, where they were listed as a bountied predator, hunters killed more than 12,000 of them between 1907 and 1963—an average of 215 a year. In 1963 they went from bountied to non-game animals and quotas were lifted so they could be shot year round. Then kills rose even higher.

In 1972, California governor Ronald Reagan suspended this trophy hunt, a halt that later became law. Not that it did much good. In recent years, according to a study done by the Mountain Lion Foundation, the premier cougar conservation organization in the United States, "humans have killed more mountain lions in the American West than at any other time in the past century—greatly exceeding even those years when mountain lions were the target of bounties and government eradication efforts." From 1997 to 2005 nearly 30,000 mountain lions were slaughtered in eleven states, roughly 3,600 a year. It's an increase of 400 percent since 1970. There may be 5,000 cougars left in California, there may be less. Because of this, the World Conservation Union has reclassified the mountain lion from a "species of least concern" to "near threatened."

As far as I could tell, apologies were in order.

So yeah, I got in that cage and held that head. It was a nowhere-near-the-top-of-the-food-chain moment. I was stepping back in time courtesy of a creature that evolved specifically to hunt the likes of me. The feeling was electric. Once again I was rubbing against pure wildness, and once again I got that sense of deep time and archetypal connection. I knew immediately that this was why Doc could live without the cuddle factor. This was a bigger payoff.

The feeling lasted until after we got the second syringe into the cat and got him loaded on the truck. It was already dark when we were done. In the early morning we would leave for the Aldo Leopold Wilderness, where this cougar would once again be set free. Until then, I was heading home, stinking of sweat and mountain lion. I'd gotten only one step past my front door when the dogs got a whiff of me, spun on their heels, and ran.

34

Aldo Leopold was born in Burlington, Iowa, in 1887, graduated Yale Forestry School in 1909, and was made supervisor of the Carson National Forest in New Mexico in 1912. A decade later he developed the funny notion that wilderness should actually contain large tracts of undeveloped land. He successfully petitioned for the 1924 establishment of New Mexico's Gila Wilderness—300,000 hectares of protected landscape that became the first official wilderness area in the United States. Afterward, Leopold transferred to the University of Wisconsin, Madison. In 1933, when his book *Game Management* appeared, defining his fundamental techniques for the conservation and restoration of native wildlife populations, he became chair of the country's first game management department. Two years later, with the help of three friends, he founded the Wilderness Society, the quartet saying of their goals: "All we desire to save from invasion is the extremely minor fraction of America which yet remains free from mechanical sights and sounds and smell."

Leopold died fighting a brush fire on a neighbor's farm in April 1948, just a few months shy of the publication of his now legendary *Sand County Almanac*. In the *Almanac,* he laid bare his land ethic: "All ethics so far evolved rest upon a single premise: that the individual is a member of a community of interdependent parts. His instincts prompt him to compete for his place in that community, but his ethics prompt him also to co-operate (perhaps in order that there may be a place to compete for). The land ethic simply enlarges the boundaries of the community to include soils, waters, plants, and animals, or collectively: the land." In 1980 Congress set aside another 200,000 hectares of New Mexico directly adjacent to the Gila and named it the Aldo Leopold Wilderness, after the man now considered the "Father of American Wilderness." It seemed a fitting place to set a mountain lion free.

Driving from Chimayo to the Aldo Leopold Wilderness is a journey into a different world. The dusty interior of the state is a stretch of small towns and ghost towns and general strangeness. Years back, I knew a woman from California whose definition of good fun included taking a couple of tabs of acid and trying to convince tourists to hop in the back of her pickup for what she called the "Redneck Tour of San Francisco." She also fought forest fires. She'd worked as a smokejumper on and off for the better portion of a decade, mainly in Montana and Idaho, but was once down in New Mexico for a blaze at the Leopold, an experience she recounted as "a whole other breed of weird." And coming from her, that was saying something.

We found proof of this outside the town of Kingman, snake-twisting our way through the Black Mountains. Tadz had joined me for this excursion. We were caravanning behind Doc, her husband, and the mountain lion. They were supposed to stay right in front of us, but between the altitude gain, the hairpin turns, and our need to stop and piss, we'd lost sight of them. We found them again, doors open, truck empty, in a pullout atop a steep cliff. There was an old Honda parked nearby, piled floorboards to headliner with bric-a-brac, but no driver. Besides one very agitated tabby cat, the Honda too was empty. We were only a few hours from Roswell.

"Alien abduction?" asked Tadz.

"Alien abduction," I concurred.

We found them—Doc, her husband, and some guy we'd never seen before—on the other side of the guard rail, standing a few feet down that cliff. As best as we could reconstruct, the guy had lost his job and his house and his wife had died, and all that was left was an old Honda, a bum leg, and a pair of tabby cats. He'd pulled off the road to stretch the leg and one of those cats darted out an open window. The first portion of the cliff was a steep downslope ending in a hundred-foot drop. Just above the drop was a small ledge, upon which his cat had decided to perch.

Somehow the guy had managed to work his way down to the ledge, but getting back up with a bum leg and cat in his hand was impossible. He'd started screaming for help. A few miles before this, Doc's truck had lost third gear. She was crossing the mountains in second, going slowly enough that she heard his shout. We arrived about five minutes later, at the tail end of the rescue operation, just in time to catch a bit of this guy's lonely backstory. Somewhere between "these cats mean the world to me" and "I really love animals, especially cats," Tadz mentioned that Doc too had a cat in her truck.

"He's a little bigger than yours," he explained.

"I don't know," said the guy. "Muffin's pretty chubby."

Doc's truck had tinted windows, so you had to press your face right up to the glass to see inside.

"Go ahead," she said, "take a peek."

We had darted the mountain lion the night before, because part of releasing an animal back into the wild is ensuring that the animal goes back into the wild. You need it wide awake and preferably agitated by the time you reach the release site. Since our cat had now been wide awake in a small cage in the back of a truck for five hours of bumpy, winding roads, it was seriously agitated. The amygdala is a tiny almond-shaped structure in the brain governing basic emotions such as fear and rage, as well as the formation of memories shaped by those emotions. Among the oldest portions of the human brain, it's old enough that the reactions to certain dangers have become hardwired instinct. Our get-me-the-hell-out-of-here responses to snakes, spiders, and the bloodcurdling roar of a big cat in a bad mood are fine examples of this process at work. That fine example knocked this guy flat on his ass.

"Yup," he said, picking himself off the dirt afterward, "definitely bigger than my cat."

35

In his essay "Why Look at Animals," John Berger writes: "To suppose that animals first entered the human imagination as meat or leather or horn is to project a nineteenth-century attitude backwards across the millennia. Animals first entered the imagination as messengers and promises. For example, the domestication of cattle did not begin as a simple prospect of milk and meat. Cattle had magical functions, sometimes oracular, sometimes sacrificial."

The transformation from magical creature to domesticated livestock that Berger's describing required a certain separation from nature, a distancing scholars believe emerged with our transition from hunter-gatherer to agriculturalist. Much has been written on the topic, with general conclusions tending toward the idea that we abandoned our mystical reverence because the brutality of farm life required maintaining a serious emotional distance from the wild. Language was where this battle first played out. Once-sacred creatures were relabeled. Plants became weeds or crops. Animals became pests or pets.

James Serpell describes this process more exactly in his *In the Company of Animals*:

Traditional hunters typically view the animals they hunt as their equals. They exercise no power over them, although they hope to persuade the animal to be more easily captured by means of certain magical or religious practices. This essentially egalitarian relationship disappeared with the advent of domestication. The domestic animal is dependent for survival on its human owner. The human becomes the overlord and master, the animals his servants and slaves. By definition, domestic animals are subservient to the will of humanity and, for the majority of species involved, this loss of independence had some fairly devastating long-term consequences.

Among those consequences are the ways we've learned to justify subservience. "If one accepted the Cartesian view that animals were soulless, insensate machines, then one could do what one liked to them without any moral compunctions whatsoever," says Serpell, later explaining further:

The myth that humans were entitled to lordship over the rest of creation was a useful cultural adaptation that greatly facilitated agricultural and domestic expansion. It allowed domestic animals to be regarded as objects and merchandise, and it encouraged an aggressive, exploitative attitude to the natural world. Wild animals which were deemed to be useless, or which made the mistake of competing with man on his own ground were universally classified as vermin that needed to be exterminated at every possible opportunity. And uncultivated areas, such as forests, moorlands and heaths, were viewed as bleak and hostile wildernesses that harbored blood-thirsty wolves and legendary monsters. It was man's duty to tame such areas; to subjugate them and bring them under the yoke of human domination. In other words, the myth was important, and defended vigorously, because it had immense survival value.

Sometimes this plays out in strange ways. As mentioned, one of the first duties assigned to the "domesticated" wolf was that of babysitter. Mommy and Daddy would go off hunting and gathering, leaving Fido and friends to mind the fort. We can argue that primitive societies held their offspring in lesser regard than we do ours—that is, if we're willing to deny a whole lot of biology along the way. Instead, we argue about wolves being allowed back into Yellowstone. "They're pests," was a frequently heard rancher's response during those debates, "dangerous pests." Those pests used to babysit our future generations—so how's that for bizarre?

Also bizarre was our need to drive all the way across New Mexico to liberate a cat that once called the entire supercontinent home. Another difficulty was the game warden. State law requires one to be present at all releases, and ours seemed to believe himself a direct descendent of the Marlboro Man, complete with cigarettes, mustache, and double-barrel shotgun. What the Marlboro Man wanted most was not to be bothered. Mountain lions are solitary by nature and require a lot of space to remain that way. Their home ranges starts at twenty-five miles and can extend up to three hundred. The plan had been to drive as far into the Gila Wilderness as possible, but the Marlboro Man was in charge. He led us three miles from the freeway and called it quits.

We parked atop a low peak, in the middle of an alpine forest. It was dusky afternoon, the light not all that different from the color of the lion's coat. Doc was on the roof of her truck. She had modified the cage so that its gate could be lifted with a hook from the roof, an important safety feature when working with an animal that can sever an artery with the swipe of a claw. The warden took up a position not far away, trousers hitched up, stance wide-legged. He had his shotgun locked, cocked, and blocked.

I once asked Doc if there was an animal that was dangerous to release. "Grizzlies are deadly," she said, "but I've never seen a bear stick around long. Open the cage and it's boogie, boogie, boogie. I've turned rattlesnakes loose and had them try to bite me. Rattlesnakes hold grudges, it doesn't matter what you do, but I think they're the only grudge species I've met in my life."

And what about mountain lions?

"Mountain lions are a different thing. They're incredibly efficient killers. If you survive a mountain lion attack, it's because they let you live."

Doc wasn't taking any chances. Tadz and I were told to stay in our truck until the cat was gone. Then she got the gate open. Nothing happened. The lion stayed inside the cage, inside the truck, just looking at all of us. We looked back. Time passed. More time passed. Eventually he stuck out a paw and slunk to the ground. He glanced right, then left, then strolled to a small clearing about twenty feet away—and stopped. This was not the way things were supposed to go.

The warden had been itching to fire his shotgun all day, and finally got his chance. It should be mentioned that so fond are people in New Mexico of their guns and so stupid in their operations, that the police find it necessary to go on television before every major holiday to remind folks there are laws against firing a gun straight into the air. Specifically, the law of gravity: what goes up must come down. Pets and people being the usual casualties in this tragic scenario. Our warden must have missed that message. He shot straight up into the air.

The shotgun blast was supposed to scare the lion into bolting. He did not bolt. He turned again, that massive head, to look back at us. Then he hissed once and bounded off into the underbrush. No one could find him for a moment, and then we saw him, stalking a wide circle around our position, finally pausing in some trees directly behind us.

"He's fucking with us, right?"

"Yeah," said Tadz, "he's fucking with us."

The last we saw of him was when he lifted that head for a final look. Then he was gone, retreating in the underbrush, leaving only the specter of that gaze behind. I had the very serious sense this cat had been trying to tell us something. The look was pretty unmistakable. I asked Tadz about it later, and he'd seen the same thing I did. What was that look? It was disgust.

Not fear. Not hatred. Just disgust.

36

Life started to change as our second autumn in Chimayo began. By then, we'd been in New Mexico long enough to have assembled a decent-sized network, which meant that we were having an easier time finding homes for our dogs, which also meant we were adding more dogs, which really meant that we always had a couple of animals around that we just didn't know too well. Back in Los Angeles, new adoptees had come through a screening process of sorts—either Joy had picked them out from a shelter or someone very close to Joy had done the choosing—but in trying to establish ourselves in Chimayo, trying to develop relationships with different vets and different shelters and the few other rescue operations around, we didn't yet get to be that discerning. If someone asked for help, we went out of our way to help. Because of that, we ended up with a number of dogs who had been described to us as "in need of socialization," which turned out to be a euphemism for "just about feral."

Feral dogs bite first and ask questions later. They're scared of humans and avoid humans, and the only way to socialize ferals is to let them do the socializing. We don't talk to them, don't try to pet them, don't even look at them. The entire relationship sits in their court. We let them make all the moves, and they don't always make them quickly. Joy had warned me this process can take months, sometimes years, and in the interim we were left in a peculiar situation: sharing our home with essentially wild animals.

Henry David Thoreau was the first in a long line of environmental philosophers who both understood the difference between "wildness" and "wilderness"—wildness being a state of mind, wilderness being a place—and stressed the importance of the former as much as the latter. Thoreau's most famous line, "In wildness is the preservation of the world," is both a statement of moral purpose and fighting words. His embrace of the wild put him in opposition to an entire line of thinkers dating back to Plato who felt that taming the wilderness outside and the wildness inside were among the greatest human responsibilities. Whether or not this is the case is less important here than the effects of such thinking on contemporary life.

When I lived in the city, I thought of wildness in mostly binary terms. The coyotes who prowled the canyons of Los Angeles were wild; the house pets they were hunting were tame. When I did have actual contact with wildness, it was always because I sought it out—I went hiking, I went climbing, I went camping—but in dog rescue, wildness was neither binary nor something I had to seek out. Wildness was there when I woke up in the morning and there when I went to bed at night. In fact, it was often there in the bed with me at night.

I don't mean this metaphorically. The socialization of feral dogs is a multistage process. The initial stage occurs when the dog in question comes inside the house for the first time. This usually takes place quickly. Dogs watch other dogs for cues, so when new dogs, even completely feral ones, realize both that the comfortable places to lie down—couches and dog beds and such—are inside the house and that the rest of the pack moves inside and outside without human intervention, they tend to do the same. After about a month of this, as these feral dogs begin to habituate to our presence, they'll occasionally want to sleep in our presence. This happens because the bed serves as the dog's den, and even feral dogs are instinctively drawn to the den. But again, it's a slow draw. In the beginning, while they might wander into the bedroom, if they choose to sleep there, it's usually in the closet. A few weeks to a month later, they'll move to a far corner, tucking themselves beneath a night table, perhaps under a chair. After two months or so, they may begin to sleep on the floor near the end of the bed. As even more time passes and they get slightly braver, they'll climb onto the bed, but only if they're sure it's safe, which is to say only after Joy and I have fallen asleep. But here's the key fact: these dogs do all of this long before either of us has actually touched them, long before they would consider letting either of us actually touch them, when any attempt at contact would still be met by snapping jaws and painful wounds.

This put me in a strange situation. I am an early riser, often awake long before the sun has come up. My routine is to get out of bed, head down to the goat shack, and start working, but that second summer in Chimayo, that routine was dented by a half dozen dogs who had yet to let me touch them but had no problem sleeping in the same room as me. Since it's dark in the bedroom, getting out of bed every morning involved first trying to guess who was sleeping where and then solving the rat's maze of avoiding them on my way out of the house. Bumping into one of these feral dogs in the dark, even if they happen to have fallen asleep directly beside me or, as often happens as they start getting more comfortable, on top of me (dogs in the process of habituation like to sleep on human feet because they know we can't move without first moving them), was enough to get myself bitten. Which meant that everything from getting up in the middle of the night to piss to getting up in the morning to go to work involved negotiating that gray area between tame and wild, a gray area that I hadn't even known existed back when I was living in California.

There is an art to living in this gray area—one that took getting used to. My home was now an environment where some level of danger and unpredictability—two of the defining characteristics of wildness—were part of the basic package. Oddly, I found that mountain lion experience somewhat helpful. That look of disgust had made me keenly aware of the imbalance in power between animals and humans. The truth of the matter is that humans have chewed up so much wilderness and devalued so much wildness that the mountain lion had gotten hit by a car while moving through what was essentially his "living room." That now struck me as completely unfair. So the fact that I might get bitten by a wilder animal on my way to the bathroom, while it wasn't quite tit-for-tat, at least it was a start.

My perspective started to change as well. Before this point, dogs and mountain lions were not even in the same category. Dogs were common components of a human world and in no sense wild. Mountain lions were the opposite. But once those feral dogs arrived, these divisions started to fall apart. I started to see all animals on a continuum: leash-walked, suburban-raised toy poodles on one end, man-eating big cats on the other, my own dogs somewhere in the middle. And once I thought of my dogs on the same wildness scale that I used to think of mountain lions, something as seemingly insignificant as affection became much less insignificant.

All that had really happened was that I had stopped taking my good relationship with dogs for granted, but once freed from this myopia a number of other facts became readily apparent. Imagine how careful you would be cuddling a giraffe—but the ratio comparison is the same when a Chihuahua snuggles up to a human. And that's a full-sized Chihuahua. I am seventeen times the height of Gidget and thirty-two times her weight. When she decides to run up on my chest and dance her dance, it's now not lost on me just how much trust she would have to feel to be willing to behave like that. And once up there, she's not even skittish. Her eyes close, her jaw drops, her head sways, and she looks a lot like Stevie Wonder playing the piano. It's a state of wild abandon, despite being the rough equivalent of a normal-sized human climbing onto a slightly undersized *Tyrannosaurus rex* to do the fandango.

And this pales significantly when compared to befriending a wild dog for the first time. Since most of us don't live with animals we can't touch, we don't see contact stretching across the border of species as extraordinary. But share a home with feral dogs for a few months—dogs that run out of the room when you enter and bare their teeth if the exit happens to be blocked—and when they finally do decide they might be willing to be petted, well, extraordinary isn't the half of it.

Not surprisingly, all of this had a pronounced effect on the rest of the pack. What I mean is that all our dogs have preferences. Some like me best; most prefer Joy. Some of the ones who prefer Joy had never really warmed to me. But as those feral dogs started to get over their fear, some of those our other dogs did as well.

Farrah was among them. A few years before we met, Joy found her at the South Central shelter in Los Angeles eight hours before she was scheduled to die. Normally, on a dog's last day, shelter workers would be desperate to find a home for the animal. Not this time. Joy was strenuously advised to let them put her down. Farrah was just too broken to mend. She was a puppy mill reject, born in a box, dumped at the pound. Mange had claimed most of her fur; what was left was pink, raw, and reptilian. And mean. She bit everyone. She was just Joy's type.

Farrah came home with Joy, and home is where she stayed. Once her hair grew back she turned out to be a looker, meriting her full name—Farrah Fawcett Minor—and the attention of others. Joy placed her on three separate occasions. None took. Farrah screamed nonstop whenever deprived of Joy's company. Since Farrah's screams sound like those of a cartoon duck, having her do that non-stop is a bit like being trapped in a hell of Walt Disney's design.

For the first year Farrah was with us, she steered clear of me unless Joy was out of the house. Even when Joy was gone, unless I picked her up or there was a thunderstorm—which terrified her enough that she would run to just about any available human for comfort—we rarely had any contact. But after those feral dogs started to come around, Farrah did as well. First she liked me, then she really liked me. She was clingy and constant, and when I got the flu a couple of weeks after getting back from the mountain lion release, apparently she was concerned. In wolves and a number of other species, it's common to return from feasting on a kill to regurgitate leftovers for young pups. Sometimes a male wolf will vomit up food as a show of affection while attempting to woo a female. Occasionally vomit will be offered to a sick pack member or as a gift to a friend. This is the only explanation I've been able to come up with for what woke me that morning, ripped from deep sleep and pleasant dreams by the unforgettable sensation of Farrah puking in my mouth.

Emotions are thought to serve three fundamental functions in humans, with the first being known as *signaling*. Fear signals impending disaster, as does disgust. When humans feel disgust it's an innate response to a bitter taste or noxious odor that often warns of a lethal toxin. Researchers have discovered that disgust can be masked but not extinguished. Trained psychologists can always spot it, as it's just too basic and powerful to hide. A dog puked in my mouth—certainly a morality tale against the dangers of snoring—but instinctive reaction or not, I didn't feel disgust. I just spit the crap out, availed myself of more mouthwash than is normally required, and turned to address Farrah. "I worry about you too" was the extent of that conversation. Which also might be a morality tale about the perils of wanting to find a life with more meaning—though not reacting to the vomit might be proof that I'd already found one.

I was talking to my friend Michael a few days later and he didn't agree.

"Are you *meshugenah*? A dog puked in your mouth and you think you've found the meaning of life?"

I tried to explain it was less about discovering what I was looking for and more about moving in the right direction, but never got that far. It was too far to go. Michael lived in a place where the gorgeous intimacy of an animal wanting to share a meal with a human was nothing close to gorgeous. In his land, a dog puked in my mouth and that was cause for revulsion. In mine, a dog puked in my mouth and somehow I had come to see this as astounding.

As I was thinking about how recently I would have shared Michael's opinion and—as the instinct that says beware of vomit is a fairly powerful one—how far I must have come to have changed my mind, I was struck by another peculiar realization: I had come this far without ever really wondering about my choice in direction. I had gone looking for a life with more meaning, but why was I sure I'd find that in dogs? Why not pigs or snakes or raccoons? If Thoreau was right and it was just about embracing the mysteries of the wild—well, I hadn't really considered dogs as wild at the time I decided to move to Chimayo. Certainly, if you had asked me back then, I'd probably have said there was something powerfully sacred about dogs, but what something would I have been talking about? What is anyone who talks like this talking about? I knew most rescuers considered the work they do to be spiritual in nature, and I would probably agree, but hearing this from the outside and seeing it from the inside were two different things. What exactly did I find profoundly spiritual about cleaning up shit on a daily basis? The more I thought about it, the more I was sure I'd moved into the ashram knowing nothing about the guru.

And when I backed this line of inquiry up, trying for a bit more perspective, I found even more puzzles. Every archaic religion in history was built around animals—but why were they sure that animals were sacred? And why do so many of us still consider animals sacred? Why are some animals more sacred than others? Is this cultural bias, spiritual preference, or biological adaptation? If it's actually biological, if animal sacredness is some sort of evolutionary adaptation, is it found only in humans, or do the animals feel it too? Do animals think animals are sacred? Do animals think some animals are more sacred than others?

"You got all this cause a dog puked in your mouth?" asked Michael.

"So what do you think—do dogs have spiritual experiences?"

"I'm hanging up now."

He did hang up, but that wasn't the end of it. I got a little obsessed. And when I said that life started to change at the tail end of that second summer, I mean that I started trying to find some answers.

37

Scientists have spent the past two centuries trying to find these same answers. The earliest attempt was *totemism*, an idea that began when two late nineteenth-century philosophers, Herbert Spencer and Rudolf Otto, tried to define religion. Both decided that religion was fundamentally about the notion of the supernatural. "This means any order of things beyond our understanding," later wrote the father of sociobiology, Emile Durkheim, in his 1912 *The Elementary Forms of Religious Life*, "the supernatural is the world of mystery, the unknowable, the incomprehensible. Religion would then be a kind of speculation on all that escapes science and clear thinking in general."

Durkheim disagreed with their ideas. He felt the supernatural presupposed a natural, an array of "natural laws" that exist in opposition to this mysterious realm. Anything that violates those natural laws is thus beyond nature and, according to Otto and Spencer, the basis for religion. But religion is rarely about the miraculous; it's mostly about the mundane. God showed Moses a burning bush not so he could learn how to start fires with his mind but so he could pass along the Ten Commandments and provide rules for daily living. Moreover, these miraculous events are geographically specific, so the rules that emerge vary across cultures—in India the cow is a sacred animal, while in America it's our lunch. Therefore religion can't actually be about the nouns—the persons, places and things labeled as supernatural or, as Durkheim prefers, "sacred." Instead, he says, "religion is a unified system of beliefs and practices relative to sacred things, that is to say, things set apart and forbidden."

He came to see the essential component of religion as the dichotomy between the sacred and the profane, but this doesn't explain why we consider animals to be sacred. Durkheim felt that the best way to solve that problem was to simplify it. He decided to strip away Western culture and modernity and start with the most "primitive" religion he could find, so based his answer on the beliefs of Australian Aborigines. Essential to the Aborigines are totems—sacred emblems of the clan's spiritual connection to their world and worlds beyond. The Aborigines were hunter-gathers, and most of their outside-the-clan social life revolved around animals. Because animal behavior so frequently falls into that ambiguous category Otto and Spencer called "supernatural," the animals became symbols for the supernatural—and critically important, Durkheim thought, for the cohesion of hunter-gather society.

Shared sacred symbols serve a purpose, according to Durkheim. The sacred is a psychic glue holding a community together. By bonding the collective, religion makes individuals feel connected and protected and thus fulfills significant psychosocial needs. Totems, then, are a way of extending that glue's bond beyond the clan and into the environment, which essentially contained a bunch of inexplicable phenomena that had long proved dangerous. Totems connected humans to a wider unknown—the idea again being with connection came protection—and this made those clans feel safer. Thus, Durkheim concluded, animals are sacred because we need them to help us feel safe in the world.

But this raised a different question: why are some animals more sacred than others? Why worship the eagle and ignore the beetle? If the goal is security, why even make these divisions? It was anthropologist Claude Lévi-Strauss who unraveled this puzzle by examining those divisions as they pertained to food restrictions. Some foods are forbidden, aka sacred, others are not—but why? Lévi-Strauss discovered that people are neither hunting protein nor avoiding poisons, that it's neither dietary nor gastronomic criteria that makes certain foods taboo. "Animals which are tabooed are chosen," explained anthropologist Mary Douglas in *The World of Goods*, "because they are good to think, not because they are good to eat."

So what does this mean and why is it true? As John Berger famously explained in *About Looking*: "The essential relation between man and animal was metaphoric. Within that relation what the two terms—man and animal—shared in common revealed what differentiated them." This was important to Lévi-Strauss because he held a different belief than his predecessors about his study subjects: he didn't believe primitive people were stupid just because they were "primitive." He figured they were just like us, just as preoccupied with the question of what it means to be human. And Lévi-Strauss believed that animals are good to think because that was how these peoples answered the question. Animals were what we thought with about ourselves. They were our first grounds for comparison, and became our first way to define our species: we are like animals this way, we are unlike them this way, that is what it means to be human. And the more we used a particular animal to think with in our daily lives, the more taboo it became come dinnertime.

This "thinking in animals" was no small step. It was the beginning of symbolic thought, an amazing leap forward. Aldous Huxley explains why:

Man is an amphibian who lives simultaneously in two worlds—the given and the home-made, the world of matter, life and consciousness and the world of symbols. In our thinking we make use of a great variety of symbol-systems— linguistic, mathematical, pictorial, musical, ritualistic. Without such symbol-systems we should have no art, no science, no law, no philosophy, not so much as the rudiments of civilization: in other words, we should be animals.

But Huxley also points out that our transformation was less a metamorphosis than a magnification:

The result is that we have been able to commit, in cold blood and over long periods of time, acts of which the brutes are capable only for brief moments and at the frantic height of rage, desire or fear. Because they use and worship symbols, men can become idealists; and, being idealists, they can transform the animal's intermittent greed into the grandiose imperialism of a Rhodes or a J. P. Morgan; the animal's intermittent love of bullying into Stalinism or the Spanish Inquisition; the animal's intermittent attachment to its territory into the calculated frenzies of nationalism.

This same process of magnification helped turn the surreal into the supernatural. We don't always understand animal behavior, but because we were hunter-gathers, understanding that behavior was critical to finding dinner, so we spent a lot of time thinking about it. Since symbolic magnification is our habit, one abstract idea led to another, and the profane became the sacred. And perhaps, we hoped, this same chain of abstraction applied to us. Because we're unlike animals, animals are linked to the supernatural. But we're also like animals, so maybe we too are linked to the supernatural. Thus the animals are sacred because they make us feel sacred too.

Why is this a good thing? Because we know we're going to

die, and this is a problem for most. Many thinkers considered this knowledge the main differences between humans and animals, which is why the problem is called the *human condition*. A long line of scientists have proven the need to cure this condition—to control our mortal terror—which is among our most powerful biological urges. In 1973, Ernest Becker won the Pulitzer Prize for arguing that death denial is the basic motivation for all human behavior—both the foundation of society and the reason we created society in the first place. A long line of scientists have also pointed out that there is only one way to cure the condition: attach the finite self to an infinite other. This, many believe, is the origin and purpose of religion—a way to cure our fear of death.

The Judeo-Christian cure works by adhering the mortal now to the immortal next via the medium of the soul. Eastern religions come the other way round: death is the illusion; we are instead infinite beings taste-testing a finite experience. There are older strategies as well. Archaic peoples didn't quite understand animals and so viewed them as liminal, hovering between the explainable and the unexplainable, serving as "an aid to bridge the natural and the supernatural, awakening the realities of both within the environs of . . . [our] own lives," as Ted Andrews put it in his quirky compendium on the subject, *Animals Speak: The Spiritual and Magical Powers of Creatures Great and Small*. Because animals are like humans in a number of ways, maybe humans too are hovering between worlds, immortal as well as mortal. Animals, then, are an effective strategy for denying death, our first such strategy: archaic, almost forgotten, almost but not quite. And perhaps this is the reason we still think animals are sacred; perhaps a part of us remembers.

PART EIGHT

It is slightly galling to think that we live in a universe that, for the most part, we can't even see, but there you are.

—Bill Bryson

38

Beyond pondering the sacred, I also spent a lot of that second autumn trying to exhaust the big dogs—which eventually amounted to the same thing, but that took a while to figure out. In the beginning, it was mostly about stamina. Once Igor discovered how to bank turns up and down the walls of the riverbed, he didn't want to stop. He soon mastered the gradual curve and moved on to the dead vertical, trying to learn how to run straight up the sides of the arroyo. If the sides got too steep to run, he'd attempt to cat-leap to the top. Igor, like most bull terriers, cat-leaped about as well as he did long division. Bella, on the other hand, could do almost anything she tried—and this drove Igor crazy.

Often when Bella pulled some stunt Igor couldn't duplicate, he'd just disappear from sight. There were days when I would call and call and he wouldn't come. One morning, I decided to stop calling and instead tried to find out what he was doing. I found him hard at work on a different cliff, practicing Bella's moves. That day, Bella had used a climbing method straight out of a Spider-Man. She'd run up the side of the arroyo and onto a protruding boulder. She used the boulder like a springboard, launching herself across the arroyo, executing a neat half-twist in mid-flight to land paws first on the other side.

Igor was giving it his best, but his best wasn't Spider-Man. He went up the wall and flew sideways and missed and smashed and a few times hard before he got it one time right. There's some basic science to explain why Igor would want to hide these practice sessions, much of it having to do with any show of weakness being a great way to get demoted in pack order—something you often see when dogs injure a paw and try to mask the limp—but in this case I think it was pure embarrassment. Igor was a klutz. He took some bad falls. That he wanted to take them privately seemed perfectly reasonable.

His embarrassment faded when Bucket got hip to the cause and started trying to run up the walls too. Bucket is small and squat and about as aerodynamic as a wheelbarrow. For a little while there the Five-Dog Workout became the Cirque du Soleil Reject Hour. And when Igor realized he wasn't the only klutz out there, he stopped trying to hide his efforts. Bella would pull some acrobatic feat, and Igor and Bucket would spend the rest of the hike falling all over the place trying to learn the trick.

In 1976, a chimpanzee researcher named M. J. A. Simpson witnessed something similar in rhesus monkeys. He noticed them practicing difficult leaps between tree branches, varying branch size, leap distance, and acrobatics often enough that Simpson took to describing these sessions as "projects." Marine biologist Karen Pryor observed the same in dolphins: "I have seen a dolphin, striving to master an aesthetically difficult trick, actually refuse to eat its 'reward fish' until it got the stunt right." But what I saw was more than stunt mastery. It was, as the behaviorist Patricia McConnell told me when I rang her up, "a fairly high level of imitative behavior."

I was also told to make a videotape of it, "just so someone might believe you."

"What do you mean?" I asked McConnell.

"What you're describing, a lot of people just don't think it's possible."

The reason most people believe imitation impossible for dogs begins with domestication. Since this is a process of neurological contraction—brain size shrinks in domesticated animals—the thinking has been that domesticated animals are dumber than they used to be. Because dogs were once wolves, we assumed they were dumber than wolves. Dumber how has been a matter of some debate, but most researchers put imitative behavior high up on the list of things that were lost in the process of domestication.

In the 1980s, assumption turned to conviction when scientists found wolves could open a latched gate after watching a human do it once, while dogs remained confused after repeated exposures. Yet something about this experiment always bothered Hungarian ethologist Vilmos Csányi. Csányi had dogs. His seemed smart enough for the job. He began to wonder if the dogs in that experiment weren't just being polite—they weren't opening the gate because they were waiting for their owner's permission to open the gate.

In 1997, with a team at Eötvös Loránd University in Budapest, he tried to find out. In their first experiment, a group of dogs had to pull long handles to get at plates full of food. During the initial trial, dogs that were allowed inside their owner's house fared worse than dogs that were always kept outside. But during the second trial, when all the owners first gave their dogs permission to get the food, the gap vanished. Maybe, Csányi thought, dogs aren't dumber than wolves, only more attuned to human desires.

Over the next few years, Csányi looked at other kinds of imitative behavior. He discovered that dogs, with little training, can copy humans bowing, moving around a room, running in circles, waving their hands (paws) in the air, finding the shortest distance between two points, or even operating a ball-dispensing machine. He also discovered that dogs can understand pointing, nodding, and staring—three things chimpanzees have a very hard time doing. More recently, he retried a variation of that first wolf experiment.

Dog puppies and wolf cubs were raised in identical environments for three months, then, with handlers in the room, were given a chance to remove a chunk of meat from a cage by pulling on a rope. Both dogs and wolves solved this pretty quickly. Then the rope was tied down, so pulling it to get the meat became impossible. The dogs gave it a few tries, failed, and looked at the humans for help. The wolves ignored the humans and pulled until they were exhausted.

Csányi believes this proof that unlike wolves, dogs have an innate ability to pay attention to people, an ability sculpted by millennia of cross-species cooperation and communication. "This idea," says UCLA professor of psychiatry and biobehavioral sciences Marco Iacoboni, "is slightly revolutionary. In the nineteenth century, every good naturalist believed animals learned by imitation, but it's hard to get real imitative behavior in a lab. So in the behaviorist-dominated twentieth century, there was a backlash. Scientists dismissed the possibility almost outright."

They stopped dismissing it outright when researchers found the portion of the brain responsible for imitation. This happened in 1995, when a neuroscientist named Giacomo Rizzolatti and a team at the University of Parma in Italy were studying grasping, an action that, as Iacoboni once told reporters, "doesn't sound like much until you try to leave the house without turning the doorknob." Rizzolatti had wired the frontal lobe of a macaque so that whenever the monkey reached out to grab an object a monitor would record his brain's firing pattern. Then a graduate student carrying an ice cream cone stopped by the lab. The macaque stared at the ice cream. The student lifted the cone to take a lick, and the monitor went crazy, as if the monkey had lifted the cone. But the monkey hadn't moved—he'd only thought about moving.

Rizzolatti discovered a new breed of neuron that fires both when an animal performs an action and when an animal sees another perform the same action. These neurons mirror the behavior

of the other animal, thus earning them the name "mirror neurons."
Shortly thereafter, scientists discovered mirror neurons in humans,
only ours are smarter, more flexible and more highly evolved than
those in monkeys. Since then, they've shown up in other primates,
elephants, dolphins, dogs, and songbirds, and are now theorized to
exist in all mammals.

According to V. S. Ramachandran, director of the Center for
Brain and Cognition at the University of California, San Diego,
knowledge of mirror neurons provides the basis for understanding
far more than mimicry. "'Mind reading,' empathy, imitation, learning, and even the evolution of language," he wrote in an article for
Edge.com, can all be explained by mirror neurons. "Anytime you
watch someone else doing something (or even starting to do something), the corresponding mirror neuron might fire in your brain,
thereby allowing you to 'read' and understand another's intentions,
and thus to develop a sophisticated 'theory of other minds.'" The
ability to read another's mind, to put ourselves in that person's place,
is the basic requirement for empathy. Because mirror neurons seem
to be the brain's empathy facilitator Ramachandran calls them "Da-
lai Lama neurons" or "Gandhi neurons," his reasoning being, as he
recently told the *New Yorker*, "they're dissolving the barrier between
you and me."

We also know that the bridge between species can be crossed
in the same fashion. In August 2009, Annika Paukner, a researcher
at the National Institute of Child Health and Human Development, gave humans and capuchin monkeys—chosen because of
their highly social nature—wiffle balls to play with. When the
monkeys got the balls they began poking them with their fingers,
pounding them against hard surfaces, and putting them in their
mouths. Two human researchers were sitting with the monkeys at
the time. One would mimic their actions, poking or mouthing or
pounding a ball of their own whenever the monkey did so, while

the second would intentionally do the opposite—if the monkey pounded the ball, the researcher would mouth it instead. Afterward, the monkeys wanted to spend time with the researcher who imitated them, while spending none with the researchers whose behaviors were opposite of their own. In a second task, the monkeys were given a token they could exchange for a food treat. Both researchers had treats, but the monkeys consistently choose to exchange their token with the researcher who had been imitating their behavior, while ignoring the other. All of this means that, just like in humans, animals match behaviors as a way of bonding.

How sophisticated are the mirror neurons in dogs is an ongoing mystery, but like everything else, the more exercise they get, the stronger they become. As my dogs imitated each other, their mirror neuron systems got stronger, and their legs as well—stronger, faster, and more able to run straight up those canyon walls. Afterward, they were significantly less inclined to stay in the river beds. When I got tired of arguing, I started practicing.

Our runs became a giant game of follow the leader, only considerably more retarded. When Bucket had point he preferred the low curves of gentle arroyos, Igor the skate park of the canyon walls, while Bella went straight no matter what was in her path. I fell down a lot. The soft dirt made it possible. It was soft, sticky, and carvable, which thankfully meant sharp turns were possible. Those turns were needed because the dogs ran like wolves, as a tight pack. Trying to stay upright while paying attention to where they were was impossible, but ignoring them was dangerous. "Part of the pleasure of being around dogs is a sense that we are participating in rituals that go back to atavistic pack behavior," wrote Jeffrey Moussaieff Mason in *Dogs Never Lie About Love*. Absolutely. One day as we were coming down a steep cliff, Igor cut me off. I tripped, he crashed, and Bella came down with us. Together we cartwheeled over a boulder and into a cactus. Pleasure was had by all.

But after a little while, no one tripped. No one fell. We moved completely in synch with one another, less individual entities than one elegant hybrid. Maybe this was our mirror neurons working; maybe even older habits were surfacing. Psychologist Carl Jung used the phrase *collective unconscious* to describe "the storehouse of latent trace memories from man's ancestral past," then later broadened the definition beyond the borders of species, including our "pre-human or animal ancestry as well." And while I've never been exactly certain where to find the collective unconscious, there were more than a few times when the dogs sure seemed to know the way.

There was a day we were running a ridge above a series of fluted cliffs, Bella leading, Bucket next, then me, with Igor bringing up the rear. Bella dropped over a three-foot rock ledge and shot down a steep flute. About thirty feet down, the flute bottomed out in a riverbed. Bucket followed her down, and I followed Bucket. When I hit the bottom, dirt and rock started raining down on my head. I looked up and realized that Igor had chosen a different line, one that was way too steep. He had slipped and was trying to arrest his fall by stretching out, forepaws wedged into one side of a flute, back paws against the other. But the flute spread farther apart the lower it dropped. Right about the point I looked up, it had become too wide from Igor to stem. He was about fifteen feet off the deck and falling straight down. Somehow, without missing a beat, I put out both my arms and caught him in stride. Which is something I've learned from dogs: sometimes the lessons are deep ecology, sometimes they're Laurel and Hardy.

39

Deep ecology is a term coined in 1972 by Norwegian ecophiloso-pher Arne Naess to describe an environmental ethos—an "ecoso-phy," as he called it—that is both fundamental to the world of dog rescue and a worldview thoroughly departed from the anthropo-centric. This ecosophy is built around the central idea that every species has intrinsic value whose worth cannot be measured by its usefulness to mankind. It is a philosophy of *biotic egalitarianism*: "The right of all forms to live is a universal right which cannot be quantified," says Naess. "No single species of living being has more of this particular right to live and unfold than any other spe-cies."

Deep ecology is "deep" because it forces us to ask penetrating questions about our species' place in the world. Who are we? Why are we here? How should we live properly? The current view holds humans as separate from our environment—as either stewards of nature or masters of nature—but Naess feels we should see our-selves as we most certainly are: as *part* of the nature, no different than any other part. Tulane philosopher Michael Zimmerman puts it this way: "Instead of identifying with our egos or our immediate families, we would learn to identify with trees and animals and plants, indeed the whole ecosphere. This would involve a pretty radical change of consciousness, but it would make our behavior more consistent with what science tells us is necessary for the well-being of life on Earth. We just wouldn't do certain things that damage the planet, just as you wouldn't cut off your own finger." Or, as Naess says: "It's a vision of the world in which we protect the environment as part of ourselves."

In positioning humans as "of the earth" rather than "on the earth," deep ecology is seen as the purest antidote to Cartesian logic. Humans cannot be a special case because there are no special cases. All life is responsible for the health and well-being of all life because—and this is another idea core to deep ecology—all life is interrelated, interconnected, and ultimately one. For this reason, deep ecologists do not favor short-term environmental fixes—like, say, recycling—rather preferring to completely redesign society based on, as the literature for the Foundation for Deep Ecology states, "values and methods that truly preserve the ecological and cultural diversity of natural systems." In his essay "The Viable Human," cosmologist and cultural historian Thomas Berry explains further: "Rather than be concerned about how to raise automobile production, this ethic would be interested in solving the problem of human mobility in a way that would not require the disruption of highways, roads and parking lots."

Joy gets more than four hundred e-mails a day from other rescuers. Each is a plea for help, containing a personality description, backstory, medical update, and the worst part: a photo of a dog about to die. For more than a hundred years, ever since the founding of organizations like the ASPCA, humans have been trying to solve problems of animal welfare with short-term fixes like leash laws, dog licenses, and public awareness campaigns. None has been very effective. Millions of dogs are still being euthanized in America each year, to say nothing of the rest of the world. Since most rescuers feel roughly the same for dogs as most humans feel for children, dealing with this "e-mail problem" is one reason why rescuers prefer deep ecology.

Another reason is scientific. Most philosophies of interconnection are spiritual in nature and thus require a leap of faith along the way. Deep ecology, though, is built upon factual insight. So while Naess's thinking appears an updated version of everything from Lao Tzu's *Tao Te Ching* to Aldo Leopold's land ethic, its most critical antecedent was actually the planet Mars.

In 1962, NASA hired British scientist James Lovelock to solve a hard problem. The agency needed an easy way to detect life on the Red Planet. Lovelock took a top-down biochemist's approach. Life requires chemical reactions. We breathe in air and exhale carbon dioxide. Lovelock reasoned that if Mars was lifeless, then the planet's atmosphere would be free of these reactions. It would be stable, in a state of chemical equilibrium, which Voyager 1 and Voyager 2 later confirmed. The earth's atmosphere, on the other hand, should be incredibly unstable because life would have a noticeable impact on its equilibrium. This did not turn out to be the case—and Lovelock wanted to know why.

How is it that life's delicate balance remains so well maintained on earth? The exact chemical combination of our atmosphere is very specific and very unlikely, yet the entire system remains perfectly hospitable and, oddly, self-regulating. Lovelock found examples of this homeostasis everywhere. The earth's temperature has remained virtually constant for more than three billion years, yet during this same time frame the sun's firepower has increased by 30 to 40 percent. Both the chemical content of the earth's atmosphere and the salinity of her oceans have also remained stable, despite entropy, the second law of thermodynamics, saying things should work otherwise.

Lovelock decided there might be a good reason for all this self-regulation, which he explained first in journal articles and later in his 1979 book *Gaia: A New Look at Life on Earth*: "The entire range of living matter on Earth, from whales to viruses, and from oaks to algae, could be regarded as constituting a single living entity, capable of manipulating the Earth's atmosphere to suit its overall needs and endowed with faculties and powers far beyond those of its constituent parts." In Lovelock's view the earth was a "super-organism," a cybernetic feedback system that "seeks an optimal physical and chemical environment for life on this planet." At the suggestion of his neighbor, author and screenwriter William Goldman, he called the system Gaia after the ancient Greek Earth goddess.

There has been a long and nasty battle surrounding Gaia, with quasi-religious overtones and lots of belligerent name-calling. Heavyweights like Richard Dawkins and Stephen Jay Gould led the charge against it. Nature lovers everywhere rushed to support it. Most animal rescuers seem to treasure it, as these days do a troupe of top scientists. Thirty years later, after a ton of computer modeling, much corroborating research, and some error correction on Lovelock's part, what was once derided as a "New Age cult" has become almost legitimate theory.

For error correction purposes, Lovelock removed all taint of teleological language—anything that said all of this happened for a reason and that life is directed by this reason—and replaced it with language in which life's delicate balance is an emergent property, an apparently much more acceptable idea. Emergence comes from complexity theory, which used to be chaos theory, which was once catastrophe theory, and all are built around the observation that as systems become more complex they begin to create coherent patterns. Sometimes these patterns are greater than the sum of their parts. Sometimes much greater. The collaborative behavior of millions of individual ants in a colony being one example, the evolution of human consciousness from the cooperative firing patterns of a billion neurons being another. A third would be the seemingly impossible idea that on planet Earth, all life maintains all life.

Naess and his supporters view deep ecology not as a theory but as an accurate description of reality and a call to action: we protect the planet as we protect ourselves. The philosophy now underlies a significant portion of the environmental movement and much of the cause of dog rescue. Naess has said this means "not thinking of the dog as an instrument for your pleasure" instead as an intrinsic part of the earth's web of life, as important as any other. And this is an importance rescuers cling to, because they often find themselves confronting others who feel otherwise.

Around our second autumn in Chimayo, a close friend, whom I'll call Karen, got extremely upset when she saw the conditions of the Santa Fe animal shelter. Karen had a brother I'll call Aaron who'd spent twenty years as a junkie on the streets of Portland. When Aaron's need for medical care outweighed his need for heroin, he finally agreed to move in with his sister. When Karen went to pick him up, the incredibly inadequate facilities the state of Oregon uses to house their homeless became apparent.

About five days after Aaron arrived in New Mexico, Karen decided that adopting a dog would speed his recovery. Since we didn't have one who fit their needs, Joy drove them to the Santa Fe shelter to help make Sophie's choice. The Santa Fe shelter is one of the better ones in America. This doesn't just mean the dogs get toys to play with and space to roam, it also means music is piped into the kennels to keep the animals calm. This infuriated Karen. "Why do street dogs get such great treatment when my brother spent twenty years homeless and never had a place to sleep so nice?" In her mind, the fact that money was being spent to help dogs when there were humans in need was a criminal injustice, a kind of systemic sociological failure that was beyond any acceptable explanation. Unfortunately, it was Joy she asked for an explanation. Like most dog rescuers, Joy favored biotic egalitarianism. She doesn't privilege human life above animal life, nor does she hide her opinion. Which is not the first time that dog rescue has cost her a friendship.

It probably won't be the last.

40

If we're ever going to stop having this argument then we need to make up our mind about the value of animals. If biotic egalitarianism is to win, if we're ever going to afford animals the same rights as humans, if people are ever going to stop begrudging dogs their standards of care and instead fight for their survival as we fight for our own, then we need to find a way to completely obliterate our Cartesian hangover. Some see this as an ethics question, but mostly—at least going by legal precedent—the answer will come down to biology: if animals are like us, then they can have their rights; if they're unlike us, then they're not our problem.

Richard Granger, head of the Brain Engineering Laboratory at Dartmouth University, has spent much of his career investigating this problem—specifically looking for areas in the human brain that might actually distinguish us from other animals. "The first thing you need to know is you can count the neurological differences between humans and animals on the fingers of both hands. Mostly they're tiny, inconsequential blips. None of them account for things like language, for any skill we would put under the Cartesian heading of 'human specialness.'"

What accounts for those skills, according to Granger, is brain size. If brains are computers, then both humans and animals have the same hardware and the same software; ours just comes in a bigger box. Because of that bigger box, our neurons have more space to make more connections with other neurons. In the wiring diagram of the brain, we have more wires. And this bigger box and these few more wires are the source of our superpowers.

Granger is currently trying to isolate the moment those superpowers develop, which is essentially the point we stopped being "them" and started being "us," but openly admits that finding it may be years away. Until then the similarity camp holds more of the cards, perhaps because they've come from at the question from the opposite direction.

In 1982, a professor of human ecology at Pitzer College in Claremont, California, the late Paul Shepard, extended deep ecology's ideas of interconnection into the realm of the psychological. In his book *Nature and Madness*, he makes the case that if there are profound and innate links between the planet Earth and the human species—the kind of links Lovelock tried to establish with his Gaia theory—then those links should extend to the human mind. And we should be able to find them.

Shepard starts with the idea that evolution shaped the brain to shrink complexity by categorization. To this end, our brains slot everything into small boxes. Part of this is our primate ancestry where divisions between "us" and "them" were critical to survival, and part came about during the development of language, when the act of giving names to things required us to first put them in categories. Since those categories were based on what we saw around us, early language acted as our bridge to the natural world. We still *bat* our lashes, are *dog* tired, and clutter our homes like *pack rats*, but in older times, the comparisons went farther. Our letter *A* is derived from the Hebrew letter *aleph*, which in turn comes from a word that means "ox." Which is why, when you turn an *A* upside down, you get a pictograph of an ox head.

In *The Others*, Shepard explains it this way:

Category making based on animals, linked to speech, was at the center of the evolution of the human mind and the beginning of language itself. Subsistence peoples today continue to extend and enlarge their repertoire of taxonomic groups avidly—indeed, we might speak of them as hobbyists or naturalists. Tribal peoples around the world know hundreds of plants and animals by name and natural history. The Nuba of Africa identify more than forty species of locusts (biologists recognize only ten) and twenty-seven varieties of sorghum which are botanically but three. "In the two preliterate societies in which I have carried out field research," says one anthropologist, "knowledge of the biological world constitutes—I would claim—a greater chunk than all of types of knowledge combined." He calculates that primitive tribes have an average of 1,000 to 1,200 kinds of plants and animals in their vocabulary, and he goes on to point out that familiarity with this great diversity of organisms is not primarily because of their economic usefulness.

Shepard was interested in the psychology of categorization and how it affected the development of human intelligence. He realized it wasn't just language that was built upon the natural world, it was everything else as well. Humans spent 99 percent of their history as hunter-gatherers, which means the entire architecture of the brain has been built atop the scaffolding of the natural world. Because of this, Shepard worried about the effects of ecological destruction on our psychic stability; specifically, he's worried about what happens when the very things that taught us how to think disappear.

This is not a new fear. A hundred and fifty years ago, Chief Seattle worried about the exact same thing. "What is a man without the beasts? If all the beasts were gone, man would die from a great loneliness of the spirit. For what happens to the beasts, soon happens to man. All things are connected." Nor, as it turns out, is this an irrational fear.

In the wake of Hurricane Katrina, according to research conducted by the Hurricane Katrina Advisory Group, the rates of mental illness doubled among those who lived in the area. On the opposite side of that coin, scientists at the University of Illinois recently discovered that a twenty-minute walk in the woods outperformed all the drugs currently on the market for the treatment of attention deficit-hyperactivity disorder in children. It was psychologist Erich Fromm who first coined the term *biophilia*, but Harvard sociobiologist Edward O. Wilson borrowed it to describe "the connections that human beings subconsciously seek with the rest of life." And after ten years researching the topic, Richard Louv, in his 2005 *Last Child in the Woods*, agrees. He coined the phrase "nature-deficit disorder" to describe why children lacking contact with the outdoors—that is, kids whose biophilic instinct remains unnourished—have been found significantly more prone to anxiety, depression, and attention disorder. But if you really want to find direct links between the natural world and the human mind, as psychologist Stanley Coren pointed out in a 2009 blog entry on the *Psychology Today* website, the best place to look is dogs.

> The possibility that dogs can produce major psychological and health benefits for their human companions has been a subject of much recent serious psychological research. . . .
>
> A recent study published in the *Journal of Psychosomatic Medicine* not only confirmed these effects, but showed

changes in blood chemistry demonstrating a lower amount of stress-related hormones such as cortisol. These effects seem to be automatic, they do not require any conscious efforts or training on the part of the stressed individual. Perhaps most amazingly, these positive psychological effects are achieved faster—after only five to 24 minutes of interacting with a dog—than the result from taking most stress-relieving drugs. Compare this to some of the Prozac or Xanax-type drugs used to deal with stress and depression. Such drugs alter the levels of the neurotransmitter serotonin in the body and can take weeks to show any positive effects. Furthermore, the benefits that build up over this long course of medication can be lost with only [a] few missed doses of the drug. Petting a dog has a virtually immediate effect and can be done at any time. Recently, researchers extended this research by looking at a group of people aged 60 and older, living alone, except for a pet. Non-pet owners were four times more likely to be diagnosed as clinically depressed than pet owners of the same age. The evidence also showed that pet owners required fewer medical services and were more satisfied with their lives.

Not only does Paul Shepard appear to be correct about the existence of profound and innate links between the human mind and the natural world, but as the only species to coevolve with humans, dogs might be our strongest connection to that world: a superhighway to our archaic past courtesy of the one animal who was along for the whole ride.

But the longer I lived with dogs the more I became certain the real question is what else we might discover if we follow that path back further. Almost all archaic cultures speak of an age when humans and animals spoke the same language. Some still do. The Dreamtime of the Aborigines is the most well-known example, but the Zuni still begin all their ancestral tales with the phrase "A long time ago, when the animals could speak . . ." In his seminal *Shamanism,* University of Chicago professor of the history of religion Mircea Eliade addresses it this way:

> Finally, we must take into account the mystical solidarity between man and animal, which is a dominant characteristic of the religion of the paleo-hunters. By virtue of this, certain human beings are able to change into animals, or to understand their language, or to share in their prescience and occult powers. Each time a shaman succeeds in sharing the animal mode of being, he in a manner reestablishes the situation that existed *in illo tempore*, in mystical times, when the divorce between man and the animal world had not yet occurred.

Shape-shifting, as the process of changing into animals is known, language sharing, occult powers—this is pretty much the point where most rational inquiries into such matters conclude. Perhaps that's where things should have ended for me, but I had spent the past two years having experiences with animals that most scientists dismissed as impossible. Empathy, altruism, homosexuality, imitative behavior, moral behavior, intelligence, abstract intelligence, language skills, laughter—this list goes on. So while shape-shifting sounded ridiculous, less than thirty years ago the vast majority of scientists thought that the idea of personality in dogs was ridiculous. At least, I thought, I should keep an open mind.

Along those lines, I had also been doing a little more research and found a passage from Carlos Castaneda's *Journey to Ixtlan* that details an encounter the anthropologist had with a coyote while studying the shamanic practice known as "stopping the world," under the ever peculiar tutelage of Don Juan:

> I sat down on the rocks and the coyote stood almost touching me. I was dumbfounded. I had never seen a wild coyote that close, and the only thing that occurred to me at that moment was to talk to it. I began as one would talk to a friendly dog. And then I thought that the coyote "talked" back to me. I had the absolute certainty that it had said something. I felt confused but I did not have time to ponder upon my feelings, because the coyote "talked" again. It was not that the animal was voicing words the way I am accustomed to hearing words being voiced by human beings, it was rather a "feeling" that it was talking. But it was not like a feeling that one has when a pet seems to communicate with its master either. The coyote actually said something; it relayed a thought and that communication came out in something quite similar to a sentence. I had said, "How are you, little coyote?" and I thought I had heard the animal respond, "I'm all right, and are you?" Then the coyote repeated the sentence and I jumped to my feet. The animal did not make a single movement. It was not even startled by my sudden jump. Its eyes were still friendly and clear. It lay down on its stomach and tilted its head and asked, "Why are you afraid?" I sat down facing it and I carried on the weirdest conversation I had ever had. Finally it asked me what I was doing there and I said I had come there to "stop the world." The coyote said, "Que bueno!" and then I realized it was a bilingual coyote.

Up until that moment I had assumed "speaking with animals" was a more metaphorical idea than a physical reality. But what

Castaneda was describing was the full Doolittle. I have to say, after spending the past two years talking mostly to dogs, the possibility that they might start talking back was just a little too intriguing to pass up.

41

If you want to explore the mystical experiences at the heart of sha-manic practice, there are four phenomena to focus upon. The first is the fundamental experience of solidarity between all living crea-tures, or unity, as the sensation is often called. Unity is not just a shamanic notion, it's a ubiquitous proposition showing up in al-most every religion that exists or has existed on earth. The idea is so popular that Aldous Huxley dubbed it the "perennial philoso-phy," and Harvard philosopher and psychologist William James agreed: "This is the everlasting and triumphant mystical tradition, hardly altered by differences of clime or creed. In Hinduism, in Neoplatonism, in Sufism, in Christian mysticism, in Whitmanism, we find the same recurring note, so that there is about mystical ut-terances an eternal unanimity which ought to make a critic stop and think, and which brings it about that the mystical classics have, as has been said, neither birthday nor native land."

Despite this omnipresence, for most of the twentieth century, the weight of rational materialism kept scientists from treating unity seriously. This began to change in the early 1990s, when an older generation of researchers began vacating posts and the younger ones who took those places were not quite as hostile to metaphysical questions. Simultaneously, George H. W. Bush de-clared the 1990s the "Decade of the Brain" and money flooded into neuroscience. The cash arrived at almost the same time as a new generation of high-powered brain imaging technology—for the first time giving scientists interested in so-called mystical experiences the tools to actually study them.

At the forefront of this work sits Dr. Andrew Newberg, director of the Center for Spirituality and the Mind at the University of Pennsylvania. In the late 1990s, Newberg, alongside the late University of Pennsylvania anthropologist and psychiatrist Eugene D'Aquili, began placing an assortment of Catholic nuns and Tibetan Buddhists inside a single photon emission computed tomography (SPECT) scanner to take pictures of their brains during moments of *ecstatic meditation*, a slippery-sounding term with a very concrete meaning. For the Buddhists, this state is known as *absolute unitary being*—the state of being one with everything—and for Catholics as *unio mystica*—a state of oneness with God's love. Either way, both are descriptions of the experience of unity.

The SPECT scan showed a number of things, but critical to this discussion is the effects of meditation on the right parietal lobe. Often called the orientation association area (OAA), the right parietal lobe is the part of the brain that helps us orient ourselves in space, allowing us to judge angles, curves, distances, and body position. Specifically, this is the part of the brain that helps define the boundary between self and other. People who suffer a stroke or brain damage to this area have difficulty sitting down on a couch because they are unsure where their leg ends and the couch begins. What Newberg and D'Aquili discovered is that intense concentration temporarily blocks the processing of sensory information from this area. When this happens, because the OAA defines the end of the "me," as Newberg explained in *Why God Won't Go Away*, "the brain would have no choice but to perceive the self is endless and intimately interwoven with everyone and everything the mind senses. And this perception would feel utterly and unquestionably real." Newberg believes this explains the sense of unity felt by

Buddhists and Catholics, but when I called him up to ask him, he also felt it works just as well to explain that mystical solidarity between human and animal.

The next three shamanic phenomena—the sharing of occult powers, shape-shifting, and speaking the same language—have been much tougher nuts to crack. The closest anyone has yet come is British biologist Rupert Sheldrake, the former director of cell biology and biochemistry at Cambridge University and a Royal Society research fellow, who has spent the past two decades examining the possibility that animals—especially dogs—possess occult powers. Sheldrake's work remains deliriously controversial, so much so that a few years ago, when speaking in nearby Santa Fe, Sheldrake was stabbed in the thigh by an audience member who, to quote USA Today on the matter, "was disturbed" by the contents of his lecture.

That controversy started in 1996, when Sheldrake delivered a lecture at the Cambridge Veterinary School reporting that dogs seemed capable of predicting the future, specifically detecting when their owners were heading home even when those owners were far beyond the range of canine senses. He had conducted a lengthy study "in which pets had been videotaped in their homes, as their owners, away at their place of work, were preparing to leave work." Despite the fact that these owners purposely deviated from their normal routines, he discovered that forty-six percent of the dogs in his study group knew their masters were coming home up to an hour before they arrived. This study has been repeatedly duplicated, both in Britain and America, with fifty-one percent being the mean average for prescient dogs. Beyond knowing when their owners are coming home, Sheldrake has also reported canine anticipatory powers extending to other areas. In further experiments, he's found dogs great at predicting everything from illness and death to natural disasters such as earthquakes and floods. All of this is still being vigorously debated, but his experiments have been fairly rigorous and his results undeniable. Personally, while I've never seen prescient behavior in my animals, after experiencing the peculiar sense of connectedness that occurred during the Five-Dog Workout—the improbable coordination of movements, the hive mind mentality (me catching Igor midstride being only one example)—Sheldrake's claim that there is an "invisible connection," like a "stretched elastic band," linking humans to dogs seems as good an explanation as any I've yet encountered.

I still didn't know what to make of the last two categories—shape-shifting or language sharing—but neither does anyone else. In recent years researchers such as Newberg have made great inroads into understanding the neuroscience of mysticism. Out-of-body experiences, near-death experiences, trance states, stigmata, speaking in tongues, and a dozen other similar phenomena are now seen as the product of standard biology. In less than twenty years the paranormal has become the normal, but despite all this progress no one has yet produced a plausible explanation for most shamanic phenomena. Maybe, I thought, it was time to go back to the source.

One of the advantages to living near Santa Fe is being able to find shamans in the phone book. I found half a dozen, called each, left messages. Ken Robinson was the only one who called me back. With an undergraduate degree in philosophy, a graduate degree in liberal arts, and a second in counseling and psychology, Robinson has worked as a teacher and environmental advocate and then the director of a wilderness camp for children before moving into more traditional counseling for adults. Along the way he became friendly with the Lakota tribe, who introduced him to the Hetaka, an ancient Amazonian people, and thus began Robinson's shamanic education. "Just being human, that is the sacred task," he said, quoting the Hetaka, summing up the whole of that education.

Robinson and I talked for a while. I learned the Hetaka not only believed in a mystical time of human-animal solidarity but agreed with Chief Seattle that unless we discovered it again there will be problems. I also found out the Hetaka do not practice shape-shifting, so Robinson couldn't tell me much about that. I asked about speaking to animals, and he told me not to be dazzled by language.

"Most people hear words like *shaman* and *mystical experience* and expect fireworks. Shape-shifting and speaking with animals are just modes of consciousness and methods of communication. They sound like magic, they may look like magic, but they feel perfectly normal."

Which is when the puzzle pieces started to slide together. I'm not sure if it was just a wild coincidence, but this was the second time in a month I'd heard those exact words. A few weeks before I spoke to Robinson, a writing assignment had sent me down to Patagonia. Toward the tail end of that trip, I was in a car full of people heading north on the Carretera Austral, when we crested a hill and rounded a bend and screeched to a stop. The Carretera is Augusto Pinochet's madman's highway through the Andes. He built it as a sign of Chilean modernity, so laid it atop ancient animals paths and herding trails. But the gauchos, those fabled Patagonian cowboys, are a proud, stubborn bunch who aren't going to let something as unimportant as progress change their ways. So they continue to drive their cows down the old roads, even if the new ones were specifically designed to end the practice. We screeched to a stop to avoid crashing into a herd of cattle spread out across a quarter mile of highway.

There were easily five hundred head. Our car was quickly surrounded. Cows snuggling up against windows, cows hugging bumpers. Whatever was going to happen next was going to take a while. It didn't take a while. One of the gauchos made a tiny circling motion with his finger, and four dogs went to work. In less than thirty seconds they had closed the ranks and shored up the line. After the animals were bunched, the dogs looked at their gaucho for further instruction. If I hadn't spent the past two years with dogs and wasn't staring right at them at the time, I never would have noticed their motion. It was just the slightest of hesitation, the tiniest of glances. Then the gaucho responded in kind. He darted his eyes to the left and twitched a finger to the right, and the dogs split the herd in half. In less than ten seconds, they had created the perfect driving lane and we were back on our way. A glance and a twitch was all it took, that was the extent of the conversation.

My friend Kristina was in the car at the time.

"What the hell?" she said afterward. "How did that happen?"

"He twitched his finger," I said.

"He twitched his finger and the dogs parted the Red Sea?"

"Dogs are really good at reading our body language."

Kristina spun around in her seat, glanced back at the cattle, and shook her head.

"I don't know about that," she said. "The whole thing looked like magic to me."

42

What actually constitutes real magic is a difficult question to answer, though the longer I lived with dogs, the more comfortable I became with the undeniable thaumaturgical nature of our nonverbal communication. Then again, considering what we now know about this talent, perhaps that's none too surprising. The most famous investigation into an animal's ability to read human body language took place in Berlin at the turn of the twentieth century. A horse named Hans, owned by a man named Wilhelm von Osten, learned to solve simple math and language problems, tapping out answers with his hoof. He performed in public and became something of a sensation, earning the moniker "Clever Hans" and the consternation of Cartesians everywhere. The whole matter was thoroughly investigated by a University of Berlin psychologist, Oskar Pfungst, who discovered that Hans could only answer questions when the questioner knew the answer and the horse was in the same room as the questioner.

Hans didn't read German or solve arithmetic, but was fully capable of detecting tiny, mostly unconscious changes in body language that revealed those answers. Clever Hans has since become Cautionary Hans, as this story has become apocryphal for those wishing to attribute fantastic attributes to animals. But Hans performed for a whole lot of people intent on stumping him—not co-conspirators, rather intentional confounders. Everybody wanted to

Pfungst the horse, so everybody tried to keep their faces blank and body language hidden. Hans still got the message

Horses were domesticated in 4000 BCE. It took them six thousand years to become this attuned to human body language. But horses have nothing on dogs. Man's best friend has been perfecting this skill for more than a hundred thousand years. Dogs are now considered the all-time champions at detecting human emotion and intention. Some researchers say they can read us better than we can read ourselves.

This skill took a little while to perfect. In the beginning, dogs scoured our bodies for nonverbal cues, but after a little while their gaze drifted north to our faces, the real fount of information. Most of what we know about this topic comes from former University of California Medical School in San Francisco psychologist Paul Ekman. In the 1960s, Ekman got curious about face reading, specifically about the messages being read. Psychologists once believed that facial expressions were culturally derived and thus different in different parts of the world. Ekman suspected otherwise. He thought facial expressions might be an evolutionary adaptation with universal commonalities. So he took pictures of people feeling different emotions—anger, sadness, joy, et cetera—and traveled the world showing them around. It didn't matter if he was in the rainforests of Brazil or the cities of Japan, everybody knew exactly what they were looking at. Facial expression appeared universal.

After Ekman returned from his trip, he wanted further confirmation. He got his hands on film of two tribes from Papua New Guinea: the South Fore, a sanguine, happy clan, and the Kukukuku, a nasty, murderous group whose male elders had a habit of turning teenage boys into sexual courtesans. Working with Wallace Friesen, Ekman had been sorting the footage for months, cutting out everything but close-ups of facial expressions. His plan was to compare both tribes. That plan got dashed when his mentor, the psychologist and famed face reader Silvan Tompkins, paid a visit to his lab—a story wonderfully recounted in Malcolm Gladwell's *Blink*:

> As Ekman set up the projector, Tompkins waited in the back. He had been told nothing about the tribes involved; all identifying content had been edited out. Tompkins looked on intently, peering through his glasses. At the end of the film, he approached the screen and pointed to the faces of the South Fore. "These are a sweet, gentle people, very indulgent, very peaceful," he said. Then he pointed to the faces of the Kukukuku. "This other group is violent, and there is lots of evidence to suggest homosexuality." Even today, a third of a century later, Ekman cannot get over what Tompkins did. "'My God!' I vividly remember saying, 'Silvan, how on earth are you doing that?'" Ekman recalls. "And he went up to the screen, and, while we played the film backward in slow motion, he pointed out the particular bulges and wrinkles in faces that he was using to make his judgment. That's when I realized, 'I've got to unpack the face.' It was a gold mine of information that everyone had ignored. This guy could see it, and if he could see it, maybe everyone else could, too."

To unpack the face, Ekman and Friesen decided to catalogue all its possible motions. They did this by researching the underlying muscles and identifying the forty-three movements these muscles can make. They spent months practicing, learning how to move each independently, then spent years learning to layer all these movements atop one another. It took years because two muscles moving in conjunction produce three hundred possible combinations; three muscles took the total up to four thousand. Seven years later, Ekman and Friesen had worked through five muscles and ten thousand variations. They discovered a lot of mishmash, but about three thousand of these movements had meaning. And these three thousand are what Gladwell described as "the essential repertoire of human facial displays of emotion."

That repertoire is heavily lopsided. The left hemisphere of the brain both governs emotion and controls the right side of the face. Important signals such as fear, joy, and anger are all handled here. For face reading, the right side of the face is far more salient than the left. When we meet a stranger our gaze shifts to the right side of their face because that's how we figure out if the person wants to kiss us or kill us. The whole process is called "left-gaze bias," and it's a survival instinct that dogs have learned as well.

In 2007, researchers at the University of Lincoln, in the United Kingdom, led by Dr. Kun Guo, showed a series of dogs images of people, other dogs, monkeys, and inanimate objects. When the dogs saw another animal or an inanimate object, their gaze moved evenly across the image. When they saw humans, their gaze moved directly to the right sides of the faces. Guo believes this was the critical evolutionary adaptation that was originally driven by a dog's desire to avoid getting kicked by a pissed-off master. And for a skill that started small, it sure got important quickly.

Over seven years of research, Ekman and Friesen spent a great deal of time labeling and practicing the micromovements of different facial expressions. They had been working their way through anger and disgust for weeks and the whole time had been feeling anger and disgust. "When this first occurred," Ekman told Gladwell, "we were stunned. We weren't expecting this at all. And it happened to both of us. We felt terrible. . . . when I lower my brows . . . and raise the upper eyelid . . . and narrow the eyelids . . . and press the lips together . . . I'm generating anger. My heartbeat will go up ten to twelve beats. My hands will get hot. As I do it, I can't disconnect from the system."

No one can disconnect from the system. What Ekman and Friesen discovered is that our facial expression are hardwired into our emotions. We cannot feel any other way. "Whenever we experience a basic emotion," writes Gladwell, "that emotion is automatically expressed by the muscles of the face." And this is not only how we feel our feelings but also how we feel for another. Mimicking facial expressions is how empathy works.

In 2003, Marco Iacoboni and a team at UCLA used advanced neural imaging techniques to examine people copying other people's facial expressions. The researchers made a groundbreaking discovery, finding far more activity in the emotional centers of those people's brains than showed up in the brains of people merely watching others make facial expressions. "For years, scientists have observed the reflexive mimicking of a wince when someone suffers a painful injury, and the infectious nature of joy or anger," said Iacoboni. "Our finding show for the first time how these reflexive facial expressions prompt our brain to heighten our empathy for the feelings of others."

It's not just human faces that are hardwired to emotions; the same holds true for dogs. If those original wolves couldn't read our faces, if their own facial expression didn't share similar emotional hardwiring, then any real level of cross-species communication would have proved extremely difficult. Domestication would have been impossible. Coevolution could not have happened. But it did happen. Along the way, a mutual interdependency was created. This most likely began as an equal partnership, but once we started to control dogs' food supply, the power structure tipped. Then, because supper was at stake, dogs' face-reading skills became even more acute and—because face reading is a subset of pattern recognition—dogs with better pattern-recognition skills were better face readers and had better relationships with people and consequently got more food and safer living conditions, and so had larger litters. Pretty soon it didn't matter that our two species didn't share a common language. Dogs could read our emotions, and empathy became another fundamental tool for their survival.

It's also what University of London researcher Atsushi Senju discovered while studying yawning. Yawning is an involuntary action practiced by almost every species on the planet. The meaning of a yawn is still a matter of debate, but we do know that its primary purpose is to convey information. In social animals, the information is important enough to group dynamics that yawning is deadly contagious, that is it's a mutually shared feeling powerful enough to trigger a mutually shared behavioral response. Humans yawn when we see another human yawn. We yawn when we see the word *yawn*. Contagion also crosses species lines. Chimpanzees yawn when they see a human yawn. Senju wondered if the same thing happened with dogs. He tested this by putting them in a room with strangers. Once eye contact had been established, the stranger yawned. As a control, Senju did a second trial where the stranger's mouth merely opened and closed. Twenty-one out of twenty-nine dogs yawned when the stranger yawned. None responded to the open mouth.

One of the main symptoms of autism is a lack of empathy. Researchers call this *mindblindness*, the inability to know the mind of another. This happens because mirror neurons in the brains of autistic individuals do not respond to the actions of others. This hampers their ability to learn imitative processes like language. Because facial muscles are hardwired into emotions and autistic individuals can't imitate those movements, they can't really empathize with others. For the same reasons, people with autism don't have a left-gaze bias nor are they susceptible to contagious yawning. On the other hand, dogs have left-gaze bias and are incredibly susceptible to contagious yawning because they're incredibly prone to copying our facial expressions. And this led Senju to conclude that dogs are also fully capable of empathizing with people.

Which might explain why older pets tend to look like their owners—a bit of long-standing folklore that was recently validated in two separate studies. Researchers at the University of California, San Diego, discovered this tendency between purebreds and their owners, but not in people cohabitating with mutts. Christina Payne, at Simón Bolívar University in Venezuela, got the same results and attributed them to *assortative mating*. Characterized as "self seeking like," assortative mating is an inborn trait that helps an animal find a genetically similar mate without fomenting inbreeding. Payne believes it also shows up when we choose a dog.

Yet assortative mating only begins the process. We learn to communicate with our dogs by face reading and face mimicking, and vice versa. The skin is elastic, but only to a point. Any action repeated over and over again will eventually leave a mark. Wrinkles, creases, and smile lines are those marks. The reason couples who have been married for a long time start to look like one another is because couples are emotionally resonant. They tend to feel similar things at similar times, so their faces wear in the same way. And the same thing happens between humans and dogs. In the process of trying to understand one another, we're slowly reshaping our faces to resemble one another's.

Even more important is that once dogs began reading our faces and mimicking our expressions, they also begin feeling our feelings. Emotions are behavior triggers; if you feel someone else's emotions for long enough, you'll start acting like them too—which is the reason pets often take on the personalities of their owners in addition to their appearance. And shared emotions are only the entrance to this rabbit hole.

Stress is a killer because the nervous system is hardwired into the immune system. And this holds true in most vertebrates. When Joy and I fight, our dogs start vomiting and shitting. This happens because they get scared and stare at our faces, trying to understand the problem. If the problem doesn't end quickly, in the way that dog problems tend to, they keep staring. Face reading becomes face mimicking becomes emotional contagion, which affects their immune system. Pretty soon Joy and I are not only annoyed, but we're mopping the floors to boot.

Chief Seattle said all things are connected, though failed to mention that it was our mirror neurons doing the connecting. He did say there would be consequences if we didn't honor this fact, and perhaps he was right about this as well. That first winter in Chimayo was cold. We were broke and scared and then Ahab's death sent me spiraling. I spent my days in a rocking chair; my dogs spent their days trying to figure out how to help. In doing so, they were flooding themselves with the stress hormones that matched my mood. We have some very old dogs with some very serious health problems. Under the best of circumstances, it doesn't take much to start a slide into illness. A cold night or a change in pack order is often enough. I stayed depressed for months on end, and that had to have an impact. We lost six dogs in six weeks after Ahab died. So I have to wonder—how many went from natural causes, and how many did my mood kill?

43

Certainly the mirror neuron system is fantastic, though perhaps not quite the mythic land of shape-shifting and language sharing the shamans describe. But how far away is it, really? Empathy, like all of our emotions, exists on an sliding scale. At one end are sociopaths, people incapable of feeling any empathy. Next come people with autism, who experience very little. Then those with Asperger's, a disease that allows for more than autism, though not quite what most of us experience. Moving toward the other end, there are hippies, humanists, and other folks who feel for our whole species; beyond them are the animal rescue community, the die-hard environmentalists, Earth Firsters, tree huggers, and other biotic egalitarians. At the far pole are those who see no separation between self and other: the meditators who experience occasional unity, the mystics who experience nothing but.

And maybe somewhere along this chain, hidden away for centuries, tucked between the *all things are equal* of biotic egalitarianism and the *all things are one* of cosmic unity, might be a place where some things are more equal than others. Where some things are one. A place reached when boundary of self extends beyond the confines of skin, not as far as the entire universe, only as far as the parts of it that most remind us most of ourselves—the animal kingdom, which, as both Claude Lévi-Strauss and Paul Shepard figured out, has always been our most accessible link to universal mystery anyway.

The shamans say that humans and animals can speak the same language, though they didn't specify what that might be. But could it be that we are holding out for the miraculous when the biological works just fine? Humans and animals already share the common tongue of emotion, which is perhaps why Castaneda didn't hear that coyote talk—rather he *felt* it talk—because the only way for this language to be spoken is through empathy.

Let me put it another way: St. Francis is the most celebrated animal mystic of all time. If we can believe the hype, birds dug him, rabbits came to sit in his lap, and fish stuck around for his sermons. His most famous trick involved a wolf who'd been terrorizing the town of Gubbio, Italy, eating livestock and killing people. Francis decided to help the villagers by going to meet the wolf. Hunters who had done the same had not returned. His friends begged him not to go. The townsfolk begged him not to go. He went anyway, and the wolf charged at him. According to the AmericanCatholic .org version of the story, this is what happened next: "Francis made the Sign of the Cross toward it. The power of God caused the wolf to slow down and to close its mouth. Then Francis called out to the creature: 'Come to me, Brother Wolf. In the name of Christ, I order you not to hurt anyone.' At that moment the wolf lowered its head and lay down at St. Francis' feet, meek as a lamb."

All that God power and hand waving sounds impressive, I know, but plenty of rescuers get the same job done using far less fanfare, and with pit bulls, no less—which are wolves plus a long history of selective breeding for aggression. After a few years of this work, even I can manage a version. In Chimayo there are a lot of wild dogs and a lot of unchained, unfenced, attack-everybody-who-comes-along dogs. At least once a week, some neighborhood bad-ass comes charging at me, and I do the same thing every time. I turn and half-shout "hey" to get their attention. This usually slows their charge. Then I start talking to them like an old friend, calm and assertive, my first question usually "So what's up with the ruckus?" It took some practice, but these days, by the third question, the dog has usually quieted down or gone elsewhere. Calm and assertive are also the same two qualities that dog whisperer Cesar Millan claims are his secret. But St. Francis had a better card up his sleeve: empathy.

Yawning is contagious, for the same reason that emotions are contagious, because mirror neurons make the process happen automatically. And for the same reason that seeing a symbolic representation of a social signal—the word *yawn*—can make you yawn, seeing the word *empathy* can make you feel for another. But you don't need to see the word *yawn* to trigger the action; just thinking it is enough to make it happen. And because mirror neurons link us to our nervous system, thinking the word *yawn* will also make you tired. The same holds for empathy. Thinking about empathy creates more of it. And thinking about empathy is most of what St. Francis did.

St. Francis's prayer is all about altruism, its key line being "for it is in giving that we receive." It's also about how to live altruistically, which Francis felt meant cultivating empathy. Right before the giving and receiving line comes his formula: "O Divine Master, grant that I may not so much seek to be consoled as to console; to be understood as to understand; to be loved as to love." Every one of those is an action involving a switch in perspective, moving from the egocentric to the allocentric, not just accidentally face reading and feeling for another but intentionally trying to put yourself in their shoes, really striving for the experience. In making empathy the cornerstone of his faith, Francis was inadvertently hypertraining his mirror neuron system.

Mirror neurons are the neuronal architecture involved in this process, but as Jaak Panksepp pointed out, there's also neurochemistry to consider. In the early 1980s, Washington University in St. Louis geneticist and psychiatrist C. Robert Cloninger began to unravel this puzzle. Cloninger wasn't interested in mirror neurons, rather in mental illness. He knew that assessing the Big Five personality traits alone could not predict vulnerability to mental disorders; for that, he discovered, character traits are needed as well. These traits are nurture, not nature. They are, as Immanuel Kant once said, and as Cloninger repeats when asked to define character, "what people make of themselves intentionally."

Cloninger found there are three character traits that govern mental life and can be used to measure its stability: *self-directedness*, or how goal-oriented you are; *cooperativeness*, or how much you're willing to play nice with others; and *self-transcendence*, the most important one for this discussion. Self-transcendence describes spiritual feelings that are independent of traditional religiosity. "It gets to the heart of spiritual belief," says National Institutes of Health geneticist Dean Hamer in his book *The God Gene*, "the nature of the universe and our place in it. Self-transcendent individuals tend to see everything, including themselves, as part of one great totality. They have a strong sense of 'at-one-ness'—of the connections between people, places, and things."

Self-transcendence, Cloninger also found, is also a blend of three traits, or subtraits, that "hang together." That is, in personality profiles, if you test high for one, you'll usually test high for all three. These are *mysticism*, a willingness to believe in the supernatural; *self-forgetfulness*, a willingness to get lost in the moment; and *transpersonal identification*, again the most important one for this discussion. Hamer explains it this way:

> The hallmark of transpersonal identification is a feeling of
> connectedness to the universe and everything in it—animate

and inanimate, human and nonhuman, anything and everything that can be seen, heard, smelled, or otherwise sensed.
People who score high for transpersonal identification can
become deeply, emotionally attached to other people, animals, trees, flowers, streams, or mountains. Sometimes they
feel that everything is part of one living organism. . . . It may
inspire people to become environmentalists. Although there
are no formal survey data, it is likely that members of the
Sierra Club and Greenpeace score above average on this
[trait].

In other words, transpersonal identification is the character trait
one develops as empathy extends beyond self and species and into
the wider world; it's the biophilia instinct at work, without which
there could be no cross-species altruism, no Rancho de Chihuahua,
and, as we'll see in a moment, perhaps no mystic experience of the
shamanic variety.

Dean Hamer is the one who discovered the gene responsible for
self-transcendence. Technically, it's called VMAT2 and regulates
the flow of serotonin, dopamine, and norepinephrine, but Hamer
calls it the "God gene" because these three neurochemicals both
govern self-transcendence and have long shown up in the brain
during so-called mystical experience, including the experience of
unity Newberg described. Since that experience is kinesthetic—we
feel one with everything—then unity might be described as the ultimate social emotion. And if unity is an emotion, then, given the
correct prerequisites, it should be like any other emotion: it should
be contagious.

Take wolves. They're a social species who, like dogs and humans, have a long history with mirror neurons, as face reading is a
technology needed to live in packs. Serotonin, dopamine, and norepinephrine, meanwhile, are found in all mammals, as is the right

parietal lobe. So wolves have the neuronal architecture to be able to experience unity. We don't know if it's part of their common repertoire, but we do know it's possible. And this brings us to a slightly different version of the story of St. Francis taming the wolf.

In this version, the wolf charges at Francis, who goes into his power-of-God routine. Wolves are innately curious, so this gets the animal's attention. He slows his pace to gather more information. He starts face reading to do so, and his mirror neurons get in on the act, and pretty soon the wolf is feeling Francis's feelings. While we'll never know what Francis was feeling, his faith was about unity, and his methods were of empathy. Most likely, he was feeling what Westerners call love and Easterners call compassion: a pure empathetic reverence for all life, the end result of well-trained mirror neurons, the feeling of unity. So why did that wolf lie down at Francis's feet? Because wolves have mirror neurons too and unity is contagious, and why bother attacking yourself?

This is science, for sure, though perhaps also sorcery. Arthur C. Clarke famously said, "Any sufficiently advanced technology is indistinguishable from magic," and face reading is a seriously advanced technology. Even after hundreds of millions spent on research and decades of international effort, we can't duplicate it. Andrew Newberg's research suggests real-world correlates for mystical experiences, and mostly that's what scientists have found once they started looking. Shamanic experiences shouldn't be any different. Maybe the mystic time where humans and animals swapped consciousness and spoke the same language is less a magic act than a function of neurons and neurochemistry, a wondrous bit of biotech mostly forgotten in our rush toward Nintendo. Maybe this explains that talking snake in the Bible. Maybe our exile from Eden is really a bad case of cognitive decline, the cure for which is still available to anyone who bothers to cultivate empathy.

One thing is certain: it's always about how you tell the story.

From the right angle, it's all archetypes. Man leaves behind frivolity of the city and seeks meaning among the beasts. Along the way he meets a holy woman who smokes sacred plants and communes with donkeys. His journey becomes arduous. He survives ruffians on the road, evils spirits disguised as bobcats, being caged with a mountain lion. He enters the dark night of the soul. The torrent drives him into wilderness. He goes up the mountain. The great dog spirit saves his life and grants him the gift of vision. His return to society is celebrated with the sacred sharing of puke. Alas, he must leave again. One final quest to a distant land. He encounters more danger, meets a wizard in the road, some bit about cattle. Finally, triumphantly, our hero returns to civilization with the power of Dr. Dolittle: he can talk dirty to the animals.

Seriously, does any of this sound familiar?

PART NINE

The obscure we see eventually. The completely obvious,
it seems, takes longer.

—Edward R. Murrow

44

Stilts arrived one day in January, a California transplant, short-haired, coat mostly black, spots of tan, a pinched face, long nose, wide eyes, a few teeth left, missing half an ear, all his tail, standing about two feet high, with the torso of an armadillo, the legs of a giraffe, and it kind of worked for him, and kind of made him look like a stilt-walking hobbit with an eating disorder—thus his name. His demeanor was half what J. D. Salinger once called "shy, reclusive Pennsylvania Dutch lesbian who Wants To Write" and half Woody Allen lost in a Stephen King novel. Or something like that. He was pretty quirky.

And really, he didn't much like his first day with us. Meeting a new pack is the canine equivalent of switching high schools. We take it slow. We have ambassador dogs who are always welcoming to strangers, and, go figure, our best ambassadors are our gay dogs. Thus Smash and Hugo always come out first. Our real tyrants are the bull dykes, thus Dagmar and Squirt stay hidden away until the very end. In between, we tend to work things around size. Big dogs meet big dogs first, small dogs meet small dogs first. And this was a problem with Stilts: he was significantly bigger than the small dogs, significantly smaller than the big dogs—which is sort of like being that same new kid except black while everybody else at the school is either white or Asian.

After introductions came what usually comes: collapse. In

recent times, Stilts had gone from person to person, shelter to shelter, state to state, and who knows what else. He needed to sleep off the shock. Two days is typical, but Stilts stayed in bed for a week. When he got out of bed, he just switched rooms. A month later he hadn't much moved from a pillow under a table. Attention, affection, good food, great pack, general silliness, long hikes, lots of freedom, lots of love—these were our standard arsenal, and none was working. When I took Stilts on walks, he would wander off and hide. It was a little frustrating and a lot heartbreaking. How to get this dog to bond was the mystery. And then I went mountain biking and got an idea decided to push him off a cliff.

I'd been mountain biking with a group of strangers in the mountains outside of Santa Fe. One of the obstacles in our path that day was a giant boulder. On either side of the boulder were long drops, so the way forward was straight over and don't waver, a technique referred to as "point and pray." So we pointed and prayed, and afterward we stood in the middle of the trail hand-slapping and back-slapping and giddy as hell. This happens because, besides adrenaline, an adrenaline high includes endorphins, dopamine, and norepinephrine. These chemicals are critical for high-risk situations because endorphins mitigate pain, while norepinephrine and dopamine are performance enhancers that speed up reaction times. But endorphins also produce social bonding, and dopamine and norepinephrine do the same for romantic love. So potent is this combination that after a two-second ride over a rock we were all acting like college kids in a new relationship. So maybe, I thought, if I could get Stilts to do something dangerous with the pack, maybe that would help.

I had the perfect something in mind. Ever since I started the Five-Dog Workout, one route—a crazy-looking ridge run that dumps over a series of small drops and then over a large cornice and on down a gorgeous sandstone cliff—had my attention. Every time

I walked that way, I stared at that route. Was it even doable? The cliff looked too steep, the drop off the cornice too big. But something about it made me want to try, and something about it kept scaring me away. I suppose I was waiting for a sign.

I got one a few days before Stilts arrived. Igor, Bella, Bucket, and I were out for a hike, climbing a tall ridgeline just before sunrise. The route I'd been eyeing was directly across from us, though it was early and the cliff was mostly shadow. A few minutes later, we topped the ridge as dawn swept down the mountains and the whole valley lit up. And there, suddenly visible in the middle of my route, sitting fifty feet below the cornice like he'd been waiting for us, was the biggest coyote I've ever seen.

He was bigger than any of our dogs, as big, pardon the pun, as a wolf. He looked like a wolf too, thick fur of silver, paws like salad plates. He noticed us immediately, and I expected that would be the last we saw of him, but instead of running away, he stayed exactly where he was, staring at us. We stared back, five minutes, ten minutes. Then Igor barked once. The coyote nodded once, stood up, and was off. Rather than running down the cliff, he went in the other direction, bounding up the route in six strides, maybe seven, then over the cornice and gone. It was like a three-hour ballet condensed into a moment. It was amazing. When it was over, the route had a name, I had my sign, and there was no real choice in the matter.

We ran Coyote's Line that day. Turns out Bucket is scared of heights and had to be carried over the small drops. Igor and Bella jumped those drops and jumped the cornice as well. Bucket took one look over that edge and found another way down. I thought about going with him but knew I'd regret it later, so five-four-three-two-one and point and pray. There was a bit of hang time in the air and a bit of a hip check on the landing, but soft, moist dirt and after I bounced back to my feet, momentum took over. My job was one foot in front of the other and nothing more. A few steps later the dogs were at my side and we were bounding down together, falling five feet with every step, falling deeper in love with every step, falling deeper into each other along the way—which seems exactly the point.

In *Play Together, Stay Together*, Karen London and Patricia McConnell point out that "the type of play we engage in with our dogs is relatively rare in the world of animal behavior . . . the fact that dogs and humans stay playful as adults is uncommon, and is a significant part of the relationship we share. To some degree, play isn't what makes our relationship with each other better, play is what creates the relationship in the first place." I'd come the long way round to this conclusion, but this is also, I have decided, the real reason I think dogs are sacred and dog rescue a viable path toward enlightenment—because it's a path where play is not only encouraged but rewarded.

A few months later, after coming back from that mountain bike ride inspired, I returned to Coyote's Line with the same crew of dogs, minus Igor, plus Stilts. Stilts didn't have much trouble with the ridge but wasn't so sure about the cornice. Once again Bucket took one look and went off to find another way down. Stilts tried to follow, but I put my hand on his back and spun him toward the drop. So much for good intentions. Five-four-three-two-one—but what was I thinking? There was no way I could push him off a cliff.

I apologized to Stilts and let him go, figuring he'd follow Bucket down and, who knows, maybe that would do some good. I decided to show him what he was missing so gave a whoop and jumped the cornice. Bella jumped with me. We landed about the same time and bounced down the slope like pinballs, coming to a flatter section where she kept going and I slid to a stop to check on Stilts. He was still there, still staring off the edge. At first I thought he was frozen in terror and I would have to climb up after him, but then he did something I've never seen a dog do before: he reared up on his hind legs and kicked his feet in the air like a stallion. He did it twice in a row and then started barking, and barked straight off the cornice. He stuck the landing and kept barking all the way down the cliff, barking into the arroyo, where, without breaking stride, he smashed into Bella and bounced into Bucket and they all rolled into a game of bitey-face—the first playful contact Stilts had with another dog.

Immediately I felt that huge rush of helper's high. I was suddenly in the zone, happy in my flow. The dogs must have gotten a contact high. We immediately scampered off down the canyon, playing follow-the-leader as we went. I ran after Bucket for a while, then Stilts—who turned out not to run like an overweight hobbit—and then Bella took the lead. Her style had not changed. She still prefers going up and over and across whatever's in her path. Normally, because I can't duplicate her acrobatics, this is when I drop out of the game. But I was in a groove and Stilts was having fun, and before I could make up my mind we ran into a wall.

The arroyo had taken a sharp right turn and Bella had stuck to old habits. She went straight, leaping from the ground onto the backside of a juniper root sticking out of the wall. It was about five feet up, a big jump for me, but without even thinking about it I leaped up after her. Bucket came up after me, then Stilts after Bucket. And we did it again and again. The moment Bella lifted off her perch, I would land on it. And the perch I had just vacated was instantly filled by Bucket, and Bucket's old spot by Stilts. Bella went rock to crack to root, and we went after her. It was like team hopscotch, only played vertically. As we leaped up the wall, I felt my entire sense of self begin to blur. For a few moves it felt like my perspective had expanded, as if I had somehow merged with the dogs. There was a voice in my head—my own, a dog's, it's hard to say for certain—letting me know that as long as I did exactly what they did I would make it up that wall. Eight moves later, that's exactly what happened. The whole pack had run straight up the side of a cliff. This was more than a contact high.

45

Csikszentmihalyi uses the term *group flow* to describe the potent conjoining of consciousness and extremely heightened awareness that results from a bunch of individuals finding themselves in a flow state together. Basketball great Bill Russell, in his 1979 autobiography *Second Wind*, described it this way: "During those spells I could almost sense how the next play would develop and where the next shot would be taken. . . . My premonitions would be consistently correct, and I always felt that I not only knew all the Celtics by heart, but also all the opposing players, and that they all knew me."

This can happen when a band plays a great show or an orchestra a great concert. When sports announcers talk about a team "coming together" or "momentum shifting" in a game, group flow is often responsible. And ever since Jimmy Johnson credited Csikszentmihalyi for the Dallas Cowboys' 1993 Super Bowl victory, this state has become one of the most sought after on earth. Both President Bill Clinton and Prime Minster Tony Blair have sung its praises. In 2007, *Fast Company* pointed out: "In the past few years . . . many major companies, including Microsoft, Ericsson, Patagonia, and Toyota have realized that being able to control and harness this feeling is the holy grail for any manager."

Running up that wall felt just like group flow, except I wasn't sure it possible for the experience to cross species lines. A few days later I called Patricia McConnell to find out. She thought it more than possible. "Good herders find themselves in flow states with their dogs all the time," she said. "It's most likely what makes them good herders." Which, among other things, explains a great deal about what I'd seen with those cows in Patagonia. I next sent Csikszentmihalyi an e-mail asking what he thought. "Well," he wrote back, "I don't see anything nonsensical about what you describe. I myself wrote about running circles with my dog as an example of how we found mutual flow."

How group flow works is essentially face-reading writ large. Instead of needing to see faces, though, concentration is so peaked and the pattern recognition system so primed, that almost any bit of body language is enough to convey information. The best example of this comes not from group flow but from flocking. When a thousand geese all change direction simultaneously, this is flocking. Versions are found in bacteria, ants, bees, fish, and any animal that travels in herds, including humans in crowds. The problem was that when researchers looked for a way information was getting passed through the flock, the speed of group coordination significantly outpaced the speed of sensory communication. So how does a swarm of bees simultaneously bank left when they're turning faster than the signal can travel? How do a million individual fish react instantly, as a well-coordinated school, to the sudden appearance of a predator?

For a while the thinking was that animals might have a sense organ we don't, but in 1986 animator and computer modeler Craig Reynolds realized one might not be required. He built a computer simulation called Boids (bird-oids) by starting from the obvious idea that, as he told the *New York Times*, "the synchronization speed is pretty astounding. And since birds aren't mental giants, they can't be doing deep thinking as they fly along. They must use fairly simple rules." So his Boids program used only three: separation, alignment, and cohesion. Separation is a short-range repulsion that helped individual boids, known as "agents" in complexity-speak, avoid their neighbors. Alignment meant these agents would steer toward the average heading of their neighbors, and cohesion mean they would also steer toward the average position of those neighbors. Three was all it took.

After seeing the simulation, author Bruce Sterling described the results this way:

> individual boids meander around in an unmistakably life-like, lively, organic fashion. There is nothing "mechanical" or "programmed-looking" about their actions. They bumble and swarm. The boids in the middle shimmy along contentedly, and the ones on the fringe tag along anxiously jockeying for position, and the whole squadron hangs together, and wheels and swoops and maneuvers, with amazing grace. . . . You might say that the boids simulate flocking perfectly—but according to the hard-dogma position of A-Life [artificial life] enthusiasts, it's not "simulation" at all. This is real "flocking" pure and simple—this is exactly what birds actually do. Flocking is flocking—it doesn't matter if it's done by a whooping crane or a little computer-sprite.

These three rules are now thought to be part of the genetic coding of any animal that needs to move in packs, but it's what those rules require that helps explain group flow. Each requires pattern recognition—the birds need to determine average distances, speeds, and motions—and body language reading—the only way to determine speed, distance, and motion is to notice what your neighbor is doing—and body mimicry—for flocking to work, the individual needs to do exactly what the group does. Since humans need to move in groups, these same rules are coded into our brains—which is what's responsible for the hypercoordinated movements I discovered during the Five-Dog Workout.

The same things also happen during a group flow experience, only at a considerably more extreme level. A football team mounting a spectacular fourth-quarter comeback is a pretty good sign that group flow is at work. Think about what happens when the play breaks down and the receiver starts freelancing—running to any open spot on the field—and the quarterback still manages to get him the ball despite not being able to see him and without any real idea where he's going. This happens because the quarterback reads the body language of the person in front of him, whose body language is a reaction to another's, and so on across the field. In flocking, this keeps the group together; in football, it's how touchdowns are scored.

The same system could easily be responsible for shape-shifting. Shamanic ceremonies start with drumming, dancing, and singing—three practices known to create flow states—but move on from there. Most shape-shifting ceremonies next incorporate what Mircea Eliade called "the mystical imitation of animal behavior." The Hopi do an antelope dance, the Huichol a deer dance, jungle tribes have tiger mimes, steppe peoples do wolf mimicry, and around 1895, when American composer Louis Moreau Gottschalk blended slave rhythms with contemporary instrumentation to create ragtime, the accompanying African dances had names like the "fox trot," "chicken scratch," and "snake dip" for the same reason. As Michael Harner reports in *The Way of the Shaman*: "The initiation of shamans . . . involves nighttime dancing during which the neophytes move in imitation of animals. This is part of a process of learning how to turn into animals."

And it doesn't take much for the transformation to take place, as Andrew Newberg and Eugene D'Aquili found out when they interviewed Bill, a conservative, fifty-four-year-old businessman who went out one evening to hear some improvisational jazz sometime in the early 1990s. Bill was sitting in a pew in the gothic Calvary Episcopal Church in Pittsburgh, listening to the Paul Winter Consort play alongside the tape-recorded sounds of a howling pack of wolves. "It's enough to lift listeners out of their everyday lives, and into another world," wrote the scientists in *Why God Won't Go Away*. "And as the wolf serenade reaches its emotional crescendo, that's exactly what's happening to Bill. Quietly, unconsciously, he has allowed himself to be absorbed into the song of the wolves, lulled by its haunting rhythms and the beauty of those wild voices. He feels deeply, serenely at peace. Then, suddenly, he is seized by a surge of excitement. It rushes up from the gut in a burst of joy and energy, and before he can think twice about it, Bill is on his feet, with his head thrown back, and he is howling from the bottom of his soul."

And he had some company. As soon as Bill leaped to his feet, so did a half dozen others. In the seconds that followed, the rest of the congregation jumped up as well—more than a hundred people spontaneously and inexplicably on their feet and howling along with the wolves. The result was a profound experience of unity—with the wolves, the other members of the congregation, even the wider world, that felt, said Bill, "not *religious*, but definitely spiritual. It's hard to put into words, there's really no way to explain it."

Actually, there might be. This process works because listening to rhythmic music focuses attention. Focus hard enough, concentrate long enough, and action and awareness merge. If you're a shaman, this is the entrance to the trance state; if you're a scientist, it's the start of a flow state, but there's really no difference. As the expansive empathy that is core to this state arrives, the boundary of self begins to expand. But flow states are progressive. Keep concentrating, keep focusing, boost the whole process by further adding in imitative behavior—an exercise that not only increases attention but further engages the whole of the mirror neuron system—and things begin pushing much closer toward unity.

So what flips that final switch is a little hard to say. As of yet, no one has firmly connected the mirror neuron system to the right parietal lobe, nor have we been able to observe exactly when the orientation association area stops sending out information, so the actual trigger for unity is not yet known. But V. S. Ramachandran believes there's a relationship between the mirror neuron system and self-awareness, and this could help explain it. He recently told the *New Yorker*: "One of the theories we put forward is that the mirror neuron system is used for modeling someone else's behavior, putting yourself in another person's shoes, looking at the world from another person's point of view. This is called an allocentric view of the world, as opposed to an egocentric view. So I made the suggestion that at some point in evolution this system turned back and allowed you to create an allocentric view of yourself. This is, I claim, the dawn of self-awareness." But if this happened once—if the system turned in to look at itself once—what's to stop it from happening again?

Flow states, exactly like flocking, exactly like consciousness itself, appear to be emergent phenomena—a more coherent level of order formed out messy randomness. But what happen if you were in a flow state, if the mirror neuron system was working overtime trying to pattern match, and the system flipped again? What happens when allocentric perception turns back to look at itself after empathy has expanded our boundary of self beyond the confines of skin, when the answer to "Who am I?" suddenly depends on how far that boundary has moved? Across the football field and it's a touchdown; beyond the species and it's shape-shifting; across the universe and it's cosmic unity.

And never mind my miniature experience with shape-shifting—if animals themselves are capable of flow states, this alone has profound ramifications. It takes a combination of things—endorphins, anandamide, serotonin, dopamine, norepinephrine, luck, mirror neurons, pattern recognition, face reading, body language reading, right parietal lobe, whatever—to produce group flow, which means that dogs have all these parts and know how to use them. It also takes this same whatever to produce every mystical experience neuroscientists have yet examined. As far as anyone can tell, there's no difference between flow states and mystical states, and like all other peak experiences, they engage the mirror neuron system and involve a chain of empathy leading towards unity. And once I figured this out, you know, being me, this was when I started wondering if dogs believe in God.

46

Wondering if dogs believe in God was perhaps a little farther afield than I had ever intended to travel, but the question no longer struck me as nonsensical. The list of similarities between our two species is considerable and why not consider this possibility as well. After all, dogs clearly have moods. They have personal preferences, ecstatic experiences, and even vices. And while these things might not sound like the typical foundation for faith, they turn out not to be a bad place to start.

In his 1983 book *From Chocolate to Morphine*, University of Arizona physician Andrew Weil points out that children spin in circles to change their consciousness, while adults do the same thing with booze and drugs. So instinctive does this behavior appear that, Weil suspected, perhaps humans aren't the first species to actively pursue altered states. As these things go, he was correct in his suspicions. In 2006, Jane Goodall and Marc Bekoff visited the Mona Chimpanzee Sanctuary in Spain. They met a chimp named Marco who dances during thunderstorms with such abandon that, as Bekoff explains it, "he appears to be in a trance." Goodall has witnessed other chimps, usually adult males, enacting the same rituals near waterfalls. According to an article Bekoff wrote for *New Scientist*: "She described a chimpanzee approaching one of these falls with slightly bristled hair, a sign of heightened arousal. 'As he gets closer, and the roar of the waterfall gets louder, his pace quickens, his hair becomes fully erect, and upon reaching the stream he performs a magnificent display close to the foot of the falls,' she describes. 'Standing upright, he sways rhythmically from foot to foot, stamping in the shallow, rushing water, picking up and hurling great rocks. Sometimes he climbs up slender vines that hang down from the trees high above and swings out into the spray of the falling water. This "waterfall dance" may last 10 or 15 minutes.'" But dancing, while an effective method for altering one's consciousness, is perhaps the long way round.

In October 2006, National Public Radio's *All Things Considered* considered Lady, a cocker spaniel spending a suspicious amount of time down by the backyard pond. "Lady would wander the area, disoriented and withdrawn, soporific and glassy-eyed," Laura Mirsch, Lady's owner and an NPR intern, said. Then there was that one night when Lady wouldn't come back. Eventually she staggered back from the cattails and opened her mouth like she was going to throw up. She didn't throw up. Instead, recalls Mirsch, "out plopped this saliva-covered, frothy, disgusting toad." The toad was *Bufo alvarius*, a Colorado River toad whose skin contains two different tryptamines—the same psychoactive found in "magic mushrooms"—and licking *Bufo* produces heady hallucinations.

And toad-tripping dogs are just the beginning. Everywhere scientists have looked, they have found animals who love to party. Bees stoned on orchid nectar, goats gobbling magic mushrooms, birds chomping marijuana seeds, rats on opium, also mice, lizards, flies, spiders, and cockroaches on opium, elephants drunk on anything they can find—usually fermented fruit in a bog hole, but they're known to raid breweries in India as well—felines crazy for catnip, cows loco for loco grass, moths preferring the incredibly hallucinogenic datura flower, mandrills taking the even stronger iboga root.

So prevalent is this behavior that researchers now believe, as UCLA psychopharmacologist Ronald Siegel wrote in his 1989 *Intoxication: The Universal Drive for Mind-Altering Substances*, "the pursuit of intoxication with drugs is a primary motivational force in the behavior of organisms."

Siegel thinks the taste for intoxication is acquired and not inborn, though once acquired, look out.

Unlike other acquired motives, intoxication functions with the strengths of a primary drive in its ability to steer the behavior of individuals, societies, and species. Like sex, hunger, and thirst, the fourth drive, to pursue intoxication, can never be repressed. It is biologically inevitable.

But from an evolutionary perspective, this is a difficult inevitability to explain.

Many animals engage these plants, or their manufactured allies, despite the danger of toxic or poisonous effects. The stupefied bees quickly become victims of predation. The carcasses of "drunken" birds litter the highways. Cats pay for their addiction to pleasure plants with brain damage. Cows poisoned with range weeds may eventually die. Inebriated elephants destroy much property as well as the lives of other animals. Disoriented monkeys ignore their young and wander from the safety of the troop. Human beings are no different.

According to Italian ethnobotanist Giorgio Samorini, in his 2001 *Animals and Psychedelics*, the risk is worth it because intoxication promotes what psychologist Edward de Bono once called *lateral thinking*—problem solving through indirect and creative approaches. Lateral thinking is thinking outside the box, without which a species would be unable to come up with new solutions to old problems, without which a species would be unable to survive. De Bono thinks intoxication an important "liberating device," freeing us from "rigidity of established ideas, schemes, divisions, categories and classifications." Both Siegel and Samorini think that animals use intoxicants for this reason and do so knowingly.

Just like us, animals take specific drugs for specific purposes. Among the Navajo, the bear is revered for teaching them about *osha*, a root effective against stomach pains and bacterial infections. Wild carrot, as we learned from birds, repels mites. Horses in pain will hunt for willow stems because they contain salicylic acid, the substance aspirin comes from. In the Gombe National Forest in Tanzania, chimps with digestive troubles swallow sunflower leaves whole. When Michael Huffman, from Kyoto University in Japan, took a closer look he found the hairs on sunflower leaves scrape worms from digestive tracts. These days, when companies such as Shaman Pharmaceuticals sends researchers into the Amazon to study the "old ways," what they're really after is medical information originally gleamed from watching animals.

Hallucinogens are no different. Psychedelics are really chemical defenses—toxins manufactured by plants to avoid predation. Fungi, among our most prolific source of psychedelics, evolved six hundred million years ago, not coincidentally at the same time as plant-eating animals. Herbivores may have first ingested these psychoactives when the threat of starvation gave them no other choice, but later on sought them out for different rewards. "For example," writes Siegel, "morning glories, which contain the same alkaloids as ergot [the basis for LSD], are eaten by rats, which feed regularly on the plant's vines and fruits. The rodents tend to avoid the larger concentrations of alkaloids in the seeds. Yet, when disturbed by severe weather conditions, a rat will occasionally snack on a single seed, then display the characteristic head-twitches of intoxication." He also noted mandrills eating the hallucinogenic iboga root and then waiting two hours for the effects to kick in before picking a territory fight with a rival. Even Lady knew what she was doing. After her initial spate of toad-licking addiction, she learned to party only on the weekends.

Tune in, turn on, and drop back even further, and we can also thank animal planet for the Age of Aquarius. The animals taught us to trip and, to borrow a phrase from Oscar Wilde, "we never had the courtesy to thank them for it." In Mexico, the Huichol Indians often use the same word for "peyote" as for "deer," which also explains the fourth-century ceramic pipe found in Guatemala—in the shape of a deer, with a peyote button between its teeth. The shaman of the Russian steppe, from where the word *shaman* descends, have a fondness for *Amanita muscaria*—a serious psychedelic mushroom that the reindeer turned them on to. From watching reindeer eat piss-soaked snow, these shaman also learned to drink urine after taking mushrooms to boost the high. And, perhaps, going from the sublime to the ridiculous, *A. muscaria* is red and white and looks like a chubby, bearded guy poured into a mushroom costume. Scholars have pointed out that Santa Claus, flying reindeer, pine trees, and the giving of gifts were the original components of an *A. muscaria* harvest festival. Christmas may have become Christ's birthday, but it began as Siberian Woodstock—except, you know, with no Jimi Hendrix and plenty of reindeer.

Meanwhile, jaguars in the Amazon chew the bark and leaves of the *yaje* vine, better known as ayahuasca and containing DMT, arguably the most powerful hallucinogen on earth. *Yaje* also makes you puke violently—so why did anyone bother following this example? Shamans, writes Siegel, teach that "by using the vine they too will be transformed into a jaguar." Which means the animals taught us to trip and we tripped to become animals—which, from a psychological perspective, is one surefire cure for loneliness. But there is one psychological problem far worse than loneliness, far worse than all others, a problem that requires significantly more lateral thinking than anything else we must confront—and this, it appears, may be the real pull of hallucinogens.

In 1963 Aldous Huxley asked for an injection of LSD on his deathbed, believing the drug could facilitate a "good death." The next year Stanislav Grof found that psychedelics reduced existential anxiety in late-stage cancer patients. Most of this research ended when Nixon declared war on drugs, but lately scientists have picked up the thread. There are currently a half dozen ongoing studies at major institutions such as Harvard and UCLA using hallucinogens for the same purpose. Most were initiated after researchers at Johns Hopkins University conducted a four-year investigation into the similarity between psilocybin and mystical experiences (published in the journal *Psychopharmacology* in 2006 with a follow-up in 2008), which also found that psychedelics could be a fantastic tool for alleviating existential anxiety.

Relief comes, according to Bill Richards, one of the scientists involved in the study, because trips tend to follow the same three-stage process. The first stage is what people typically associate with the drugs, a swirl of lights and colors and sounds. The second stage is a catalogue of faiths—users see Jesus, Buddha, Greek gods, Egyptian gods, and so many others that this stage has become known as the "archetypal realm." But it's what comes next that make psychedelics so effective against mortal terror. "After the archetypal realm comes the mystical state," says Richards. "There's a dimension of awesomeness, of profound humility, of the self being stripped bare. In the psychology of religion, mystical experience is well-described—unity, transcendence of time and space, noetic knowledge, sacredness, ineffability . . . It's the sacred dimension of revelation, but it can be what Kierkegaard called 'fear and trembling'—incredibly profound and powerful terrain to travel." Hallucinogens then do the same job as religion—they provide proof of unity, which is still the only known cure for fear of death.

So if you want to know if animals believe in God—that is, whether they seek the comfort of unity—you need to answer two questions: Do animals share our fear of death? And do they actively seek ways to assuage that fear? As far as the second question, Ronald Siegel once saw a mongoose chewing morning glory seeds not as a routine part of his diet but rather as a reaction to the death of his mate. "Morning glory seeds are used by modern Mexican Indians to console themselves in times of trouble; perhaps the animals are doing the same," he says. But morning glory seeds are a potent psychedelic known by the nickname "heavenly blue" for a reason, so maybe that mongoose wasn't just trying to numb his grief temporarily; maybe he was trying to nullify it completely, seeking in psychedelics the same thing we seek in psychedelics—proof of membership in infinite collective, proof that death is not the end.

We can also say for sure that animals know this end is coming. In her *Coming of Age with Elephants*, biologist Joyce Poole describes a mother elephant grieving for a stillborn baby—crying, slumped over, days on end spent desperately trying to revive her child. On another occasion she saw a troop moving through the forest when one of them fell over and died. The elephants spent a long time trying to revive their companion before moving off into the jungle, only to return the next day for further ceremony. Marc Bekoff has observed both magpies and llamas grieving. Chimpanzees too go through elaborate, multiday rituals with the corpses of dead relatives—though they casually discard those relatives once they start to rot. In 2008, the Internet was flooded with photos of Gana, an eleven-year-old gorilla at the Münster Zoo in Germany, who refused to let go of the dead body of her infant son for several days, prompting *New York Times* science writer Natalie Angier to explain: "Gorillas, and probably a lot of other animals as well, have a grasp of their mortality and will grieve for their dead and are really just like us after all."

It was a dog named Foghat who settled the issue for me. As for her name, well, she had stringy white hair that stuck straight out from her head and—you guessed it—made her look like a dog wearing a hat made of fog. This was gallows humor for certain. Foghat was a mostly feral dog far beyond saving. She was a Rancho de Chihuahua special, utterly untouchable, blind and deaf and arthritic, could barely walk, had dementia, barked at phantoms, bit everyone and everything that brushed her fur. I once watched her attack the couch after accidentally bumping into it. All the other dogs just stayed out of her way, and she returned the favor. As for the humans, neither Joy nor myself was entirely certain she'd even met our species before. It wasn't just that Foghat ignored us; it was that she lived in a world where we didn't exist.

For a while we tried to bridge that gap. If she passed close by, we would reach down for a quick pet. But for a dog that could barely walk, she could certainly spin her head around with alacrity. Normally, with biting, we have a three-strikes-and-you're-out rule, but Foghat used those up her first afternoon. Euthanizing her immediately felt like adding insult to injury, so we broke our rule. Plus, Foghat had starved on the street for so long that when food appeared before her—and *appeared* is the right word, as we learned to stand across the room and slide her food dish to her like a shuffleboard puck—she was deliriously happy. We figured this was the first time she'd had this particular feeling, and why not let her have it for a little while longer.

At least, that's what we figured out loud. No dogs had died since the previous winter, and Joy was worried about what would happen to me when the next one did. She wasn't alone in this concern. Everything I'd been doing in the interim had only increased my empathy for our dogs, which only made me that much more susceptible to heartbreak. I had become a better rescuer, perhaps, maybe kinder, more patient, but definitely not tougher. Coming to terms with the dogs dying felt like my last hurdle. "The closer you get to the gate, the fiercer the lions," say the Buddhists, and seriously, it's a little annoying how often these guys are right.

Foghat lasted longer than we guessed. The betting pool hovered around six weeks, but after eight she was still around. Around the ninth week, the phone lines went out again, and because I was on deadline, Joy and I switched offices—I started working up at the house, she moved down to the goat shack. I have always been a morning person, but living in the country has made it a sickness. Most days I'm up around four. A wonderful time. The universe is quiet, the dogs are quiet—or usually quiet.

One morning I got to my desk a little early, dead-of-night time. But no sooner had I arrived than something brushed against my leg. I looked down and saw Foghat looking up. I yanked my leg away as fast as I could, certain she was about to bite me. She didn't bite me. Instead, she took a few steps forward and brushed against my leg a second time. I remember very clearly thinking, It's too early and Joy's not going to like having to drive me to the emergency room if this goes bad, but it sure seemed like Foghat wanted to be petted. I hemmed and hawed for a few minutes, then put my hand on her back and hoped for the best. Instead of attacking, she leaned into me, putting her full weight against my fingers. I kept scratching. She kept leaning. After ten minutes she walked away, but came back the next morning for more. By the third day she was in my lap. By the fourth, she was there most of the day. On the fifth, she climbed up to lick my nose; even with our burgeoning relationship, having her teeth inches from my eyes was more than a little alarming, but again she'd come in peace. Foghat licked me for a few moments, then laid back down and started purring. She purred for two hours straight and only stopped when her organs began to fail.

Foghat died in my lap later that day. We buried her not long after. Her grave is beside Vinnie's; who knows, maybe they can snuggle if it gets cold. After the funeral, Joy and I walked back to the house in silence. On the porch she gave me a hug, and this time she did say, "Don't worry, everything will be better in the morning." In this, as in so much else, she was absolutely correct.

The great Bengali polymath Rabindranath Tagore once said: "Through the rise and fall of empires . . . through the creation of vast bodies of symbols that give shape to his dreams and aspirations . . . ; through his forging of magic keys with which to unlock the mysteries of creation . . . through it all man is marching from epoch to epoch towards the fullest realisation of his soul. . . . Yes, they are coming, the pilgrims, one and all— coming to their true inheritance of the world; they are ever broadening their consciousness, ever seeking a higher and higher unity." More and more, I was coming around to his opinion.

So whether animals are aware they're going to die and whether they are willing to do something about it are no longer things I wonder about. While I can offer no counter to Descartes's idea that dogs have no soul, it does appear that they have all the right equipment to have the same spiritual experiences as we do and that they actively seek out such experiences. I guess we could go back and forth about whether they believe in God, but one thing is certain: if you're looking for similarities as a reason to make moral decisions about animal welfare, there's one in particular that should give you pause, and that is that dogs, humans, and possibly a great many other species all consider the exact same things holy.

47

The last time I ran Coyote's Line was the day Igor died. It was April 2009, almost our three-year anniversary in Chimayo, but this story starts over a year earlier, in February 2008, on the occasion of a different marker: the one year anniversary of Ahab's death. I had wanted to do something in his memory. Almost everything I've learned and done and become began when he showed up on my friend's doorstep. He'd been my best friend and the reason I first jumped into this infinite game in the first place. I wanted to say thank you.

I decided to take the dogs to the Thumb. This was another destination I'd been staring at for a while, always wanting to get closer, always afraid of what I might find. Wind and weather had shaped sandstone into a massive fist with an extended thumb, technically called a "fairy chimney," "tent rock," or "hoodoo," but none of those terms quite captured its size. The Thumb is colossal, three hundred feet of red rock sitting atop another two hundred feet of rubble. When viewed from a distance, it appears the last vestige of some gargantuan hitchhiker looking for a cosmic ride out of this place. But I wanted a closer look.

It was cold and clear and Sunday morning. I had Bella, Bucket, Igor, and Poppycock—a shepherd stray who'd showed up around Christmas and never left—with me. The first hour was spent crossing wide plains on wide trails. By the second hour, we'd moved into a slender arroyo that narrowed into a slot canyon that soon became a maze. There were side slots and dead ends and it took a long while to find our way through. The exit was at the top of a steep hill, where we got our first good look at the Thumb—but no sooner did we sight it than it vanished.

Flurries had been drifting down for a while, but suddenly it was dumping. Visibility became ten feet at best. The wind was blasting through the canyons. I rounded a corner and found myself standing at the mouth of a wide arroyo as the entire riverbed sprang to life. It might have only been wind-swirled snow, but it didn't look like that. The image that stayed in my head afterward was of Chinese emperor Qin Shi Huang's Terracotta Army, eight thousand clay soldiers all waking up from a long nap, donning armor, gathering weapons, preparing for some great battle. But there was no battle. Just as quickly, the wind calmed, the ghosts vanished, and a great silence returned. The real voice of the desert. The whisper that's always there, the message just below all others, not really audible, but someday, perhaps, we'll learn how to listen.

We didn't listen that day—and we should have. Instead, we just kept clomping forward, post-holing through ever deepening drifts. It took another hour to get to the bottom of the rubble pile, and, just as oddly, the moment we arrived, the storm abated. The sun poked through the clouds and I got my first good look at another grand mystery. Up close, I knew immediately, this place wasn't my business. It was ominous, precarious, the whole balancing act impossible. I stood beneath it with my neck craned back, all that rock, all that deep time, a bad feeling starting to rise in my stomach. I felt like I was trespassing, violating some covenant written eons ago, another promise somebody had forgotten to keep.

I ignored the promise, just like I'd ignored the blizzard. I had come this far and would not be denied. So up we all went. The escarpment was steep and crumbly and it took ten more minutes to scramble to the top. As we reached the Thumb, at the eerily exact moment my young flesh touched its old stone, the storm returned. Biting cold, howling wind, dumping snow. Visibility vanished. I could barely see the dogs beside me. Somewhere in front, I knew, the whole of the valley floor unfurled. I wanted to take in the good view and didn't want to try climbing down in a blizzard, so hunkered down to wait out the blow.

I chose a tiny ledge, tucked just out of the wind, but no sooner did I sit down than the bad feeling in my stomach got worse. At first I thought adrenaline, maybe a touch of vertigo caused by so much looming mass above me. Then the feeling became a stronger vibration, which soon became a hard quaking—like someone was slapping a conga beat on my belly. I was getting queasy. Whatever this place was, I wasn't sure I wanted anything more to do with it. And neither were the dogs.

What usually happens if I sit down anywhere in the backcountry is that the dogs run over, give my hand a lick—their way of establishing connection to their secure base—and head off exploring. Maybe they're back in five minutes, usually about ten. That day, as soon as I sat, the dogs didn't just lick me, they crashed into me. First Poppycock clipped my back with her hips as she ran past in a tizzy. I decided this was because she was new to the pack. Then Bella did the same thing, only harder, and after Truchas Peak she'd been extremely careful whenever heights and ledges were involved. Bucket didn't smash into me; instead began whimpering and trying to hide under my legs. Igor, the only one who'd gone off to look around, returned two minutes later, looking seriously demented—and moving at a full gallop.

I had a moment to wonder what had spooked him so badly, but only a moment. The next second, Igor tried to dive into my lap. Seventy pounds moving at twenty miles an hour was more than enough to rip me off my perch. Bucket and Igor ripped with me. I'm not sure what happened to them, but I spun sideways into the air and landed backward on the ground. My shoulder hit rock, my neck and head next. I backflipped down the slope. It was only the fresh snow that kept bones from breaking. For the next couple of weeks there would be a bruise down my left side that looked as though someone had taken a sledgehammer to the rings of Saturn. Right then, there wasn't time for the pain.

Bucket and Igor had crash-landed on either side of me and all of us were now tumbling down the slope. We kept tumbling for a little while too, though eventually got our feet back under us. As I popped upright I saw Bella and Poppy beside me, also running full tilt. There was now no turning back. We all went boing-boing and pell-mell and straight down. We bottomed out and kept going across an arroyo, and that's when I noticed Igor was missing. He had been beside me only a moment ago, but how long ago was that moment? Two seconds? Ten seconds? A minute? I stopped and called and waited and called and ran up and down the canyon and then did it again and still no Igor. I tried to backtrack using paw prints, but the snow was coming down too hard and there was no trail left. Igor had gotten lost before once and headed home. Maybe, I hoped, it had happened again.

But he wasn't at home. So Joy and I hiked back to the Thumb. The storm grew worse. By morning there'd be twenty inches of fresh snow, but for the moment we were hunting a white dog in a whiteout. It took another two hours to retrace the route, but there was no sign. We went back home, then struck out once more, getting nervous. Bull terriers are badly adapted to the cold. Their coats are too thin to protect them, and their pain tolerance high enough that they often don't notice themselves freezing to death until too late. We hunted all day and into the evening, the temperature dropped below zero. We never found him.

It was a bad night: the uncertainty, the helplessness, the sense that perhaps I'd been given fair warning but chose to ignore it. We had promised the dogs that their last memories would be of love. I had visions of Igor dying alone, scared and cold and missing his family—the exact opposite of my vow. Joy found me the next morning sitting at my desk in the goat shack, though I didn't remember even walking out there. It didn't matter. She had come down to tell me we needed to put up flyers around the neighborhood.

"You're kidding—this neighborhood? Our last hope is a community that doesn't give a fuck about dogs?"

And that's where I was wrong. Utterly and completely wrong. Everywhere we went people cared about dogs. Strangers helped tack up flyers. Gang bangers came out of their houses to lend us a hand. Some went back inside to call their friends and ask them to keep a lookout. Others told us stories about times their pets had gotten lost and returned weeks later unscathed. Even the heroin dealers sent our search parties. I was looking for a miracle. Igor hadn't shown up yet, but it certainly seemed like we'd found one.

And then we found Igor.

When we got home from putting up flyers there was a message on our machine from a guy who lived about five miles down the road. The message said Igor was standing on a cliff across from his front door. We jumped in the truck and flew over there. Almost immediately we spotted him on that cliff. I pulled the truck over and jumped out. Igor saw me then, but didn't move. Instead, he shook his head back and forth, lowered his gaze, and started trembling. I wasn't sure what to do, so dropped down to my knees. He stared at me for a long time, then finally came over, his head still low, his tail tucked deep. He looked like he had done something very wrong and was very sorry. He might have been sorry, but he was never the same.

Igor had frostbite on his paws and slashes across his belly and back. He was also exhausted, needing about three days to sleep it all off. But when he awoke he was a different dog. At first, whenever we walked into the backcountry, he'd wander off, find a high perch, and gaze at the Thumb. It was spooky, perhaps, but understandable. Pretty soon he was just wandering off. He'd started losing interest in the pack, and in me. I tried to lure him back by running cliffs, hoping for a repeat of the Stilts experience. It didn't work. Whatever had happened to him out there was too much for simple neurochemistry to cure.

Then the change crept into his home life. Bucket was his best friend and they liked to wrestle, but somewhere Igor had misplaced his self-control. He was hurting Bucket, throwing him around too much, biting him way too hard. Then he bit me. I was walking down to the goat shack one day and Igor ran up behind me and took a chunk out of my thigh. It didn't seem playful; he broke skin and did damage. It seemed intentional.

It happened again later that week—and this time there was no accident involved. I was sitting in my rocking chair, and stood up and took a step toward the house. Igor came out of nowhere and snapped at my arm, catching my fingers, doing even more damage. The following day, I tried to climb into bed with Joy—Igor and some other dogs were lying next to her at the time—and he attacked. Joy grabbed his collar before he made contact, but it was the first time in a long time I'd been scared by a dog.

I didn't know what to do. I didn't know what had happened. I told a couple of people the story, and they both said the same thing—that it's a different world in the badlands, and maybe we'd met something out by the Thumb.

"Met something?"

"You know—*something*."

And I did know. But what that something could be was not a question I could answer. Maybe my shaman could. So I called Ken Robinson back and told him the story.

"Well," he said afterward, "you met a land spirit."

"Uh-huh," I said. "Absolutely. I met a land spirit."

He thought an offering of good tobacco would smooth over the situation. I didn't even hesitate. I tried the tobacco. I would have tried anything.

Joy and I both have favorite dogs. It's not intentional, but it's useful. When all the other dogs are making us crazy, on days the couch has been ripped open, the garbage upended, the shit piles strewn across the house, when our nerves are frayed and tether ends reached, these are the dogs we head toward. These favorites help us remember why we're in this game. Ahab was always my guiding light, but once he died, it was Bucket who replaced him. Once Otis was gone, Smash took that top spot for Joy. And it was Smash whom Igor attacked next.

We'd all been hanging out in the living room when a friend stopped by the house. I went out to the gate to greet him, leaving Joy alone with the dogs. By the time I returned, she was crying, Smash was shaking, and there was blood all over the place. In my absence, Igor had jumped to his feet and leaped on Smash. He'd bitten his face, punching incisors through cheek, going for the bone beneath. Bull terriers have incredibly powerful necks to go along with their incredibly powerful jaws. Igor used both to lift Smash straight up in the air and start whipping him back and forth, trying to snap his neck. Two more seconds, maybe five, and he would have succeeded. Joy got them apart before that happened, but it was the beginning of the end.

Because of the inbreeding required to produce all-white bull terriers, they're prone to epilepsy, and because of the epilepsy, they're prone to rage syndrome—which is like an epileptic fit, only with a berserker rage instead of the shakes. Whatever had happened to Igor on the Thumb had flipped that switch. There was no way to flip it back, no treatment for rage syndrome. The disease is progressive.

Fits last longer, violence escalates. In Mexico, Joy once lost half of her face to this same escalation. So no, the good tobacco did not smooth over the situation.

We called our vet, scheduled euthanasia for the next morning, and had another very bad night. I got up early to take Igor for one last Five-Dog Workout—the very game I'd invented for him in the first place. I brought Poppycock and Bella and Bucket. We ran Coyote's Line again that day. I wanted it to be magical, I wanted it to change everything. Igor and I leaped the cornice and landed and bounded down and together and for those few seconds of primordial reenactment—just a man and a dog at play—everything did change, the way it always has. But then the moment was gone. There was no magic out there that day, only disappointment.

By the time we got to the bottom I was too sad and my heart wasn't in it. I slowed to a walk. I couldn't even look at Igor. Then I couldn't even walk. I just sat down in the dirt and buried my head in my hands. When I glanced up again, Poppycock was gone. She'd never run away before. I called and called and searched and searched, but it was getting late and the vet would be at our house any minute. I knew it was a bigger danger having Igor around the other dogs than it was having Poppycock lost in the badlands—but what kind of decision was that? Should I stay and hunt? Should I go keep Igor's appointment with death? Maybe Singer had it right—try to do the greatest good for the greatest number regardless of species—but some days, there's just no good to be done.

48

It was a long trudge out of the badlands. Having to hike out of the backcountry to go euthanize a dog and turn around and come back to hunt another is the kind of heartbreak only animals can provide. But I also knew it wasn't going to kill me. I was having a crap day, but that was about where it would end. Animal rescue might be a game of death, but isn't everything? Tomorrow I would wake up and try to save some more dogs regardless, and the day after that as well. Joy was right—this is what we did. So yeah, if dog rescue was a cult, then I was now a full-fledged member,

And right about the time I realized that, I spotted Poppycock. She was hovering right at the edge of the badlands, standing beside a juniper bush, acting the way dogs act when they've just buried a bone—like there was something to hide. The other dogs weren't paying too much attention, but there was a tingle down my spine and the hair on the back of my neck stood up. I took about ten steps forward and glanced behind the bush and my jaw dropped open. Sitting there, sitting less than ten feet from me, was the coyote, *that* coyote, the coyote in Coyote's Line.

In person, not separated by a canyon, he was enormous, well over a hundred pounds. His face wide, his shoulders broad, his coat two-toned, the top layer a thick gray shag, beneath it a thinner tan. He was glorious, yet off somehow. He looked like a hybrid, like a dog, wolf, and coyote all rolled into one. He looked like the standard-bearer for the entire canid line. And we got a good look because he wasn't running away, in fact didn't even appear afraid of us. Instead, his face broke into a giant grin and he sat straight up, positioning his torso directly over his hind legs and then—I shit you not—he started hopping on those hind legs, hopping just like a kangaroo.

It was among the oddest things I'd ever seen an animal do. I didn't know how to react, so stood there gaping. The coyote hopped a wide half-moon across the desert, his great jaws hanging open, his tongue flopping, his toes tapping. Later Alan Beck, head of the Center for the Human-Animal Bond at Purdue University, explained that hopping is what coyotes often do instead of bowing. It's how they initiate play. Then the coyote stopped hopping.

When he stopped, we were all standing in a long line: the coyote at one end, Igor at the other. He'd stopped a few feet from Poppycock but ignored her and started walking toward me. He passed me and then Bella and Bucket, and halted in front of Igor. They stood a few inches apart for what seemed like an eternity. Then he leaned in close and rubbed his head against Igor's neck—the same adopting-into-the-pack gesture I'd seen in wolves. They stood together for about twenty seconds and then, with some silent signal I never detected, the ceremony ended. In three quick lopes, the coyote was gone, vanishing in the distance, melting into the landscape, becoming, as I soon discovered, another backcountry apparition, another story no one quite believes, yet no one entirely doubts.

Trickster, shape-shifter, and transformer is how most cultures view the coyote. He is the keeper of magic, the bringer of death, the gateway to renewal. His presence, according to many, carries with it specific lessons. Ted Andrews explains, "The coyote teaches the balance of wisdom and folly and how both go hand in hand. The image of the wise fool has been used in the lore of many societies. This is the individual who seems to be a simpleton and yet the words and actions have a much greater wisdom than is initially rec-ognized. Are you not seeing the wisdom of your life and its events? The coyote will help you."

I needed the help. Igor was dead within the hour. Joy made it through okay, I took a couple extra days to get right again, but Bucket, well, he hasn't been the same since. All things, as they say, are connected—but that doesn't make them any easier. Or any more comprehensible. Mirror neurons might explain unity, flow states might explain shape-shifting, but neither is much help with land spirits. Neither kept Igor alive. As for the coyote, well, that's going to have to be tomorrow's mystery. But if the past is any way to judge the future, eventually something will help solve that puzzle. And there will be another puzzle beneath it, because there always is an-other, because the great gift of the natural world is that of mystery.

Perhaps with enough "solutions" we'll rethink our relationship with the animal kingdom. Perhaps it'll happen sooner. Eventually our morality and our technology will catch our problem. We no longer believe the Bible when it tells us stoning children to death at the city gates is a good way to punish rebellion, just as we no longer believe a few other tales. Our need for inegalitarian ecology has lessened as well. Within a few years, researchers tell us, we will be placating carnivores with meat grown from stem cells. Materi-als science can now weather the elements far better than hide and hair, artificial skin needs only a legislative push to put cosmetic-testing bunnies out of business, and we are a truce with the breed-ing clubs away from national spay-and-neuter laws—the universally accepted first step for transitioning to no-kill dog sheltering. But do we really need to wait?

Not too long ago, scientists and philosophers examined the facts and could not find reason why our closest biological relatives did not deserve legal rights, so a Spanish court granted them to great apes. A Swiss law now protects the "dignity" of all organisms.

And no matter where you look nor whose testimony you hear, you'll find none who have hunted the meaning of life in the world of animals and returned wanting. This alone should pique our curiosity. Many argue that our inability to consider animal welfare from an alternative perspective is for failure of will and weakness of vanity, though I see this cross as a lack of imagination. The shamans speak of a time when humans and animals could speak the same language. I don't know if we could ever find it again, but considering everything I've seen along the way, I would certainly like to look.

Perhaps the best way out of this dilemma is to again to check the scorecard. In her 1792 *A Vindication of the Rights of Woman* Mary Wollstonecraft felt it necessary to remind us, "If the abstract rights of man will bear discussion and explanation, those of woman, by a parity of reasoning, will not shrink from the same test." This is timely since the last election saw a woman run for president of the United States and end up as secretary of state. She replaced an African American woman who not long ago was considered unfit for office, being wrong in both sex and skin color. Two centuries ago her people were leashed and caged and factory-farmed; today Barack Hussein Obama is our president. I don't know what happens if we begin to treat dogs as our partners. I only know what the scorecard says—that every other time we've tried equality the results have been spectacular.

Acknowledgments

Human: Once again, I'm deeply grateful to my agent, Paul Bresnick, my editor, Kathy Belden, and everyone at Bloomsbury. For their tremendous help with the dogs: Elise Durant, Tiffanie Hauger, Madena Bennett, and Dr. Trina Hadden. For their tremendous help with the adventure: Joshua Lauber, Burk Sharpless, Rick Theis, Joe Donnelly, and Thaddeus Kortubala. A lot of very bright scientists were extremely patient with me along the way: Alan Beck, Lorri Greene, Marco Iacoboni, Marc Bekoff, Patricia McConnell, Patricia Wright, Steven Guerin, Jim Olds, Rick Granger, and Andrew Newberg. My thanks to Dr. Kathleen Ramsey for her unending generosity, to my parents and my brothers and their families for their support, and most of all to my amazing wife, without whom none of this would have been possible.

Canine: Ahab, Otis, Corky, Igor, Vinnie, Jake, Gidget, Damien, Bella Chupacabra, Poppycock, Bucket, Smash, Squirt, Pony Girl, Maus, Elton, Rio, Shy-Shy, Hugo, Dagmar, Farrah, Helgar, Wookie, Leo, Chow Yun Fat, Zen Master Mishah the Terrible, Salty, Flower, Blue, Jeb, Julia, Foghat, Lux Diamond, Apple Lightspeed, Stilts, Rigel, Sprocket, Butch, Scarlett, Ziggy, Fig, Marco, Willi, Joey, Chispita, Turtle, Newton, Bug, Munchie, Elmo. Without all of you, I am most certainly lost.

ET CETERA

Rancho de Chihuahua is a registered 501(c)3 nonprofit. If you feel like making a donation, you can do so via our Web site: www.ranchodechihuahua.org.

Notes

PREFACE

viii Veterinarian suicide: see http://www.medicalnewstoday.com/articles/105081.php and http://www.medicalnewstoday.com/articles/179796.php.

viii A short note about music: most of this book was written while listening to one playlist. Here's that list. Thank you to all involved.

1. "Space Travel Is Boring," Sun Kil Moon
2. "One," U2
3. "Karma Police," Radiohead
4. "Hey Pretty," Poe
5. "Watch Them," Soldiers of Jah Army
6. "Cold Desert," Kings of Leon
7. "Conquering Lion," Yabba You
8. "Who Was That Masked Man," Van Morrison
9. "Theory of the Crows," The National
10. "Ladies and Gentleman We Are Floating in Space," Spiritualized
11. "The Seventh Seal," Groundation
12. "El Jugador," South Park Mexican
13. "Speed Law," Mos Def
14. "St. Petersburg," Supergrass
15. "Sink, Florida, Sink," Against Me
16. "Blind," Gomez
17. "Let Live," Midnite
18. "Peace, Love and Understanding," Nick Lowe
19. "How's It Gonna Be," Third Eye Blind

20. "Rocket Man," My Morning Jacket

21. "Goin' to Acapulco," Calexico and Jim James

22. "Fake Empire," The National

23. "Prayer of St. Francis," Sarah McLachlan

ix　　T. H. Irwin, *Aristotle's First Principles* (Clarendon Press, 1988).

PART ONE

3　　A lot has been written about the Sixth Great Extinction, but Elizabeth Kolbert does a really nice job in the *New Yorker*, May 25, 2009, 53.

4　　June 23, 2007, John Burnett reporting for National Public Radio.

4　　For the DEA's official version of Operation Tar Pit, see http://www.justice .gov/dea/major/tarpit.htm. For a closer look at the bigger picture, try Chellis Glendinning's *Chiva: A Village Takes on the Global Heroin Trade* (New Society Publishers, 2005).

4　　"Lessons from New Mexico's War on Heroin." Again, it's John Burnett reporting for NPR, August 18, 2005.

5　　The village is called Tesuque. The author, Cormac McCarthy, also lives there. He is on staff at the nearby complexity science think tank, the Santa Fe Institute (SFI). When asked about the nature of his job, McCarthy once told reporters: "I have two official duties, to eat lunch and attend afternoon tea."

6　　For a good Griffith Park history, see http://www.griffithobservatory.org/ obshist.html.

8　　Most feel that shelters underreport kill rates and the real number is 10 million dogs put down annually.

11　　T. S. Eliot, *Prufrock and Other Observations* (The Egoist, Ltd., 1917), line 51.

15　　http://www.wilsonsalmanac.com/book/nov16.html.

19　　Check out http://www.circuses.com or PETA's circus fact sheet, http://www .peta.org/MC/factsheet_display.asp?ID=66, for examples.

20　　Stephen Jay Gould, "Time's Arrow, Time's Cycle: Myth and Metaphor in the Discovery of Geological Times," the Jerusalem-Harvard Lectures, 1987. That said, the most poetic account of deep time is probably found inside John McPhee's *Basin and Range*, though why stop there? McPhee's *Annals of the Former World* includes *Basin and Range* (it started out as four separate books, was then combined and republished, and won the Pulitzer) is by far the most dizzyingly wonderful look at geology that will most likely ever see print.

27   If you read my last book, you probably have some understanding that musician Jim White is a vortex of weird. For example, when New York film-maker Stephen Earnhardt went down to Pensacola, Florida, to shoot Jim White's first music video, at Jim's suggestion he hired folks living at a nearby trailer park to work as extras. After the shoot was over, these same folks convinced Earnhardt to stay in Florida and help them make a horror movie about a one-armed purple gorilla who haunts the swamp behind their trailer park. They said it would take two weeks. It took three years. The movie, by the way, is called *Mule Skinner Blues* and remains one of the best meditations on creativity and culture around. But the reason I mention this here is because it was Jim who first suggested I try to track down the legend of the Conductor. I took his advice and lost three years of my life to that little quest (see that aforemen-tioned last book, *West of Jesus: Surfing, Science and the Origins of Belief*). It was also Jim who suggested I read James Carse's *Finite and Infinite Games*. Just like the last time, I took his advice and, well, it's three years later and you'd think I'd've learned by now.

28   What I mean by "well spent" is that the last time I went to see the Pogues play, Shane MacGowan passed out halfway through their first song, then woke up and sang most of the rest of the show lying on his belly, with his head hung over the edge of the stage.

29   I wish I could track down that original article. A friend sent it to me and I haven't seen it since moving to New Mexico. But here's a link to the *Independent*'s coverage of those same suicides: http://www.independent.co.uk/news/uk/this-britain/spate-of-canine-suicides-from-bridge-baffles-animal-experts-527155.html.

PART TWO

38   http://abcnews.go.com/GMA/story?id=2510076&page=1.

41   For a good look at the science behind "animal whisperers" see the section on operant conditioning in Karen Pryor, *Don't Shoot the Dog: The New Art of Teaching and Training* (Bantam, 1984).

45   For all things Wavy Gravy: www.wavygravy.net.

46   Robber's Roost: http://www.okmag.com/index.cfm?id=44&homepage id=35.

47   He truly is an exceptional photographer. See www.wray-mccann.com.

51   Jennifer Dewey wrote a children's book about Doc, *Wildlife Rescue: The Work of Dr. Kathleen Ramsay* (Boyd Mill Press, 1994). Also, I did a Q&A with Doc for *National Geographic Adventure* that can be found here: http://adventure.national geographic.com/2008/10/kathleen-ramsay-text.

51   Shevawn Lynam, *Humanity Dick Martin* (Lilliput Press, 1997).

51   Mildren Mastin Pace, Daniel Miller, and Paul Brown, *Friend of Animals: The Story of Henry Bergh* (Jessie Stuart Foundation), 1995. For a full look at the history of American animal activism try *For the Prevention of Cruelty: The History and Legacy of Animal Rights Activism in the United States* (Swallow Press, 2006).

52   "Four paws and 140 years ago": this is from the ASPCA's history page, http://www.aspca.org/about-us/history.html. They also do a nice summary of Henry Bergh's contribution.

52   Katherine Grier, *Pets in America: A History* (Harvest Books, 2007).

52   Most of this information came from personal interviews, though the Web has plenty of this information as well. The American Humane Society's Animal Shelter Euthanasia Fact Sheet (http://www.americanhumane.org/about-us/news room/fact-sheets/animal-shelter-euthanasia.html.) is a decent starting point.

55   http://www.blackpearldogs.com; "Black Pups Face Doggie Discrimina-tion," MSNBC, March 5, 2008, http://www.msnbc.msn.com/id/23472518.

55   Konrad Lorenz, *Part and Parcel in Animal and Human Societies*, in *Studies in Animal and Human Behavior*, 2:115–95 (Harvard University Press, 1971 [1950]). Also, Stephen Jay Gould does a great job in *The Panda's Thumb: More Reflections in Natural History* (W. W. Norton, 1980).

55   Natalie Angier, "The Cute Factor," *New York Times*, January 3, 2006.

57   James Serpell, ed., *The Domestic Dog: Its Evolution, Behavior and Interactions with People* (Cambridge University Press, 1996), 258.

57   Raymond Coppinger and Lorna Coppinger, *Dogs: A Startling New Under-standing of Canine Origin, Behavior and Evolution* (Scribner, 2001).

58   Coppinger, in a roundtable discussion on PBS's *Nova* (February 3, 2004), put it this way: "The idea that Stone Age people could tame and then train and then domesticate a dog is just ludicrous, as far as I'm concerned. When I think of how much time it takes to train a dog, and think that those people back there, who had their own problems, and they've got to spend weeks, months, training wolves, and the wolves are going to put up with this kind of thing, and they're going to do it generation after generation, and I'm going to breed my wolf with your wolf? I mean, wolves have very strict rules about who they breed with, and when they breed, and so on. I mean, I don't see Stone Age people sitting out there with chain-link fences and all the things that are required for me to breed dogs. They just don't have the stuff to do it with."

58   In that same *Nova* show, Coppinger explained this as well: "Imagine fourteen thousand years ago when people first get the idea of living in a village. They settle down, they build permanent houses, and around . . . those permanent houses, all the waste products of their economies build up. You've got waste food; you've got waste materials of all kinds. Now there's a whole set of animals that move in on that. We know them now: we've got house mice, we've got cockroaches, we've got pigeons, we've got all kinds of animals that are living off the human waste. One of them is the wolf. The wolf moves into that kind of a setting, that new niche, that new foraging area, and it's great. You don't have to chase anything, you don't have to kill anything. You just wait; people dump it in front of you."

58   Again, Coppinger from *Nova*: "The ones that run away the first time anybody shows up, those are the ones that are going to be selected against, they're going to go out, have to make an honest living out in the wild. They're not going to be able to get enough out of that dump. So here's natural selection in action. Any one wolf that's a little tamer than the other, who can stay there longer, get more food, he's the one that's going to win that evolutionary battle."

PART THREE

66   For a great history of altruism (without which the opening to this chapter would have been impossible) try Daniel Charles Batson, *The Altruism Question: Toward a Social Psychological Answer* (Lawrence Erlbaum, 1991).

67   There are a ton of choices if you're curious about biological altruism. Obviously, you can begin with Darwin's *Descent of Man*, but for a fast and dirty overview start with the *Stanford Encyclopedia of Philosophy* entry on the topic: http://plato.stanford.edu/entries/altruism-biological. Also, a classic (though now somewhat dated) book on the subject is Kristen Monroe's *The Heart of Altruism: Perceptions of a Common Humanity* (Princeton University Press, 1996).

69   Richard Dawkins, *The Selfish Gene* (Oxford University Press, 1976).

69   There is very little written about cross-species altruism, so if you're curious about "reputation models" you're going to have to look in other directions. One place is David Rand and Martin Nowak's article "Name and Shame" from *New Scientist*, November 2009, which examines eco-friendliness and reputation. For a bigger look at reputation issues, try Robert Frank's *Choosing the Right Pond* (Oxford University Press, 1987), which examines the question of status in society.

75   See the preface to Marc Bekoff and Jessica Pierce, *Wild Justice: The Moral Lives of Animals* (University of Chicago Press, 2009).

80   Paul Waldau and Kimberley Patton, *A Communion of Subjects: Animals in Religion, Science and Ethics* (Columbia University Press, 2006), especially "Caught with Ourselves in the Net of Life and Time: Traditional Views of Animals in Religion," 27–39.

80   C. Vilà et al., "Multiple and Ancient Origins of the Domestic Dog," *Science* 276 (1997): 1687–89, or Robert McGhee, "Co-evolution: New Evidence Suggests That to Be Truly Human Is to Be Part Wolf," *Alternatives Journal* 28 (Winter 2002).

81   W. M. Schleidt and M. D. Shalter, "Co-evolution of Humans and Canids: An Alternative View of Dog Domestication: Homo Homini Lupus?" *Evolution and Cognition* 9, 1 (2003): 57–72.

82   This question has lately seen much debate. Two things are worth considering. The first is that in recent years a number of prominent researchers interested in studying the evolution of ethics (Harvard's Marc Hauser is one example) have switched from studying primates to studying dogs for this very reason. That said, Rob Shumaker, a scientist with the Great Ape Trust, agrees that very little social learning took place between the great apes and humans, but he feel this may "have more to do with physical location than mental skill set." Humans and primates tended to occupy the same niches and thus competed for the same resources. Competition is the reason we didn't see more social learning between our species, not because primates are somehow "less capable" than wolves.

82   W. Schleidt, "Apes, Wolves, and the Trek to Humanity," *Discovering Anthropology*, March/April 1999, 8–10.

85   For a really good look at Erika's Friedmann's work and the relationship between health, pets, and people see the *Discovery Health* episode on the topic, available online: http://discoveryhealthcme.discovery.com/beyond/miniPlayer .html?playerId=1670048703

86 K. Allen, "Cardiovascular Reactivity and the Presence of Pets, Friends, and Spouses: The Truth About Cats and Dogs," *Psychosomatic Medicine*, 64 (2002): 727–739.

PART FOUR

96 Allan Luks and Peggy Payne, *The Healing Power of Doing Good* (iUniverse. com, Inc. 1990).

96 Mihaly Csikszentmihalyi, *Flow* (Harper's Perennial, 1990).

100 See Doug Boyd's *Rolling Thunder*.

103 Douglas Preston and Lincoln Child, *Thunderhead* (Grand Central Publishing, 2000).

110 It wasn't just that our computers broke. It was also that when we finally did get them back, on both computers our iTunes libraries, photos, and e-mails had been erased—that is, we lost the only things on our computers that truly connected us to our past.

113 http://ezinearticles.com/?Dog-Dominance-and-Dog-Aggression-%96-Which-Is-It?&id=366572.

114 http://www.statemaster.com/encyclopedia/Big-Five-personality-traits.

115 Jerry Wiggins, ed., *The Five-Factor Model of Personality: Theoretical Perspectives* (Guilford Press, 1996), 183.

117 S. Kotler, "The Most Natural Selection." *LA Weekly*, April 18, 2004.

117 Joan Roughgarden, *Evolution's Rainbow: Diversity, Gender and Sexuality in Nature and People* (University of California Press, 2004).

118 M. Takahashi, H. Arita, M. Hiraiwa-Hasegawa, and T. Hasegawa, "Peahens Do Not Prefer Peacocks with More Elaborate Trains," *Animal Behavior* 75, 4 (April 2008): 1209–19.

118 Joan Roughgarden, *The Genial Gene: Deconstructing Darwinian Selfishness* (University of California Press, 2009).

119 Jonah Lehrer, "The Gay Animal Kingdom," *Seed*, June 7, 2006.

119 The quote is from personal communication with Joan Roughgarden.

121 A good overview of the Techichi is from *Dog and Kennel*: http://www.pet publishing.com/dogken/breeds/chihuahua.shtml.

125 There's a ton written on play behavior, but Marc Bekoff and Jessica Pierce's *Wild Justice: The Moral Lives of Animals* (University of Chicago Press, 2009) is outstanding.

126 Temple Grandin and Catherine Johnson, *Animals in Translation: Using the Mysteries of Autism to Decode Animal Behavior* (Harcourt, 2005), 123.

PART FIVE

131 S. E. Hinton, *The Outsiders* (Puffin, 1967), 35.

134 The Department of Justice report on everything wrong with Rio Arriba County, "The Nature and Extent of the Problem," is available here: http://www.ojp.usdoj.gov/rioarriba/natprob.htm.

139 Taken from a presentation on the subject; transcript available at http://nursing.msu.edu/habi/Lavergne.pdf.

140 From personal correspondence with Lorri Greene. For more information, see Lorri Greene and Jacqueline Landis, *Saying Good-Bye to the Pet You Love: A Complete Resource to Help You*.

140 Mary-Frances O'Connor, Michael R. Irwin, and David K. Wellisch, "When Grief Heats Up: Pro-inflammatory Cytokines Predict Regional Brain Activation," *NeuroImage* 47, 3 (2009): 891–96; Mary-Frances O'Connor, David K. Wellisch, Annette L. Stanton, Naomi I. Eisenberger, Michael R. Irwin, and Matthew D. Lieberman, "Craving Love? Enduring Grief Activates Brain's Reward Center," *NeuroImage* 42, 2 (2008): 969–72.

141 J. Olds and P. Milner, "Positive Reinforcement Produced by Electrical Stimulation of Septal Area and Other Regions of Rat Brain," *Journal of Comparative and Physiological Psychology* 47 (1954): 419–27.

142 For more information on Patricia Wright, see a long feature I wrote about her for *Plenty Magazine*. There's a copy available on my website: http://www.stevenkotler.com/node/62. She also appears in Michael Apted's wonderful *Me and Isaac Newton* (1999).

143 Linda Spalding, *A Dark Place in the Jungle* (Algonquin Books, 1999).

145 This is Kundalini Yoga founder Yogi Bhajan's 3HO Foundation.

146 http://www.britannica.com/blogs/2007/07/thoughts-on-the-meaning-of-suffering-part-1.

149 For a further look at the hell of puppy mills, try http://www.stoppuppymills.org.

150 Whether animals get PTSD is an open question, at least for anyone who hasn't really spent any time around abused animals. A decent look at some of the research can be found in Charles Siebert's "An Elephant Crack-Up," *New York Times Magazine*, October 8, 2006.

151 Steven Lindsay, *Handbook of Applied Dog Behavior and Training*, vol. 2: *Etiology and Assessment of Behavior Problems* (Wiley-Blackwell, 2001).

PART SIX

155 Joan Didion, *Slouching Towards Bethlehem* (Farrar, Straus and Giroux, 1968), 196.

155 This is by no means the end of the list of origin stories for "This is the real McCoy." The British etymologist and writer and *Oxford English Dictionary* contributor Michael Quinion lists a bunch of further possibilities on his World Wide Words website: http://www.worldwidewords.org/qa/qa-mcc1.htm.

159 Coren writes a blog for PsychologyToday.com. You can find this story under "A Dog Whose Memory Was Too Good," published November 24, 2008, but the quotes are from personal communication.

165 Doug Star, "Animal Passions: Fido Loves You," *Psychology Today*, March 1, 2006.

165 Candace Pert, *Molecules of Emotion: The Science Behind Mind-Body Medicine* (Simon and Schuster, 1999).

166 J. Bowlby, *Attachment,* vol. 1 of *Attachment and Loss*, 2nd ed. (Basic Books, 1999); J. Bowlby, *Separation: Anxiety and Anger*, vol. 2 of *Attachment and Loss* (Hogarth Press, 1973); M. Ainsworth and J. Bowlby, *Child Care and the Growth of Love* (Penguin Books, 1965).

167 Jaak Panksepp, *Affective Neuroscience: The Foundations of Human and Animal Emotions* (Oxford University Press, 1998).

168 "Sounds of Dog's Laugh Calms Other Pooches," ABCNews.com, December 4, 2005. But if you want to hear for yourself, Simonet released a CD called *Dog Laughter* that you can play at home and watch the sound calm down your dogs.

168 B. Holland, "Express Yourself: It's Later than You Think," *Atlantic Monthly*, July 1996.

171 http://www.sfgate.com/cgi-bin/blogs/dailydish/detail?blogid=7&entry_id=35782.

174 R. Descartes, "Animals Are Machines," in *Environmental Ethics: Divergence* *and Convergence,* eds. S. J. Armstrong and R. G. Botzler (McGraw-Hill, 1993), 281–85.

174 Voltaire info comes from Jeffrey Moussaieff Masson, *Dogs Never Lie About Love* (Crown, 1997).

174 J. Bentham, *Introduction to the Principles of Morals and Legislation* (Kessinger, 2005).

175 Ibid.

175 "First Chimp Reported to Learn Sign Language Dies," Associated Press, October 31, 2007.

175 Elizabeth Hess, *Nim Chimpsky: The Chimp Who Would Be Human* (Bantam, 2008).

177 Bill Maher quote from *US Magazine,* February 1999.

177 Testimony of James F. Jarboe, domestic terrorism section chief, Counterterrorism Division, FBI, before the House Resources Committee, Subcommittee on Forests and Forest Health February 12, 2002, "The Threat of Eco-Terrorism."

177 Gareth Walsh, "Father of Animal Activism Backs Monkey Testing," *Sunday Times,* November 26, 2006.

179 American Museum of Natural History press release, April 20, 1998. See http://www.well.com/~davidu/amnh.html.

179 J. Hance, "Governments, Public Failing to Save World Species," Mongabay .com, November 4, 2009.

179 R. Manning, *Against the Grain: How Agriculture Has Hijacked Civilization* (North Point Press, 2004).

180 Joan Didion, "On Self-Respect," from *Slouching Towards Bethlehem.*

PART SEVEN

185 See the Mountain Lion Foundation, "After the Hunt: Challenges Facing California's Mountain Lion Population."

190 Mountain lions are technically not big cats because they can't roar. Instead, they share vocalization patterns with house cats—hissing, growling, and such. But they can also scream, which sounds much like a roar, only slightly more extraterrestrial.

191 J. Berger, "Why Look at Animals?" *About Looking* (Pantheon, 1980), 1–28.

191 James Serpell, *In the Company of Animals* (Cambridge University Press, 1996).

193 J. Robbins, "Resurgent Wolves Now Considered Pests by Some," *New York Times*, March 7, 2006. There are also lots of other places to read about the battle over wolves in Yellowstone, but my personal favorite is Rick Bass, *The Ninemile Wolves* (Ballantine, 1992).

197 For a great staring point for Thoreau on wildness, try his 1862 essay "Walking."

201 Farrah Fawcett-Major was the star of the 1970s TV show *Charlie's Angels*.

201 D. Mech, P. Wolf, and J. Packard, "Regurgitative Food Transfer Among Wild Wolves," *Canadian Journal of Zoology* 77 (1980): 1192–5.

202 Paul Ekman, *Emotions Revealed: Recognizing Faces and Feelings to Improve Communication and Emotional Life* (Times Books, 2003).

204 E. Durkheim, *Elementary Forms of Religious Life* (BN Publishing, 2008).

206 Mary Douglas, *A World of Goods: towards an anthropology of consumption* (Basic Books, 1979).

206 This can be found in the foreword to Jiddu Krishnamurti's *The First and Last Freedom* (HarperCollins, 1975).

208 Ernest Becker, *The Denial of Death* (Free Press, 1973).

208 Ted Andrews, *Animals Speak: The Spiritual and Magical Powers of Creatures Great and Small* (Llewellyn Publications, 1996).

PART EIGHT

212 P. P. G. Bateson and R. A. Hinde, eds., *Growing Points in Ethology* (Cambridge University Press, 1976).

212 Karen Pryor and Kenneth Norris, eds., *Dolphin Societies: Discoveries and Puzzles* (University of California Press, 1976).

213 "Why Your Dog Is Smarter than a Wolf," *Christian Science Monitor*, October 26, 2005.

214 Adam Miklosi, *Dog Behavior, Evolution and Cognition* (Oxford University Press, 2007).

214 The Marco Iacoboni quote came from personal communication.

214 Lea Winerman, "The Mind's Mirror," *Monitor on Psychology* 36, 9 (October 2005).

215 There's a ton of technical books out there about mirror neurons, but for good fun try Michael Gazzaniga, *Human: The Science Behind What Makes Us Unique* (HarperCollins, 2008).

215 Sandra Blakeslee, "Cells That Read Minds," *New York Times*, January 10, 2006.

215 http://www.edge.org/3rd_culture/ramachandran/ramachandran_index .htm.

215 John Colapinto, "Brain Games," *New Yorker*, May 11, 2009, 76.

215 A. Paukner, S. Suomi, E. Visalberghi, and P. Ferrari, "Capuchin Monkeys Display Affiliation Towards Humans Who Imitate Them," *Science* 325, 5942 (August 14, 2009): 880–83.

216 Masson, *Dogs Never Lie About Love*, 147.

217 C. Jung, *Archetypes and the Collective Unconscious* (Princeton University Press, 1969).

219 Thomas Berry, "The Viable Human," *Re-vision* 16 (1993).

220 James Lovelock, *Gaia: A New Look at Life on Earth* (Oxford University Press, 1979), 9.

221 For a great discussion of the conflict, see Lynn Margulis's "Gaia Is a Tough Bitch," available at http://www.edge.org/documents/ThirdCulture/n-Ch.7. html.

221 Steven Johnson, *Emergence: The Connected Lives of Ants, Brains, Cities and Software* (Touchstone, 2001).

224 Personal communication with Rick Granger. That said, Granger and Gary Lynch lay out the entire argument in their excellent *Big Brain: The Origin and Future of Human Intelligence* (Palgrave Macmillan, 2008).

225 Paul Shepard, *The Others* (Island Press, 1996), 54.

227 Pauline Anderson, "Hurricane Katrina Survivors Face Increasing Mental Health Problems," *Medscape Medical News,* November 15, 2007.

227 E. O. Wilson, *Biophilia* (Harvard University Press, 1986).

227 Richard Louv, *Last Child in the Woods: Saving Our Children from Nature-Deficit Disorder* (Algonquin Books), 2005.

227 This is from Coren's blog, "The Canine Corner," found on the Psychology Today website: http://www.psychologytoday.com/blog/canine-corner/200901/ dogs-therapists-the-case-actor-mickey-rourke.

229 Mircea Eliade, *Shamanism: Archaic Techniques in Ecstasy* (Princeton University Press, 1964), 94.

230 Carlos Castaneda, *Journey to Ixtlan: The Lessons of Don Juan* (Simon and Schuster, 1972), 251.

232 William James, *The Varieties of Religious Experience: A Study in Human Nature*, 1902.

233 Andrew Newberg and Vincent Rause, *Why God Won't Go Away: Brain Science and the Biology of Belief* (Ballantine, 2001).

234 Rupert Sheldrake, *Dogs That Know When Their Owners are Coming Home: And Other Unexplained Powers of Animals* (Three Rivers Press, 1999).

235 For more information about Ken Robinson and the work he does, see http://www.unseendimensions.com.

238 Oskar Pfungst, *Clever Hans (The Horse of Mr. von Osten): A Contribution to Experimental Animal and Human Psychology*, trans. C. L. Rahn (Henry Holt. 1911 [originally published in German, 1907]).

238 Mary Kilbourne Matossian, *Shaping World History* (M. E. Sharpe, 1997), 43.

239 Malcolm Gladwell, *Blink* (Little, Brown, 2005), 200.

240 Ibid., 202.

241 K. Guo, K. Meints, C. Hall, S. Hall, and D. Mills, "Left Gaze Bias in Humans, Rhesus Monkeys and Domestic Dogs," *Animal Cognition* 12, 3 (May 2009): 409–18.

241 Gladwell, *Blink*, 197–214.

242 Iacoboni said this to WebMD journalist Jeanie Lerche Davis in an April 8, 2003, article entitled "Mimicking Emotions Creates Empathy."

242 A. Senju, R. Joly-Macheroni, and A. Shepherd, "Dogs Catch Human Yawns," *Biology Letters* 4 (2008): 446–48.

243 Simon Baron-Cohen, *Mindblindedness* (MIT Press, 1997).

243 Jocelyn Selim, "Dog-Faced Humans," *Discover*, July 2004.

244 C. Payne and K. Jaffe, "Self Seeks Like: Many Humans Choose Their Dogs Following Rules Used for Assortative Mating," *Journal of Ethology* 23, 1 (January 2005).

247 http://www.americancatholic.org/features/francis/stories.asp#wol.

249 C. Robert Cloninger, *Feeling Good: The Science of Well-being* (Oxford University Press, 2004).

250 Dean Hamer, *The God Gene* (Doubleday, 2004), 18.

250 Ibid., 26.

250 Ibid., 79–89.

251 Arthur C. Clarke, "Hazards of Prophecy: The Failure of Imagination," *Profiles of the Future* (Harper & Row, 1973 [1962]).

PART NINE

255 J. D. Salinger, "Zooey," *New Yorker*, May 4, 1957.

256 S. Kotler, *West of Jesus* (Bloomsbury, 2006), 162.

258 Karen London and Patricia McConnell, *Play Together, Stay Together* (McConnell Publishing, 2008), 5.

261 Bill Russell and Taylor Branch, *Second Wind* (Random House, 1979).

261 Ann Marsh, "The Art of Work," *Fast Company*, December 2007.

262 James Gleick, "New Appreciation of the Complexity in a Flock of Birds," *New York Times*, November 24, 1987.

263 Bruce Sterling, "Artificial Life," *Magazine of Fantasy and Science Fiction*, December 1992.

264 Eliade, *Shamanism*, 93–94.

264 Michael Harner, *The Way of the Shaman* (Harper and Row, 1980), 60.

265 Ibid., 77–78.

266 John Colapinto, "Brain Games," *New Yorker*, May 11, 2009, 76.

268 Andrew Weil and Winifred Rosen, *From Chocolate to Morphine* (Houghton Mifflin, 1983), 15.

268 Marc Bekoff, "Do Animals Have Emotions?" *New Scientist*, May 23, 2007.

269 Laura Mirsch, "The Dog Who Loved to Suck on Toads," NPR, October 30, 2006.

269 Ronald K. Siegel, *Intoxication* (Park Street Press, 1989), 11.

269 Ibid., 208.

269 Ibid., 11.

271 M. Huffman et. al., "Ethnobotany and Zoopharmacognosy of *Vernonia amygdalina*, a Medicinal Plant Used by Humans and Chimpanzees," *Proceedings of the International Compositae Conference, Kew* 2 (1994): 351–60.

271 Siegel, *Intoxication*, 71.

271 Barbara G. Myerhoff, "The Deer-Maize-Peyote Symbol Complex Among the Huichol Indians of Mexico," *Anthropological Quarterly* 43, 2 (April 1970): 64–78.

272 R. Gordon Wasson, *Soma: Divine Mushroom of Immortality* (1968).

272 Siegel, *Intoxication*, 64.

272 Laura Huxley, *This Timeless Moment* (Celestial Arts, 2001).

273 S. Kotler, "The New Psychedelic Renaissance," *Playboy*, April 2010.

273 Michael Hughes, "Sacred Intentions," *Baltimore City Paper*, October 16, 2008.

274 Siegel, *Intoxication*, 71.

274 Joyce Poole, *Coming of Age with Elephants* (Hyperion, 1996).

274 Natalie Angier, "Do Animals Grieve over Death like We Do?" *New York Times,* September 2, 2008.

276 Rabindranath Tagore, *Sahana: The Realization of Life* (Macmillan, 1915), 33.

284 Linda Ward, "What Is Rage Syndrome?" Rage Syndrome Information Centre.

287 Andrews, *Animals Speak.*

A Note on the Author

Steven Kotler is the author of the novel *The Angle Quickest for Flight*, a *San Francisco Chronicle* bestseller, and *West of Jesus*, a 2006 PEN West finalist. His work has appeared in the *New York Times Magazine*, *GQ*, *Wired*, *Discover*, *Outside*, *National Geographic*, and elsewhere, and he writes "The Playing Field," a blog about the science of sport for PsychologyToday.com. Kotler runs the Rancho de Chihuahua dog sanctuary with his wife in rural New Mexico.